Advance Praise for

The Water Remembers

"Water is family and activism is generational in Amy Bowers Cordalis's moving account of the Yurok Nation's long battle to save the Klamath River and enable unprecedented environmental restoration. Her own role in that story is bravely fought and beautifully told in *The Water Remembers*, which is **a summons for more courage, connection, and community to save the places we hold dear.**"

— **Tara Lohan, environmental journalist and author of *Undammed***

"Amy Bowers Cordalis story tells us how Yurok values are lived. *The Water Remembers* details how and why she assumed her responsibility to protect our homelands and all that we value. **Her story can guide us all to meet our shared responsibilities to the world we have been gifted.**"

— **Judge Abby Abinanti, Yurok Tribal Court Judge (and first Indigenous woman licensed to practice law in California)**

"**In this moving memoir, Amy Bowers Cordalis shows what happens when ancestral memory joins forces with the law.** The fight for the Klamath River is an important fight for Indigenous and environmental justice in the American West."

— **David Owen, author of *Where the Water Goes***

"**Amy's writing sings with urgency and purpose.** Informed by her family's generational fight for fish and fishing rights, her unique and intimate perspective as an Indigenous Nation member and water rights lawyer is direly needed to save the wildness of the Klamath River and its fish, and the people of the Yurok Nation."

—**Josh "Bones" Murphy, filmmaker/director of Patagonia's *Artifishal***

"A brightly written, driving narrative of Indigenous voices and many other people...this important book is **a joyous and uplifting story.**"

— **Charles Wilkinson, author of**
Blood Struggle

"Triumphant story and ever widens the awareness of the dangers that threaten Indigenous people and their historic lands."

— **Congressman Jared Huffman**

The
Water
Remembers

My Indigenous Family's Fight to
Save a River and a Way of Life

Amy Bowers Cordalis

LITTLE, BROWN AND COMPANY
New York   Boston   London

Little, Brown
Hachette Book Group
1290 Avenue of the Americas, New York, NY 10104
littlebrown.com

First Edition: October 2025

Little, Brown and Company is a division of Hachette Book Group, Inc. The Little, Brown name and logo are trademarks of Hachette Book Group, Inc.

The publisher is not responsible for websites (or their content) that are not owned by the publisher.

The Hachette Speakers Bureau provides a wide range of authors for speaking events. To find out more, go to hachettespeakersbureau.com or email hachettespeakers@hbgusa.com.

Little, Brown and Company books may be purchased in bulk for business, educational, or promotional use. For information, please contact your local bookseller or the Hachette Book Group Special Markets Department at special.markets@hbgusa.com.

Print book interior design by Taylor Navis

Interior art provided by the author

ISBN 9780316568951

LCCN is available at the Library of Congress.

Printing 1, 2025

LSC-C

Printed in the United States of America

Dedicated to my grandmother Lavina Bowers, the bravest, most beautiful woman I know. To my parents, Bill and Diane Bowers, your love is your legacy. I am so blessed to be your daughter. To my boys, Tobiyazh, Keane, and Brooks, this was all for you.

The Government could never pay us back if [it] lived a million years...for the things they took away from the Indians. Because we had a beautiful freedom.

— Geneva Mattz, August 29, 1984

Contents

PART III: WORLD RENEWAL

Klamath Basin Map

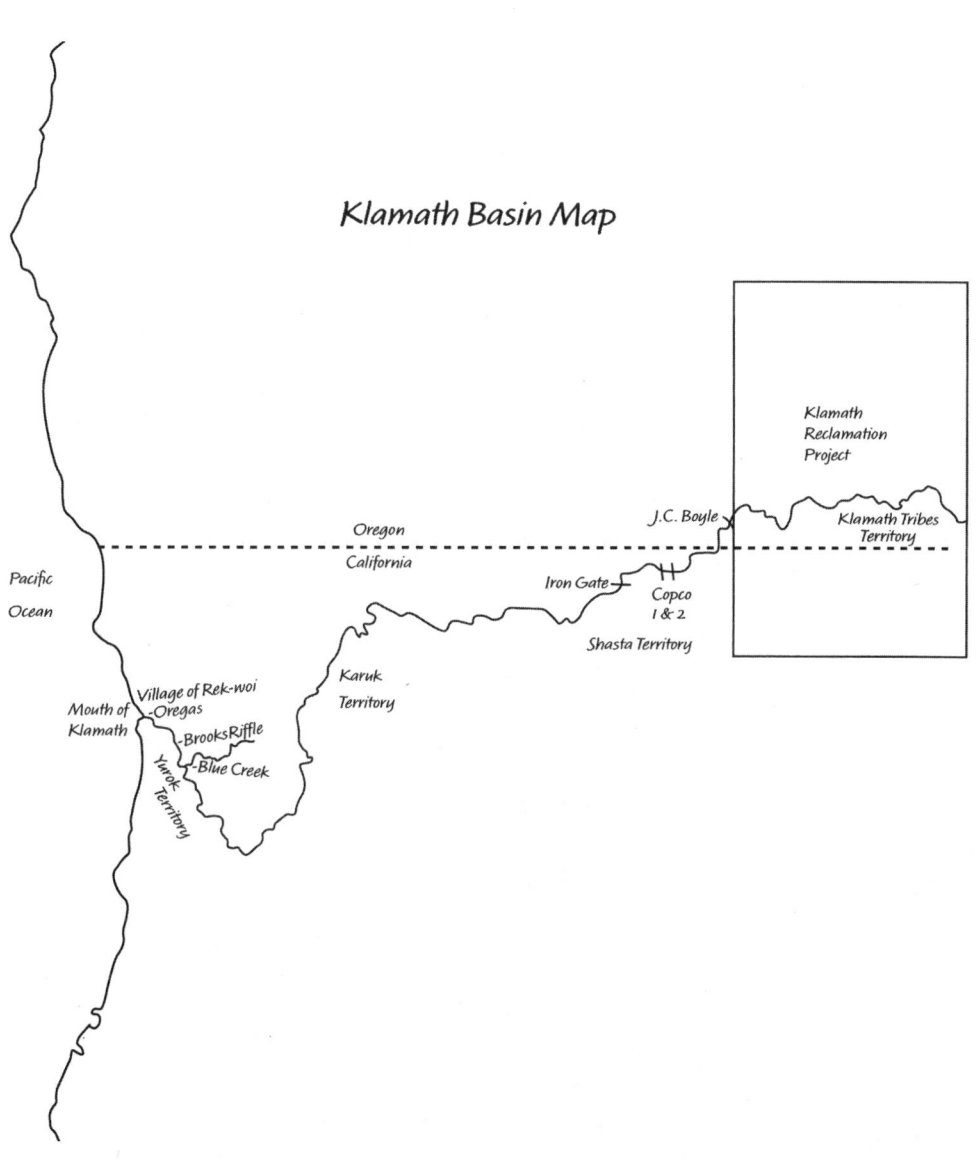

Pacific
Ocean

Oregon
California

J.C. Boyle

Klamath
Reclamation
Project

Klamath Tribes
Territory

Iron Gate

Copco
1 & 2

Shasta Territory

Village of Rek-woi
Oregas

Mouth of
Klamath

Brooks Riffle

Blue Creek

Yurok
Territory

Karuk
Territory

Mattz-Brooks Family Tree

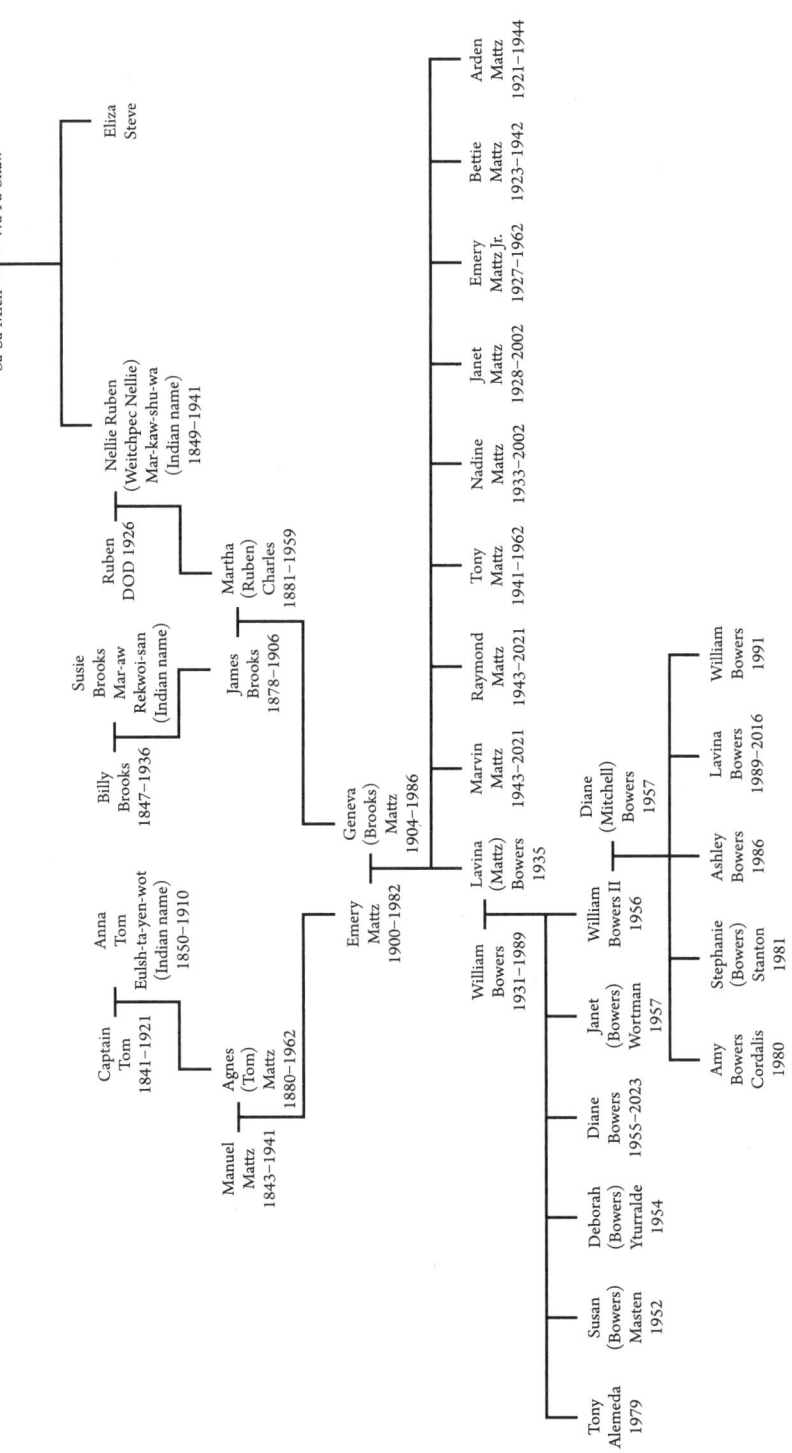

Author's Note

I am very lucky to be a member of a glorious family, community, and the Yurok Nation. Writing this book has been one of the greatest privileges of my life. I grew up hearing many of the stories in this book around my grandmother's house, on the River bar next to a campfire, and in the Yurok tribal offices. Also, in the mid-1980s theologian Helen Oppenheimer conducted interviews at the family home in Rek-woi with several members of my family. Many of the stories and much of the dialogue in this book are from these interviews. I also lived through many of the events in this book.

The stories in this book are my reflections on my family's history and my work. The book is not the Yurok Nation's official account of its work on fishing rights and dam removal, nor is it a complete account of Klamath dam removal. There are many champions of the Yurok Nation, the Klamath River, salmon, and dam removal. I adore and deeply respect these warriors and they have many different stories that I hope will be told.

This book is written in the format of Yurok storytelling. It flows circularly through time, place, and generations. I attempted to use authentic Yurok style and tone. I refer to tribal nations as nations because "tribe" was a label provided by colonizers that does not reflect the inherent sovereignty of Indigenous nations. Also, the Klamath

River is a main character in this book as it is an ancient relative. I have capitalized references to the Klamath River to give respect and reverence to the River.

Join me on the Klamath River at fish camp, sitting next to a fire, with the gill net in the River close by. As you read this book, I'll tell you a story.

PART I
Origin Story

Billy Brooks at the House of La'yeq at the Village of Rek-woi, 1910

CHAPTER 1
Ancestral Home

▲▲

2002

The spirits were moving through the universe alone.

The Creator met with the spirits, who said, "We are lonely."

The Creator said, "I will make a place for you to be together where you will have all you need."

First, the Creator started with the dirt, mixing in oxygen, air, and water to render the core of the earth. Next, to shape the landscape, the Creator filled the lower elevations with water, forming the Klamath River and the Pacific Ocean. Together, the River and the ocean dug through the soil, eddying in deep pools to soften the newly formed land. The Creator then made plants, animals, and humans, my ancestors.

This is the creation story of my Nation, the Yurok, our aboriginal territory, and my home village of Rek-woi, at the mouth of the Klamath River in what is now known as Northern California. Our aboriginal territory spreads from the rugged Pacific Ocean in Northern California up the mighty lower Klamath River and into the High Country, our sacred spiritual lands in the first coastal range of the Klamath Mountains. This is our world. It is everything.

It has everything that anyone or any creature could ever need to survive, just as the Creator promised. This extraordinary area of the world includes redwoods — the largest trees on the planet — rare freshwater lagoons, wild Pacific Ocean coastline, and the fierce Klamath River, the lifeblood of my Nation. The Yurok word for the Klamath River is Heyl-keek 'We-roy, which means the "River that comes from the mountains," named such for its geographic origins. These powerful ecosystems support many life-forms. In the River, the third-largest coho and chinook salmon runs in the continental United States, including a spring and fall chinook run and a fall coho run. Historic runs of green and white sturgeon, steelhead, trout, eels, candlefish. Along the coastline, mussels, seaweed, abalone, whales, seals, birds, crabs, and much more sea life. On land, iconic elk herds, deer, bear, cougars, and smaller animals, and acorns and all types of plants. This area is one of the most biodiverse places on the planet.

While we respect and treasure all, salmon has always been our primary food source. The Yurok word for salmon is *nepuy,* which translates to "that which is eaten."

The Creator told my ancestors, the Yurok people, that all of this was made for them. They would never want for anything if they lived in balance with this world as part of nature and by never taking more than they needed to survive.

You live this way, the Creator said, and you will thrive here forever. You will never want for anything. You'll know you are doing good because I will reward you with resources to support yourselves. Use these gifts as a guide.

The Yurok people agreed.

In doing so, we formed our first binding obligation, the first covenant between the Creator and the Yurok people. This was a reciprocal relationship with the Creator, the natural world, and the Yurok people to maintain balance in the world by living symbiotically together. We each had duties and responsibilities to uphold. The Creator bestowed on the Yurok people the inherent sovereignty to regulate the core components of society within Yurok Country to fulfill our duty to the Creator. It charged us with inherent responsibilities to steward the land, water, and Yurok's other natural resources to ensure their regeneration each year. In return, we have the great privilege of being the beneficiaries of the natural abundance of the lower Klamath Basin. The Creator would continue to care for us by providing an abundance of first foods — seafood, salmon, game, wild vegetables, nuts, and berries in the natural world. This reciprocal relationship is so sacred to us that our stories teach that if the Klamath salmon and the Klamath River die, so will the Yurok people, because there will be no purpose for the Yurok on earth.

The Nation regulated the use of natural resources through complex aboriginal law, religion, and hunting, gathering, and fishing customs and practices to enforce the first covenant. Aboriginal law restricted when and how a person could fish. It was prohibited to take salmon before the first salmon ceremony, which opened the new year's fishing season with a large gathering, ritual protocols, and a feast. Once fishing began, restrictions ensured that no one took more than was needed, allowing some fish to be caught upriver, and others to spawn. Fishing holes were owned by families that had the power to exclude, use, and regulate fishing. Rules were enforced through a payment system for violations. This system had worked for generations.

Since time immemorial, my ancestors have lived on the lower Klamath River. We continue to enjoy a subsistence lifestyle of fishing, gathering, and hunting. We are a dance family with responsibilities to host annual world renewal ceremonies, brush dances for sick children, and other ceremonies in our village. We still honor our covenantal duty to protect the River, Yurok Country, and every living thing there. Over time, complex and restorative laws, practices, traditions, and ceremonies that showed thanks for being in this place were perfected to ensure we exercised our sovereignty to advance our obligations to the Creator.

When I moved home for a summer internship in June 2002 with the Yurok Tribal Fisheries Department, my family had told me about the creation story and the first covenant, but I didn't know them well and didn't understand fully their meaning. My formal education hadn't acknowledged that Indigenous peoples still existed in the United States, and instead perpetuated myths that Indigenous peoples only existed in the seventeenth century. I did not know how the first covenant between my family and the Creator — and my corresponding responsibility to protect Yurok Country — would direct my life, like a gravitational pull as strong as the moon on the tides, propelling me on a journey, blasting through iron gates, pandemics, water wars, and a lot of fish blood.

I was twenty-two. I accepted the Yurok fisheries internship because I had always loved and felt a calling to Rek-woi, the River, salmon, and Yurok. My mother and father went to great lengths to teach me and their other four children about Yurok customs, religion, and values, taking us fishing on the Klamath River even before we could walk, attending tribal ceremonies and tribal government meetings, and spending time on the reservation. My family maintained two landholdings on the reservation: the family home in Rek-woi at the mouth of the River and the homeplace, next to Brooks Riffle up the River about twelve River miles from Rek-woi. We have always lived in these places.

Despite being raised in Yurok culture, my family was relearning how to live a Yurok way of life again after being subject to two centuries of genocide, assimilation, and oppression by the US government during colonization. Yurok aboriginal law was once about the respect we had for each other and our environment, the songs we sang, the ceremonies we kept, and the balance we maintained between humans and the more-than-human world. But in the eyes of the colonizer, we were not stewards — we were less than human, savages and criminals. The very traits that anchored us to our place — our language, our ceremonies, our fishing way of life, our presence on ancestral land and water — became grounds for execution, surveillance, suspicion, and control. US law, which promises equality, was turned against us. We were policed not for what we did, but for who we were.

I call this what it is: the criminialization of culture and the weaponization of law. It is a form of racialized state violence, where the machinery of justice is bent to mark certain peoples as threats — simply for practicing their ways, defending their lands, or refusing to disappear. When law enforcement harasses Indigenous people for gathering medicine, fishing for subsistence, or standing on their own land and water, it is not about safety. It is about power. It is about erasure.

My family had shed blood, sweat, and tears to exist and uphold its duty to the Creator to protect Yurok Country and the Yurok people through colonization. When I was born, in 1980, the wounds of their fight were still healing, and the reservation was still a dangerous place, plagued with widespread poverty in the aftermath of the war against the US government. My parents — my Yurok father and my nonnative mother — chose to raise their family in Ashland, Oregon, because of its relative proximity to the reservation, only a short drive away. They desired the stability of white communities outside the reservation, like a good education and recreational activities in a safe town with access to food, electricity, and jobs. My parents wanted me, along with my brother and three sisters, to benefit from a stable home life and good education, while also experiencing the best parts of the reservation — my extended family, the ceremonies, fishing, the River, sacred sites, and the people. They hoped we would stay clear of the lingering effects of colonization, like poverty, crime, pervasive substance abuse, and persistent sexual abuse, or, worse, being stolen by an organized crime unit, like the cartel or the Mafia, and sold into human trafficking (the Yurok Reservation has one of the highest rates of missing and murdered Indigenous women in the country). Growing up, I recall my grandmother telling me to stay close "or you'll get stolen."

Colonization deprived us of the means to provide for our families and live a Yurok way of life. The Yurok people's ability to exercise our duties to the Creator was made more difficult because most of our land, water, and access to natural resources had been taken by the colonizers. It was replaced by a type of poverty — no land, water, or animals — we had never known during our history on earth.

My family was trying to learn to live again, raising our young in a colonized world that offered conspicuous consumption and creature comforts, some of which we could afford, like boxed cereals and cable TV. When I grew up during the eighties and nineties, I was taught to believe that the American dream applied even to me, a Yurok girl whose family had been the target of the federal and state governments' genocidal policies toward Indigenous peoples for the last three hundred years.

I learned our family history through oral histories told by my grandma and other relatives, but I hadn't lived through the very traumatic struggles of previous generations of my family. While I would later understand that I have always carried ancestral anger, I have, for the most part, lived with radical joy because I am an Indigenous person. Later in life, I came to appreciate that my ancestors had mastered living in balance with the natural world and survived genocide at the hands of the strongest government in history. This realization empowered me because I carry ancestral knowledge about how people and the planet can live sustainably. I felt lucky to have this life to share that knowledge. I was unapologetically proud to be Indigenous and wanted to learn as much about my culture as possible.

I wanted to live it. The internship as a fisheries technician, counting and recording the Yurok salmon harvest, gave me the opportunity to learn more about Yurok and the tribal government, to explore the reservation, and to fish.

A week before my internship started, I moved into my family home, tended by my grandmother Lavina, located in the village of Rek-woi, which means "the end of the River" in Yurok. The village sits on a sloping hillside that overlooks the Klamath River, the Pacific Ocean, and O'-rey-gos, a once lonely spirit turned into a rock at the time of creation who cares for the area. The family house sits on a rare flat spot in the middle of the village from which you can see the full glory of the Klamath estuary and mouth. The Klamath River makes a 263-mile journey from its headwaters in Southern Oregon to its mouth at Rek-woi at the Pacific Ocean. The headwaters of the River originate in an arid desert in Southern Oregon and flow through the Cascade mountain range. As it enters California, the River runs through a canyon in the Siskiyou Mountains, with thick coniferous forest in the mid-Klamath that gives way to redwoods on the lower Klamath. The River opens up in the last few miles, stretching the land wide to allow the water to lay flat and big. A sandy beach divides the River from the ocean, broken only at the mouth of the River in a powerful exchange of River and ocean. The energy of the two meeting in one place below my ancestral home is unparalleled. This is big water.

I chose a bedroom upstairs that took full advantage of the view from the house's position on Rek-woi Hill with an unimpaired view of the Klamath estuary and mouth, O'-rey-gos, and the Pacific Ocean. From my bedroom window, I could see more water than land and I could hear the rhythmic sound of the waves pounding the sandbar just below the house in the estuary, its constant roar keeping time for the sun passing overhead. I felt like I was standing on the deck of a gigantic boat, stretched out over a wet blue expanse, like I could float away in the current and drift west miles away, to salmon's home at the farthest edge of the earth.

I was very excited to move in with my grandma Lavina. She kept the home like a family museum, which she curated like a disgruntled archivist. In her mid-sixties, Lavina still had the charm and energy of her youth. She looked like Elizabeth Taylor, strikingly beautiful, with pleasant natural features highlighted by her signature maroon lipstick, big black hair, and petite figure. Later in life, she told me had she known she was beautiful, she would have moved to New York City. Instead, she spent most of her life in Rek-woi, after a few decades in Oregon and Canada while in an abusive marriage to an air force senior master sergeant with whom she had five children. She left him and returned to Rek-woi in the late 1970s. Despite the abuse, she remained witty, funny, smart, energetic, and loving. The entire family loved her with unconditional devotion, loyalty, and joy. She was the ultimate matriarch. I felt lucky to spend the summer with her in her court.

The house was the ultimate shelter, stewarded by my ancestors and made safe for me and my family by the Creator. Under Grandma's care, the house had a way of giving us what we needed, physically and spiritually. I never knew if the house had an agenda it advanced through making things happen just so, or if the Creator moved through the house, guiding destinies, or if it was our ancestors making sure we found whatever it was we needed. Lost things had a way of finding us there. Lost pets, misplaced earrings, old books and letters, and ex-boyfriends and ex-girlfriends — they all seemed to show up at the house. Sleep there provided answers to questions, and mornings offered new beginnings in which all that was lost, was found.

My third-great-grandfather Billy Brooks built the house in 1911 next to the House of La'yeq, our family's ancestral home, a traditional Yurok redwood plank house that had been occupied by sempiternal generations of my family. The new house was one of the first modern stick-built houses in Rek-woi. My great-grandmother Geneva, who was raised by her grandparents Billy and Susie Brooks in the House of La'yeq, recalled with wonder how the boards of the house arrived in a cart pulled by horse and buggy. She had never seen trees cut up that way. The "new house," as we still call it, is more than one hundred years old.

Over the decades, the new house had become the physical headquarters of the family, home to all of us and open to family members when they needed a place to stay. Before my great-grandmother Geneva passed away, she bestowed the house on my grandmother Lavina on the condition that, if other family members needed a home, they'd be allowed to stay there. I suppose that's part of how I ended up staying there for the summer. Grandma honored that it was important to her mother, Geneva, that everyone always had a home because the Yurok people of her generation had lost everything: family homes, inherent rights to land, water, and fish, and the ability to self-govern. With a simple stroke of a pen in Washington, DC, entire Yurok family legacies had been wiped out in congressional acts they'd never even know about until white men wearing wrinkled suits, hats, and holsters came to tell the Yurok people that everything they had owned now belonged to the colonizers.

To teach children how to be Indians, our elders like to joke, you have to teach them to be outlaws by breaking the white man's laws to continue our way of life. This was certainly true for my family. We had always fought these men. Our strategy had been to resist regardless of their rules and regulations simply by staying on the land they said wasn't ours and continuing to fish on the same waters they said we couldn't. Indeed, some anthropologists claimed Yurok was the most resistant to "white law" of any tribal society in the world. Perhaps that is why those waters continue to surround us to this day: deep running water, crashing waves, dew and mist and fog, the Pacific, and the River and its estuary and mouth. The mighty Klamath.

Overlooking this water is its protector, O'-rey-gos, the formless spirit who at the time of creation wanted to be immortal.

> The Creator granted this wish on the condition O'-rey-gos protect the mouth of the River, its fish, and its people. She would be responsible for telling the salmon when to enter the Klamath River from the Pacific Ocean. O'-rey-gos agreed, and the Creator transformed her into a rock, formed in the distinct shape of a mother carrying a baby basket on her back. Twice a year when the land brightens with colors from spring flowers and fall leaves — like confetti at a welcoming party — the salmon gather in the ocean at the entrance of the mouth of the Klamath River. They wait for O'-rey-gos's signal to enter.
>
> From her vantage point, high on the hillside next to Rek-woi, she looks up the River to observe conditions. O'-rey-gos waits for the rain to swell the waters enough to enable the salmon to return to spawning grounds safely and warns them about dangerous places along the way where debris, bears, or silt might harm them or their eggs. She calls in the fog to roll up the River, covering the salmon like a blanket, protecting them from these perils. Only when conditions are right does O'-rey-gos give her signal, and the salmon begin their freshwater journey.

To this day, O'-rey-gos sits on the north side of the mouth of the River, overlooking Rek-woi, the Pacific Ocean, and the Klamath River estuary. The new house sits perpendicular to O'-rey-gos, just about five hundred feet upriver. From the house, we have watched countless annual migrations of salmon guided by O'-rey-gos's careful eye. She has served her people and her River well. Following her lead and Yurok stewardship, the Klamath River was home to the third-largest salmon population in the lower continental United States and several other keystone species.

We are a historic Yurok fishing and dance family. Specific Yurok families, including mine, are dance families with responsibilities to host religious ceremonies to maintain balance and care for the ancient and powerful fire, medicine, and rituals associated with the dances. These families are the leadership class. We followed the first covenant and have been rewarded by the Creator with resources to live well. We have tried to exercise our duty to the Creator to protect our homelands throughout time, but still, colonizers invaded our lands and waters. When Russian traders, traveling by oceangoing boat, breached the Klamath River mouth in the 1700s and attempted to debark at Rek-woi, we made them stay on their boat. We refused to trade with them because their bodies were covered with hair and white bugs that crawled in and out of their beards and body hair. Eventually, they left.

One hundred years later, European white settlers ripped the fog blanket that had protected the coast of Yurok Country, keen to extract the salmon, redwood trees, and gold of the Yurok people. We believed they would leave too. But instead, more and more came, greedy for profit. To secure their fortunes, they launched murderous raids throughout Yurok Country, killing Yurok people and plundering our land and resources. War ensued.

The federal government sent a treaty-making delegation to negotiate a peace treaty with my ancestors. My third-great-grandmother Mar-kaw-shu-wa (Nellie Ruben) and third-great-auntie Eliza Steve were toddlers, and our relatives, Sa-Sa-Mich and Wa-Pa-Shaw, signed a treaty with the US government in 1851. The treaty would have secured our land, water, resources, fishing rights, and inherent sovereignty within our refined territory, that included not all but some of our original territory.

The treaty called for a reservation spanning Yurok coastal villages from the Lost River mouth to False Klamath Cove, the lower Klamath River, prairies, and a section of the High Country in the Klamath Mountains, which are a part of the Siskiyou Mountain Range. It would have preserved our way of life, fishing the coast and River, hunting and gathering on the prairies, and praying in the High Country. The federal agents stated the treaty would stop the white people from raiding the Yurok villages and killing Yurok people. The US government made us sign papers, making a mark called a signature, a foreign concept in my culture as we didn't have a written language and agreements were verbal. We believed our homelands and ourselves were safe.

But the state of California viciously opposed the treaty. California was engaged in state-endorsed genocide, enacting laws that paid white settlers a bounty for Indian scalps and sold Indian children into forced labor. A treaty preserving Indian rights and land was contrary to the state's agenda. As a result, the treaty was never ratified. Instead, it was hidden in a locked vault somewhere deep inside the bowels of the US government in Washington, DC, not to be seen for another hundred years.

We remained under attack.

Finally, between 1855 and 1891, the president of the United States took action, signing a series of executive orders to create the Yurok Reservation, its boundaries one mile on each side of the River, from the mouth at the Pacific Ocean to forty-five miles upriver to just past the confluence of the Trinity River. To comply with a federal act that prohibited more than four Indian reservations in California, the Lower Klamath Reservation was merged with the neighboring Hoopa Reservation for administrative purposes but still referred to as the Yurok Reservation or Lower Klamath Reservation. The reservation did not include the coastal villages, the prairies, or the High Country. We lost so much without any say or knowledge. We were never consulted or even told of the executive orders.

Sadly, my Nation lost more than we won. In 1892, Congress applied the General Allotment Act of 1887 to the Yurok Reservation, which opened the reservation to non-Indians through public sale of land and allowed only small allotments to Indian families. Most of the land within the Yurok Reservation was lost to timber companies. By the time I had moved home that summer in 2002, the federal government, timber companies, and squatters had stolen 99.72 percent of our aboriginal territory.

Sitting on Grandma's couch in Rek-woi, in the less than 0.28 percent of our territory we controlled, I snuggled next to her. "Grandma, how long have you lived here?"

"Well, you know, I lived up at the homeplace at Brooks Riffle when I was a girl. It's about twelve River miles from Rek-woi." She explained that the riffle was named after my third-great-grandfather Billy Brooks because his family had stewarded it pre-colonization. The family had held on to the land through colonization, built a cabin, cleared some land for a garden and farm animals, and fished the riffle.

"I have lived here in this house at Rek-woi since the 1970s," she continued, "but the family has been here since the beginning of time living in the House of La'yeq. We have never left. You know, we are lucky because we kept our Rek-woi house, land and fishing hole in the mouth of the River, and the homeplace up at Brooks Riffle after the white people came. This has never left our family, but we had to fight for it." She looked over at me, paused, and her expression changed; she smiled. "I am glad you are here to fish. It's great the Nation gave you a job. I know you love the River. We will have fun together," she said.

I smiled at her. "I can't wait to go fish. I figure I can work my shift on the River and then go fishing."

I did not know how much each generation of my family had done to stave off genocide, assimilation, and oppression. Nor how recently they had fought these forces to simply continue our way of life in our homeland. Just a few years before I was born, my Uncle Ray's Supreme Court case challenging the state of California's authority to prohibit Yurok fishing was resolved, and the Salmon Wars over the federal government's authority to prohibit Yurok fishing ended. The racist campaigns to extinguish our rights — "can an Indian, save a fish" — had quieted. The family had fought for centuries for Grandmother and me to sit on her couch at Rek-woi and make plans to go fishing.

《《《

Two hundred and sixty-three River miles upriver from Grandma's house in Rek-woi, in an arid desert, the headwaters of the Klamath River in south Oregon flowed into Upper Klamath Lake and out into the main stem of the Klamath River, connecting into one comprehensive ecosystem as the mighty Klamath Basin, more than twelve thousand square miles of Southern Oregon and Northern California. Its name was derived from the Chinook language, a commonly used Indian jargon in the area. "Tlamatl" means "swiftness" and translates to English as "Klamath."

At the top of the basin, following the headwaters of the Klamath, was the chemical runoff from 230,000 acres of agricultural land included in the Klamath Reclamation Project. Authorized by Congress in 1905, the Klamath Reclamation Project converted the Upper Klamath Basin ecosystem into agricultural land by draining lakes and wetlands and rerouting the River. This destroyed critical ecological functions that set a trajectory toward the basin's demise in the twentieth and twenty-first centuries.

Further, the land was the aboriginal territory of the Klamath,

Modoc, and Yahooskin people, known now as the Klamath Nations, who once lived comfortably on the area's abundant natural resources until they were subject to murderous raids and the land was violently taken by the US government in the largest Indian war in the area in the late 1800s.

A treaty secured a landholding for the Klamath Nations. With the Indians removed from the land, Congress quickly authorized the Klamath Reclamation Project, auctioning off the tribal land to white farmers, along with contractual water rights to irrigate the land. The federal government tasked the Bureau of Reclamation with the administration of the water contracts and the Klamath Reclamation Project.

In the mid-Klamath, the lands of the Shasta and Karuk people were also violently taken without compensation. Here, there was no treaty or Indian reservation. Instead, the Indians were slaughtered. My fifth-great-grandmother was killed attempting to cross the Klamath River by Orleans, while fleeing a murderous raid by colonizers. Many others fell to the same fate.

After the Indigenous peoples were slaughtered, private companies seized economic opportunity. Between 1911 and 1964, in this area, four dams were built in the mid-Klamath without fish passage. Behind the dams were reservoirs that converted the River channel into more than two thousand acres of reservoir. Built without fish ladders, the dams blocked salmon and other anadromous species' access to more than 450 miles of spawning habitat, blocked cold-water springs from cooling water downriver, and prevented sediment from naturally flowing.

This violent, relatively short period was one of the most destructive for both humans and the ecosystem. The first peoples and the ecosystem of the Upper Klamath Basin had been colonized.

In the early summer of 2002, the legacy impacts of colonization were at a breaking point. There was a drought. There wasn't enough water for farmers and fish. Making matters worse, when I returned home, the chemical runoff from the Klamath Reclamation Project up-river flowed downriver and pooled in the reservoirs behind the four Klamath dams. The water and chemicals mixed and caused a massive toxic algae bloom, turning the water a nuclear bright green that leached into the waters of the Klamath main stem from the Iron Gate Dam spillway, the same waters the Creator told my family to protect.

Downriver, in the middle Klamath River, the weather was hot and the late-summer drought was starting to take its toll. Water levels were lower than ever. The riverbed was visible, which made traveling by boat treacherous, and the chinook salmon, almost en route to spawning waters, would struggle in the shallows and be exposed to the same warm waters polluted with the toxic blue-green algae bloom exploding behind the dams.

Yet, at the mouth of the River, just below my grandmother's house, the estuary showed no signs of distress. One of the largest runs of fall chinook salmon the Klamath had welcomed home in years was about to enter the estuary. O'-rey-gos eagerly waited for the right conditions to give them the signal to start their journey home. There, water raged, pushing and pulling between the River and the Pacific Ocean in a steady current of prosperous promise and stability. At least that's what the view from the bay window next to Grandma's couch looked like to me.

CHAPTER 2
Blood Memory

2002

I was born loving the Klamath River, fishing, and my home village of Rek-woi. My family tells a story about when I was two years old, and my parents and I visited my great-grandparents Emery and Geneva and my grandma Lavina at the family house in Rek-woi. It was time to leave but I wanted to stay. I hid, convinced that if my parents couldn't find me, they would leave me behind. The family started a search and the first place they looked was by the River. Eventually, they found me hiding in a closet in the house. I cried when they put me in the car and we drove away, leaving the River and village behind. Since then, my family and I have fished the Klamath more times than I can count.

Commonly our family fishing trips would start with a call from a family member in Rek-woi. My dad would take the call. I'd overhear the conversation, and before he placed the phone back in its cradle, I'd ask him, "Can I go fishing with you?"

"Sure, love." My dad has always been a good, kind father. He didn't mind that the salmon were half my size and weight, and taking me meant extra work. I looked forward to these trips like nothing else.

In the 1980s fishing trips with my dad had a standard protocol. We would go to the Klamath River to salmon fish at Rek-woi or Brooks Riffle, where my family had fished since the beginning of time, hoping to catch enough to fill the smokehouse and freezer. We took minimal gear: two tarps, a gill net, two anchors, and my dad's favorite fish-cleaning knife. His initials, "W.D.B.," were etched on the sharp four-inch blade. My dad would direct me to get my jacket, jeans, and sleeping bag (we didn't fish with waders or rain gear then). My mother would help, as she knew how much I loved going fishing with my dad. We would drive to Rek-woi in his orange-and-white Chevy truck.

Turning onto the road to Grandma's house felt like crossing a metaphorical gate to the old village site. The road starts about five hundred yards above the River, rolling steeply, switchbacking down the hillside for about a mile to Grandma's house. The view from the top of the road is breathtaking. Adding to the beauty, alder and spruce trees, various ferns and grasses, and blackberry bushes outnumber people one hundred to one. The birds were gloriously abundant — hawks, eagles, vultures, wrens, hummingbirds, seagulls, and many more. On most occasions, the sky would be slightly cloudy and fog would roll in from the Pacific Ocean, but there was always a sliver of sun highlighting the hillside.

We would park at Grandma's house to visit and pick up the motorboat we stored at her house. Often, my great-uncle Ray (Grandmother's brother) would be there and we'd ask him where he thought the salmon might be. It was customary for him to track the salmon by observing the estuary and the River through binoculars, searching for activity.

"See anything?" my dad would ask.

If the salmon were in the River, they would often pool and rest in the deep holes in the estuary and could be seen moving from one hole to the next. But if they weren't spotted, it was likely they would be upriver. Ray, an authority on Klamath salmon, would provide his report and we would fish where he said the salmon would be, most commonly at Brooks Riffle.

Dad and I would pack the boat, launch at the Requa boat ramp about a quarter mile upriver from Rek-woi, and head to Brooks Riffle. While Dad drove, I would watch for fog. Yuroks believe that fog is a blanket the salmon wear to protect themselves from predators as they travel upriver. When there is fog on the River, there is often salmon.

The homeplace and Brooks Riffle were twelve River miles up from Rek-woi. As we arrived, Dad would often say, "We made it, Famous," using my nickname. There was a sandbar we liked to camp at, in front of which the River narrowed and ran straight for about three hundred yards. Then it narrowed further, shallowed, and dropped in elevation, creating a riffle, named after my third-great-grandfather Billy Brooks. Many birds, including seagulls, blue herons, hawks, crows, and eagles, often flew down the channel. The tree line cascaded down from the mountains, the High Country as we called it, toward the River bar. Large fir, alder, oak, and young redwood trees grew.

To set up camp, we would spread out our sleeping bags and tarps next to a fire pit. Dad never took a tent fishing. We'd sleep under the stars next to the fire. We would comb the River bar for firewood. I remember being taken by the wildness of this place and recall an exchange we had one time: "Dad, I see some bear poo over here," I said, noting a large pile of scat not far from our camp.

"Don't worry," he said. "We will keep the fire going all night. That will let the bears know we are here."

There are always more bears than people here. Dad was used to being a human in this wilderness.

Next, we would set the gill net just above Brooks Riffle across from our camp, where the fish tended to pool in an eddy. I would watch my dad expertly set the gill net. A long time ago, Yurok made our nets from iris plants. Today, we use synthetic materials, but the method of fishing is unchanged. Gill nets range in size depending upon the type of fishing and are commonly twenty-five to one hundred feet long and about twelve to forty meshes deep, with six- to eight-inch squares made of nylon. The top of the gill net is secured to a cork line, which is a rope with floating white Styrofoam cubes attached about three to four feet apart, and the bottom of the gill net is secured to a lead line, a heavy rope that pulls the net toward the bottom of the River. Salmon get stuck in a gill net when they swim into the square net holes. When a fish hits the net, its gills can get lodged in the gill net squares or its body can get wrapped in the gill net, pulling the cork line and the corks into the water, alerting the fisherwoman to a potential catch.

With the gill net set, we would wait for the salmon.

Dad was born to fish. Our ancestors had fished the very same way for these same wild salmon on this exact riffle. Dad explained that the salmon and Yurok people evolved together, and by now we shared the same DNA. He had prayed, sacrificed, and worked hard, and the Creator had rewarded him with the skills he needed to support our family with fish. He once told me the most satisfying thing he could do was bring a load of salmon home to his family.

"Keep an ear out," Dad would say. "Sometimes you can hear the fish hit the net."

"What does it sound like?" I would ask.

"Like someone got in a fight with the water, lots of splashing," he replied.

We would settle into the night around the campfire. Dad had taught me to wrap the tarp around my whole body to stay dry during the night. I liked to snuggle into the sand, moving my hips and shoulders just so the sand would support my body. I would sleep well on the River bar, and my biggest concern was not the bears, but sleeping through an opportunity to check the gill net in the middle of the night.

"Will you wake me up when you check the net?" I would ask.

"We will see," said Dad.

Usually, I would wake up with the first light of the sun, having missed the night's fishing. My father would usually be awake, too, and we'd check the gill net.

The River at sunrise is remarkable. The sunlight begins to peek over the eastern ridge of the River's channel, backlighting the evergreen trees on the ridge top, giving the River a glowing crown. Yet, the dark of night still lingers in the high sky. Often the sun and the moon are still visible in the east and west. The light and dark mixing creates something new my ancestors understood well. One time, Dad shared, "The sun and moon are lovers. This time of day when the moon and sun are in the sky, they are together and happy. Their love produces a new day, a present. That's why today is called the *present*. We always must be thankful for the present day." I learned much more than how to fish on these mornings with my dad, the two of us on the boat and the only people in sight.

"Famous, grab the oars," Dad would say, calling me by my nickname, as he pulled the cork line of the gill net from the water, grabbed the fishing net, and started pulling it from the water. He would coach, "Keep the boat close to the net and row in the direction your fishing partner is pulling the net. Stay in tune with your partner." Dad had taught me to row by keeping both oars even with the water, then gently, but with force, barely tapping the surface of the water and moving the oars simultaneously. This took a while to master and I remember frequently struggling with the oars and the position of the boat. I recall my dad working the gill net quickly and methodically. When he spotted a salmon in the gill net, his motions were rhythmic as he worked to free it, unwrapping it from the net, still thrashing, water dripping off the salmon while it gasped for air, and pulling it out of the gill net. I watched closely.

He made it look so easy. He would let me try, but the gill net would become more tangled or I couldn't figure out how to free the salmon from the net. This was difficult work he did masterfully.

Noticing my awe, he would reassure me that he'd been salmon fishing his entire life and that someday I would do it as well as him.

"I hope so, Dad," I would say as I watched him pull another salmon into the boat and look up at me with a smile. I would smile back. Fishing was in our blood memory.

《《《

My early experiences on the River served me well during my internship. I had an understanding of the River and a big love for it that grew over the summer of 2002. I worked day and night shifts. When I worked the night shift, I would patrol the River, driving up and down the estuary in a boat with my work partner. Sometimes, when it was slow, calm, and clear, we'd park the boat in the middle of the estuary and look up at the stars. Each night, I watched the Little Dipper move a little bit farther northeast, following the earth's rotation. It was comforting and reassuring that the Big Dipper was always there, every night, above my head. Following the sky, it curved into the ridgeline above Rek-woi. Even after the passage of time, Rek-woi at night looked the same as it always had: no big buildings or housing developments, and just a few lights that looked like campfires from the water below the village.

I often thought of how my ancestors had observed this same view from this very spot. Perhaps in a redwood canoe on a calm, warm night, they, too, paused to notice the Big Dipper and the village below it. It filled me with wonder that transcended time, placing me back to when it was just my ancestors in this place. Did we see the same thing? The sky and village's steady presence made me feel the world was safe and sound. What luck I had to be from a family that was always here in this place, breathtakingly beautiful, abundant, powerful land and water.

The most authentic family legacy is to care for one another and your homeplace so that both improve with each generation. I believed my family had improved ourselves, the River, and the land around me. The informative nights and days spent on the River that summer and during my upbringing made me proud to be Yurok. I was from the dirt and water of this very place. My role was to protect and enjoy it.

I did my best to do both that summer. The Yurok commercial fishery had opened in August and was in full swing. A large chinook run of salmon was expected to return to the River. The fishery had always been strong, healthy, and plentiful. We could rely on it. Even when they said it wasn't ours, we could still count on there being fish in the River, and even in recent years when the runs started to diminish, there were still enough fish for subsistence needs. It had always been that way, since the Creator had made it for us.

The Nation had secured a few commercial fish buyers who had set up buying stations on the Requa Dock. Several Yurok families had returned in August to the estuary to take part, setting up fish camps through the estuary on the River bar or the RV park at the dock. The Requa Dock, at the north side of the Klamath estuary, was the port of the tribal fishery, including a parking lot, boat launch, and dock that had been built into the side of the River bar. It became a pop-up city, a myriad of buzzing activity. Boats and trucks pulling in and out. People schlepping fishing gear from truck to boat and back. Large nylon gill nets were everywhere, in car trunks and fish totes, hanging from fences and boats. Anchors tied to long, thick ropes scattered the dock. Food trucks, tribal fishery modules, a large mass-producing ice machine, and RVs lined the edges of the dock. Individual family fish camps lined the banks of the estuary, small tents, sleeping bags, fire pits, fish totes, and gill nets. The estuary was plumb full of boats, nets, and people. People were fishing hard as the buyers were paying top dollar.

The Klamath River salmon harvest was heavily regulated by a consortium of federal, state, and tribal governments called the Pacific Fishery Management Council, which worked in collaboration to set a sustainable harvest allocation and then divide that amount. Fifty percent to the Indian fishery and 50 percent to the offshore commercial fishermen, ocean sport and river sport. The Yurok Nation regulated its harvest, setting limitations on hours that could be fished, fishing locations, and more to ensure a sustainable harvest.

My job was to count how many fish were caught each day to keep a tally of the Yurok harvest, to ensure the Nation did not exceed our allocation of salmon, to prevent overfishing. I went from fish camp to fish camp by boat, or in congested areas by foot along the River bar, with a boxed clipboard to collect scale samples for data regarding type of fish, age, and origin. The Yurok Tribal Fisheries Department used the information to manage the fishery. Salmon scales are like tree rings that can be analyzed to determine the fish's age and origin. The samples were taken back to a lab in the Yurok Tribal Fisheries Department office for analysis.

When I wasn't working, I usually just stayed on the River to commercial or subsistence fish. I'd salmon fish with a gill net with a sibling, cousin, auntie, or uncle, or if I was feeling brave, by myself. Either that or I would visit with family, happy to listen to their stories and content to monitor the estuary from my grandmother's couch or her front lawn. When the salmon were running, the house served as a de facto command center, its inhabitants multiplying with fishermen and fisherwomen who expertly scouted the fish from the good vantage point overlooking the estuary. The most experienced family members knew the "big holes" in the estuary where the water was deep and cool enough for the salmon to rest. They could spot the fish from Grandma's window, based solely on how the water flowed through the estuary. They could smell the fish in the air, too, a deep, murky musk, with a twist of moss and seaweed and fish slime. The smell, which moved from the water up the hillside and through Grandma's front door, made us all a little goofy, triggering some instinctual desire to catch those fish.

One midmorning in August during the commercial fishery, through binoculars, I watched the salmon roll in. I saw so many I couldn't sit still. I had to go fishing. This could be my chance to catch enough salmon to pay my rent through the school year or fill the smokehouse with salmon to can for the year to come. I was raised fishing and listening to my family's legendary fishing stories of catching hundreds of salmon, experiencing them from a child's perspective. I had caught enough fish growing up that I would dream of catching salmon, reveling in the thrill of watching the net bob up and down full of fish, the adrenaline of pulling a salmon from the depths of the water, not knowing if a seal was chasing it or if it was going to thrash and fight in the net while you battled the beast.

Salmon can migrate quickly upriver if conditions are right, or they can find a cool patch of water to stay put and rest. This meant if I wanted to catch the fish I observed from Grandma's house, I had to move quickly. In a rush, I packed up my 1990s blue double-cab Toyota truck, hitched the rowboat to it, and drove the short distance to the dock, blasting Madonna the whole way to pump me up for the impending adventure. I was excited and enjoying every moment of the anticipation of what would come on the River. I launched the boat and started rowing to the mouth of the River; the adrenaline from the excitement caused by the potential to catch a lot of salmon flooded my body with the strength to powerfully maneuver the boat through the estuary's swift current. I headed toward the "front line," the lowest boundary of Yurok-authorized legal fishing, two hundred or so yards east of the mouth of the River. Because incoming salmon had to cross it, the front line was the most coveted fishing spot, but it was difficult and dangerous. Only the most skilled and toughest of fishing people managed to fish the front line successfully. The ocean breakers at the mouth were loud, powerful, and sneaky, and the current moved swiftly and unpredictably there. Strong enough to pull boat and woman out to sea. On top of that, there were the seals, hunting these waters for an easy salmon dinner. If you were too slow, they'd snatch your salmon from your gill net or your hand (which had happened to me one time).

When I got to the front line, several Yurok fishing people in large jet boats were already tending their nets, carefully placed fifty feet apart from one another in compliance with Yurok law. Surveying the water, I found an open spot among all the other boats and clamor. To set my gill net I started by rowing to shore. My net was placed at the bow of my boat. I tied one end of the net to a long rope with an anchor on the other end and secured the anchor on the north side of the River bar by jamming it in the sand. I began to row backward to the middle of the River. The anchored side of the net pulled tight and began to roll out of the boat into the water like a string of pearls tied to lace bouncing gingerly on the collarbone of the water's surface. I tied the other end of the net to an anchor and threw the anchor into the water. The net was set. Almost immediately, the cork line bobbed, signaling a salmon was in the net.

To catch the salmon, I grabbed the cork line attached to the gill net. I used it to pull myself toward the location in the net where I thought the fish was stuck. Arriving there, I pulled that small section of the gill net up from the water. A salmon emerged from the depths of the dark water, bright and shiny. I took a deep breath and pulled its mass from the water into the boat. It was still alive and thrashed its head and tail as it landed on the boat's floor. Its body was wrapped and twisted in the nylon, and it desperately thrashed and flopped, fighting for its life. It weighed probably fifteen to eighteen pounds, average for the fall chinook run, and was as bright as polished chrome. Its scales sparkled against the sun, a bright rainbow of color.

I squinted my eyes in the brightness, and in my head I heard my dad's voice telling me, "Start with the head and tail." I unwrapped the net's nylon squares from the salmon's lips and gills until its head was free of the net. I quietly thanked the fish for giving its life. I held on to the net, hoping for another fish.

Bent over their own nets, the Yurok fishermen and women were busy untangling their own catch, swearing and yelling at one another to pick up the pace. They were as excited as I was and as worried as I was about losing this bounty. Their livelihood was at stake, as the commercial fishery was many people's primary income. They depended upon it to feed and clothe their children and pay their bills. My cork line moved up and down again. Another salmon. I quickly moved twenty feet down the net and ran it down until the fish appeared. This one was big, maybe thirty to thirty-five pounds. Its wide belly was fat, its nose curved over its lips, likely an elder in its class as a four-year-old salmon. It fought hard and I struggled to get it in the boat, bending my knees and using my whole body to lift this massive salmon. The effort nearly knocked me over, but I finally landed the huge salmon on the floor of the boat with a loud thud.

"Dang, Ames, that salmon is bigger than you," the fisherman next to me called out.

I chuckled but didn't stop or look up. I barely heard him. I was consumed with the task of beating this monstrous beast and getting the other three salmon I had seen in the net into my boat. It was urgent business. I'd have to untangle this salmon before pulling in the rest. The fish could escape the net and I'd have to beat the seals, which I knew were already after my fish.

I made fast work of dislodging the big salmon from the net. Four nylon squares of net were caught in its mouth. I pulled two fingers below the nylon line stuck on its head, which opened its mouth and exposed a jagged row of teeth full of fishing line. I yanked out the line, and the fish spasmed. I gave it another yank, and its body rolled out of the gill net. Then I pulled up the next three salmon. Then another four. Then another five. It was exhilarating. As I pulled in one salmon after another, my muscles were alive, pumping and screaming. I felt at one with the River and in harmony with the natural world, just as the Creator wanted. I was the River. I was the natural world.

This is who you are, I thought. *This is how it's supposed to be.*

Before it was all done, I had caught more than forty salmon in less than half an hour. My hands ached, and my knees and forearms were surely bruised from leaning against the side of the boat. None of this mattered because I was catching salmon. Navigating the rowboat's position to the net and the fish was normally the work of two people. If I could manage a fish run by myself, I remember thinking, there wasn't much in the world I couldn't do.

Once the tide came in, the fishing slowed down because the salmon tended to move with the tides and rest when the tides settled. I rowed to the shore and started cleaning my catch. I sold most to the salmon buyer at the dock and took one home to Grandma.

"How did you do?" she asked.

"I did all right," I said, intentionally being vague because a fisherwoman never tells how many fish she catches so as to not be boastful or disclose a good fishing hole and lose it to another fishing person.

"Don't you try that with me," Grandma said with a grin, shaking her finger at me. She was a fisherwoman too. "How many did you catch?"

"Forty or so!" I blurted out and jumped up, unable to control my excitement. "Can you believe it?"

"By yourself, at the mouth?" Her expression was full of surprise and love.

I nodded.

"Good girl! I gotta call Uncle Ray. He'll be excited." Ray, a legendary fisherman, was always interested in the family's fishing adventures.

She sat back down on the couch and picked up the phone to call Uncle. Being at Grandma's house and sharing my catch with her and others felt rewarding. I had fished these same waters with my family my whole life. I knew they had fought for the right to be here, the right to fish and live at Rek-woi. The River, that day, taught me why they had fought so hard. We had worked together as one: one system, each part playing the role the Creator intended. The River a home for fish, I a Yurok fisherwoman, and nepuy (that which we eat) salmon, caught to feed the people. All of us working together under O'-rey-gos's watchful eye.

Throughout the rest of the summer, my grandma, the house, the River, the salmon, and I all seemed to move together as one. As a fishing family.

Unbeknownst to us, 193 miles up the River, a PacifiCorp employee adjusted a lever that caused the release of warm polluted water from the Iron Gate Dam reservoir, unleashing a flood of toxic blue-green algae that would begin to flow downriver toward Rek-woi.

CHAPTER 3

World Renewal Ceremonies

▲▲
▼▼

2002

Working with the Yurok Tribal Fisheries Department, I spent my days moving with the River from fish camp to fish camp, counting the salmon caught by families I've known my entire life, and collecting fish scales, which I scraped from salmon backs into a small white envelope.

One afternoon, while I was inspecting a catch next to the Requa Dock, a grizzly character walked up and stopped me. He was gillnet fishing off the Requa Dock. His gill net was about one hundred feet long and thirty to forty meshes deep, secured to one side of the dock and anchored on the other side in the River by a rope with corks on it to keep it afloat. I could see his twelve-foot rowboat on the water was metal and dented, and there was a stench coming from the boat — a combination of rusting metal, rotting wood floorboards, old fish blood, and beer cans.

"Hey, ain't you Billy's daughter?"

Ocean wind blew strands of his tangled black hair into his eyes. He wiped it away with his hand, which was still covered with specks of fish blood. I noticed his middle finger was severed clean at the top knuckle. I was nervous about talking with him because I didn't know his intentions. He was calloused and dirty, with scars on his face and deep wrinkles contouring his face and neck.

Yet I knew the people here were resilient. They were people who knew how to survive, despite the long legacy of federal and state dispossession of their resources and criminalization of their way of life. The taking of their land and water; the development of an economy based on extracting natural resources like gold and redwoods that robbed them of their cultural and natural resources and ruined their sacred sites; and racist laws that prohibited them from fishing when white commercial fishermen could. Stripped of the habitat and cultural resources necessary to sustain a Yurok way of life, people struggled to make ends meet doing what they had always done: hunt, fish, and gather. But the lack of access to land and water and declining fish, deer, and elk populations made survival almost impossible. The years of hard living showed in missing teeth, wrinkled brown skin, jagged scars, and the faded tattoos of the names of lost friends and family. They fished in the same clothes they wore into town, beat-up tennis shoes and worn-in jeans with holes in the knees, and almost everyone wore a hooded Yurok Nation sweatshirt, which was often a coveted door prize or gift at tribal events, and hand-knit beanies bearing Indian designs. Though their small River boats were pocked with leaks and snags, their gill nets were always clean and well tended. This could be managed without money.

"Yep," I said.

"You grew up."

"Something like that."

"I used to fish with your dad. Up round the bend of the River. We knocked out three hundred salmon one night. Stayed up all night, and then hauled 'em out the next mornin'. Your dad is a heck of a fisherman." My dad grew up fishing on the River before the salmon runs declined. He is a kind, reliable, respected fisherman within the Yurok Nation, and most people knew me as his daughter.

The wind continued downriver, carrying his scent of fish and cigarettes in my direction. I turned my head. We were standing in the large parking lot at the Requa Dock, the headquarters of the Nation's fishery. It was the middle of a commercial fishing season. The dock was busy, full of people, boats, and fishing gear. The River's estuary was to the west of us. It flowed wide and flat in almost a circle and then abruptly narrowed at the River mouth. We called it "the lips" affectionately.

While the estuary looked healthy, water temperatures were rising inexplicably. The tide was in, and the River was swollen with the water, almost to the high-water mark, noted by thick brush, blackberry bushes, and willow and alder trees. Light wind moved from the mouth of the River and the Pacific Ocean just five hundred yards west of the dock parking lot. We could hear the waves breaking against the beach dividing the River and the ocean. Seagulls, crows, hawks, and osprey flew overhead squawking, and the sea lions barked.

"What the heck you doing down here with a clipboard? You oughta be catching the fish, not counting them. I've seen you fish before with your dad."

I just nodded, still nervous about saying much to him.

"Hey, tell your family the people upriver are putting on a White Deer Skin Dance, one of the World Renewal Ceremonies. Your family should come."

The World Renewal Ceremonies are a series of three different dances at which people gather to eat, dance, sing, and complete rituals to give thanks to the Creator for providing for humans and to restore balance between nature, humans, and the Creator. I was too shy to ask him for more information as I knew Grandma had strong opinions about which ceremonies we attended because they were very powerful and hadn't been done for a long time. She was worried we might get hurt by bad medicine or improper rituals that could cause injury, bad luck, or death.

"Maybe," I said.

"Oh, here comes Ray Mattz. Must mean the salmon are running! You know he can tell when the fish are running; he can smell them," he said. "He doesn't waste time like other fishermen, setting in the water waiting for them to hit. He only fishes when they are here. I better get back to my gill net. If Ray's here, salmon are likely to hit. He is your uncle, right?"

"Yes." I nodded.

"Hell of a fishing family." He headed back toward his boat.

I walked toward the boat launch, where Uncle Ray was putting his jet sled into the water. It was loaded with two gill nets tied in blue tarps, a few anchors, and a turquoise-blue fish tote.

"Hi, Uncle, salmon running?"

"Hiya, baby girl," he said and gave me a hug. He was wearing his signature fishing outfit: a brown, orange, and pink knitted hat with Yurok designs, Levi's jeans, a fleece jacket, and fishing boots to his knees. "I saw a few rolling around from the house. Tide is going out now, they should be in there," he said.

"Where are they catching them?"

"I'm headed down to the lips. Give it a shot."

He turned on his boat motor and headed west toward the mouth of the River, the water kicking up behind him as he moved away from me, the sun shining directly on him like a spotlight following a famous star through the tribal fishery.

《《《

That night I thought about the World Renewal Ceremonies. Since time immemorial, Yurok people and the neighboring Nations have held biannual World Renewal Ceremonies that included the White Deerskin Dance, the Jump Dance, and the Boat Dance. In the 1900s the federal government prohibited the dances by law. They disappeared for some time but were not forgotten. The World Renewal Ceremonies' purpose was to maintain the balance between the natural world and its people and to thank the Creator for the many blessings it provided. In the Yurok worldview, the concept of *balance* means that all spirits, like the plants, animals, humans, water, and ecosystems, live symbiotically. Each plays a specific role to maintain a healthy environment in which every spirit thrives. Balance leads to good things happening on earth. Humans are a part of the ecosystem and have responsibilities to steward the land, water, and animals to maintain balance. The world, however, can become unbalanced if one species, like humans or another part of the ecosystem, takes too much. Then, the harmony is disrupted. When the balance is disrupted, bad things happen to the people and the planet, like drought, famine, or war. The ceremonies were meant to restore balance and thereby renew the world.

Each ceremony had different rituals, songs, medicine people, and dances. At the heart of all the dances was medicine, both plant and metaphysical. After a medicine person fasted, the plant medicines were collected in the wild and mixed into powerful healing tinctures. The metaphysical medicine is more difficult to describe because it is not tangible and cannot be seen, and there is no similar concept to compare it to.

One way to understand metaphysical medicine is to observe how it's used in our songs. Yurok ceremonial songs carry strong medicine that when combined with ritual and plant medicine can heal the sick and renew the world. We can't see where the song or medicine comes from or how it works, but we feel it. A song comes to a singer when he or she is calm and peaceful, has consciousness of purpose, and claims responsibility for that purpose. We know it's a force that enhances our prayers. The song and its medicine are a gift from the Creator, a reward for this higher level of consciousness. The medicine is not for us to understand because we are humans and it's beyond our comprehension. The medicine, singer, and Creator are in relationship to one another, all working together toward an intended outcome. As to the World Renewal Ceremonies, the singers, dancers, medicine, and Creator are in relationship working together to restore the balance between the natural world and humans. This is a powerful unseen partnership that has guided the Yurok world since time immemorial.

Dance families lived according to the original covenant between the Yurok and the Creator by living in balance with the natural world, stewarding it, treating people well, and caring for others. Their reward was the highest currency in Yurok culture: powerful medicine, regalia, and wealth. Dance families tended to maintain their status through generations, accumulating more wealth, so long as they continued to exercise their duties and responsibilities, until the colonizers came.

After the Yurok Reservation was created in 1855, the Bureau of Indian Affairs established an office and sent a federal employee deputized to manage the Yuroks' affairs called an Indian agent. A part of the federal government's nineteenth- and twentieth-century campaign to "kill the Indian and save the man" was to outlaw Indian religious ceremonies and practices and convert the Indians to Christianity. The federal government banned the World Renewal Ceremonies. Anyone found planning for or participating in one of the ceremonies would be thrown in jail. (Apparently, the First Amendment to the US Constitution didn't apply to the Bureau of Indian Affairs' dealings with Indian people.) Because of these government restrictions and local ordinances, dance families like mine had been unable to host dances. Wary in equal measure of prosecution, beatings, and murder at the hands of the Indian agent and his cronies, families hadn't hosted the dances since the early 1900s.

By the time I returned to Rek-woi in 2002, there was an ongoing push among some of the dance families from the upriver villages to bring back the World Renewal Ceremonies. Like many Nations during this era, the Yurok was experiencing a cultural, tribal, and religious revival. Bringing back language, traditional knowledge, governance practices, and, importantly, religious ceremonies and worldviews was a crucial step toward recovering from colonization. Restless, they brought back what could be remembered. They spoke to grandmothers and grandfathers, great-uncles and great-aunts, our elders — anyone in possession of even the tiniest details about the ceremonies. They cautiously worked to restore the ceremonies and themselves.

《《《

A few days after I first heard about the World Renewal Ceremonies, my auntie Sue and uncle Leonard came over for dinner. Sue was my grandmother's eldest daughter. Uncle Leonard was a member of the Hoopa Nation, the southeastern neighboring Nation of the Yurok, and a Bureau of Indian Affairs cop. After Sue returned to the reservation in the early 1970s, while she was fishing, she took one look at Leonard, who was handsome with curly hair, and declared he would be her husband. Sue inherited her mother's good looks and was strikingly beautiful, with an irresistible smile and personality. Her secret weapons were her photographic memory and political savviness. In her twenties, she returned home to represent the Traditional Indian Fisherman's Association to secure no less than 50 percent of the salmon harvest allocation. In her thirties, Sue organized the modern Yurok government and in 2002 was the Yurok Chairwoman, leader of the Yurok tribal government.

Grandma still managed the Nation's most difficult situations and personalities from her living room couch, usually while she watched daytime television. From this position of influence, Grandma watched the River and welcomed visitors, family members, and non–family members alike, who presented her with conversation and community news, which she passed along throughout the reservation, sharing stories over the phone that moved up the River faster than the wind.

For dinner, Grandma cooked salmon napes, the neck and collarbone of the salmon, which have the juiciest, best tasting meat, making it the coveted choice cut of salmon for Yurok families. She had baked it with salt and pepper, a dash of lemon, and potatoes. We gathered around the table in Grandma's dining room, and the smell of cooked salmon, slightly fishy yet warmly sweet with familiarity, came from the kitchen. The bay window offered us a view of the estuary, which illuminated the room as the sun moved closer to setting on the Pacific Ocean horizon.

"Mom, did you hear Ray had high boat last night? He knocked 'em." It was common for Uncle Ray to catch the most salmon in a night, giving him the honor of "high boat," and my family affectionately called catching a lot of salmon "knocked 'em."

I laughed a bit recalling the Yurok fisherman's comment from the other night. Uncle Ray knew when and where the salmon would be.

"Good for him," said Grandma.

We took a few bites. The salmon napes were delicious, tender and dripping with salmon oil.

"Did you hear they are doing a White Deer Skin Dance World Renewal Ceremony upriver?" asked Sue.

I was relieved that Sue had raised this instead of me. Grandma had strong feelings about what ceremonies we attended. I would never question her judgment. I looked at her to gauge her reaction.

"Who's doing it?" Grandma asked, frowning.

"One of the old dance families from up the River," Sue said.

"They don't know what they are doing."

"I don't know, Mom. They're going to do it anyway."

Grandma looked Sue straight in the eye. "Well, they don't have the right medicine. That medicine died with the old people. They don't know the rituals. It's gone now. It's too dangerous."

"They want us to go," Sue said. "We are a dance family."

Auntie Sue is the most persuasive person I have ever met. She's rarely told no.

"Well, we ain't going. It isn't safe. My momma did not go to those dances because they are too dangerous," said Grandma.

"I know, but what about world renewal? We must make things whole again. Too much is out of balance. The world's not right. How else do we fix it? We have responsibilities as a dance family," Sue replied, urging her mother with her fork still poised over her salmon.

As the tribal chairperson, Sue knew all too well the struggles of the reservation community. While the commercial fishery had provided limited income since the late 1980s, it was not reliable enough to support a family year-round. There were few other jobs available. Most tribal members made less than $11,000 a year, which was under the national poverty level for a family of four. This wasn't enough to cover a family's basic needs. It was her job to support tribal members and improve life on the reservation.

Grandma and Auntie Sue ate their napes in silence. Uncle Leonard and I observed. I was too nervous to speak up. Uncle Leonard was used to these mother-daughter standoffs. And as a two-decades-long Bureau of Indian Affairs law enforcement agent and current Yurok chief of police, he was also wise enough to know timing was everything.

Following their lead, I chewed, too, considering. I observed them like I had done in this very spot at the dinner table at Grandma's house throughout my life. I trusted them. I relied on them. They knew so much about what had been and what had happened. They were at the center of the Nation, politically, religiously, and socially. But I didn't understand this disagreement. If the dances were powerful enough to keep the world in balance, why shouldn't we do them? Wouldn't the Nation benefit from their strong medicine, even if it wasn't the same medicine my ancestors had used in the past or the rituals were slightly different?

The table stayed quiet longer than usual.

Recognizing the right moment, Uncle Leonard said, in his deep-and-slow way of speaking, "Eat your damn napes." He had a smirk on his face and a glimmer in his eye.

"Oh, don't start it with me, mister," Grandma said back at him with a grin, laughing.

Auntie Sue chuckled too.

As the tension finally left the room, I mustered up the courage to speak.

"Grandma," I asked, "why can't we go?"

"They don't know the medicine and bad things can happen, sweetie." Her voice was soft and tender.

"But, Grandma, isn't that the point, to bring back the medicine? I thought this dance was about world renewal and making things good

41

again. It sure seems like we need that around here. People are hurting. I see it every day on the River. They're trying to scrape by on what little they're allowed to have. Everything feels out of whack. Why would it be bad to bring this dance back?"

Sue nodded, thinking about what I said.

"The World Renewal Ceremonies are different from other things. I support the dance and the people who want to bring it back. I want us to do it again when it's done right, when we're ready to do it right," she explained. "The dance includes a medicine we can't see and another type, a mixture of herbs. When it's combined with fire, song, and dance, it has the power to change the future. No one has done the dance in a long time. The medicine and rituals have to be done perfectly. If done wrong, it can have harmful consequences on nature and people. I just don't want anyone to get hurt."

"What kind of consequences?" I asked reluctantly, not wanting to seem disrespectful.

Grandma frowned. She put her fork down. She turned to look at me with her chin slightly tilted down, the way she always did when she said something I needed to remember forever. I leaned in to listen.

"A long time ago, they used to do those dances up and down the River. Our family hosted them here in Rek-woi. We held the medicine, and each generation had a medicine person, who completed the ceremony. Like the medicine, the ceremonies are powerful. We lost my grandfather when he was a young man training to be a medicine man. His heart stopped. Some people said the medicine wasn't right after the white people came. After my grandfather died, we never trained anyone. Robert Spot asked the family to train him and we refused. Then the family stopped going to the ceremonies."

Grandma paused again to let me process. She had grown used to telling her stories in ways that people could remember. Her face grew a little longer and her eyes sorrowful.

"My momma promised her grandfather that she wouldn't let her family go to the dances because they were too dangerous. We already lost her daddy. And then people stopped doing the ceremonies because the feds made it illegal. If they caught you dancing, they'd beat you up or kill you, or take your regalia and throw you in jail. You know, when they first brought back other dances up there, bad things always happened. The mouth of the River closed up, and another time someone died. I don't want our family to get hurt. We shouldn't go."

Grandma let her words linger, and I felt the weight of her wisdom. I leaned back in my chair, looking at her in wonder. She knew so much about the family's history, stories I had never heard, even though I had spent hours and hours listening to her talk about our family and our Nation.

"It's going to happen with or without us," Sue said finally. "We can't control it."

Grandma shook her head.

"What have they said about it at the culture committee?" Sue asked.

The culture committee comprised Yurok elders who were cultural and historical authorities and who offered guidance to the tribal government on such matters.

"The culture committee makes things up," Grandma said jokingly, implying that the elders made up stories about Yurok history and culture. Grandma had been a longtime member of the cultural committee. Only she could joke about the truth of its guidance.

Sue and Leonard laughed. I didn't dare.

All of this made my head spin and my heart hurt. I wanted to go to the ceremony. I wanted to be a part of bringing back my culture and something that would renew the world. How could I miss it? Wasn't it better to do the ceremony, even if parts weren't right, than to not do it at all? Wasn't more than a hundred years long enough to wait?

My family had learned the hard way the power of the medicine and Grandma was determined to protect us. Others shared her concerns. As the dance got closer, I heard more and more people talking about it. Among the Nation were mixed emotions about whether it should be completed. Most people believed it should, but almost everyone understood that its medicine, both plant and metaphysical, was strong enough to change the course of the future for better or worse — and was dangerous if done wrong. This was the crux of the problem. No one, it seemed, was against the ceremony. They were afraid of what could happen if they didn't do it right, and almost no one believed it could be brought back exactly how it had been done before it was outlawed. The risk of doing it wrong was high and the consequences were dire, possibly even fatal.

The White Deer Skin Dance happened. On the first day of the ten-day ceremony, I could sense Grandma's discomfort. I knew she didn't approve of me going, but I continued to hope that she would relent and let me explore and satisfy my curiosity, even reluctantly. I dared not even consider going without Grandma's permission. Her word was gospel because she knew the old ways better than anyone. After all, she had learned from her mother, who had lived them. We all loved and respected her for many reasons, including that she always took good care of us. Crossing her word to sneak into a prohibited ceremony would be like double-crossing the Creator. I might never catch a fish again. Until the last night of the dance, I held out hope that maybe Grandma had another story she hadn't told me that would lead to me going to the ceremony. One in which my third-great-grandfather had lived through his training, the government hadn't outlawed the ceremonies, and my family had kept the medicine going hosting the ceremonies. A story that would assure me that the medicine had lived on through to the next generation of our family to fortify and push us forward, safely and in balance.

On the last night of the White Deer Skin Dance, I thought about the dancers. I opened the curtain over the window by my bed and looked out to the estuary. It was a clear night, and the full moon lit up the water. I said my own prayer for the safety of the dancers and prayed the ceremony would be done right. I prayed for world renewal. Even if I couldn't be at the dance, I could still offer a prayer.

Upriver, the poison from the Iron Gate Dam reservoir passed the dance site.

The Creator heard the dancers' songs and began to make the medicine. It saw the poison and felt the River begin to get sick. The world was gravely out of balance. Something had to be done to fix it. The Creator consulted with the salmon.

CHAPTER 4

The Fish Kill

◢◢◢◢◢◢◢◢◢◢◢◢◢◢◢◢◢◢◢◢◢◢◢◢◢◢◢◢◢◢◢◢◢◢◢◢◢

2002

W arm one today. River water flows look low," I said to Merle, my coworker for this shift. He jumped in the jet sled boat I'd been sitting in, waiting for him to join me. He moved toward the steering wheel and began to prepare the boat. "Yeah, warmer than I remember it being this time of the year," I thought aloud. "I guess it is September."

It was morning and I had returned to work but was still thinking about the ceremony, knowing that upriver the final dance would be completed at this same time, and a feast would be served. Downriver, Merle and I were preparing for our shift as fisheries technicians. We'd spend the next eight hours on the lower five miles of the River, counting the Yurok tribal salmon catch and collecting fish scales for data.

It was around 10 a.m. The sun was reaching from the east, moving upward toward the first ridge of mountains surrounding the east of the River. In a couple of hours, it would be full, beating down on the water and River bar. The tides would change, and the fish would run from the ocean up the River.

Merle turned over the boat engine, releasing a puff of smoke, which blew in the ocean breeze in my direction. I coughed and turned my head east. I looked up and observed the fishery.

Our boat was docked at the Requa boat dock. The tribal commercial fishery was in full swing; its parking lot, boat launch, and dock, built into the side of the River bar, were all busy. Yurok fishing families, including children, men, and women, were in a constant shuffle of moving boats, gear, supplies, and family members into and out of fish camps. The two fish buyers had set up camps on either side of the large crane and scale that lifted a salmon catch from a boat to the fish-buying station. The buyers' fifteen-foot-long RVs were rusty but looked like an oasis surrounded by moss, water, and River bar. There was a constant buzz of energy, people, trucks, boats, and salmon.

From the dock looking west toward the mouth of the River, family fishing camps were visible, set up on the banks of the River around the estuary. Gill nets were in the water, the corks bouncing gingerly on the surface. Fishing people were in their boats, milling around, checking and tending the nets. It was busier than it had been over the last few years. The fishing families had come home because the returning fall chinook salmon run was expected to be the largest in years. People were eager to make money and be on the River. The tribal council had authorized a commercial fishery because the tribal allocation of salmon was expected to satisfy ceremonial, subsistence, and commercial needs.

The fishing families were experts at their trade. They knew the River and the salmon and how to catch and care for them. Fishing was in their blood and was their business. Despite having aboriginal fishing rights reserved in the creation of the reservation in 1855, the Nation had only had a commercial fishery for a handful of the 147 years since, because of legal complications. While I didn't know it yet, our legal battles over a 1933 state law and a 1978 federal moratorium that prohibited Yurok fishing had ended in 1987 when the Nation's protests and my family's and other Yurok court cases reaffirmed our fishing, water, and land rights, laying the legal foundation for this commercial fishing season.

"I wonder if the bureau will release any more water. This heat will increase water temperatures, and I heard they are catching 'em. There are salmon in the River that will need water to move upriver," said Merle. Merle was young, dark, and stout. He spoke little, and only when it was worth saying the words; his statement reflected what was so commonly on all our minds and the main topic of conversation: water, salmon, and River health.

Unbeknownst to me, my internship had put me in the center of one of the worst water wars in the country. The Bureau of Reclamation (BOR) had controlled water flows on the Klamath River for almost one hundred years, since the authorization and construction of the Klamath Reclamation Project in 1905. The purpose of the project was to "reclaim" the lands from nature to make them useful to humans, but things went wrong. The federal government drained 230,000 acres of wetlands and the Lower Klamath Lake to convert to agricultural fields. Then it built a few thousand miles of canals to transport water from Upper Klamath Lake and the Klamath River to the fields, diverting water from flowing into the Klamath River. A natural reef at the bottom of Upper Klamath Lake, where it transitioned into the Klamath River, was elevated to serve as a control valve to regulate water releases to the Klamath River.

By 2002, the BOR's release of water had become a tangled web of broken promises and bureaucratic priorities it claimed was based on an attempt to balance competing interests: Indigenous reserved rights, endangered species protections under the Endangered Species Act (ESA), and agricultural deliveries. But the reality was far from balanced — or legal. The water was flowing to farmers, not the River or Lake — not to us. The Klamath and Yurok Nations' water rights were secured in the creation of their respective reservations. They included consumptive and nonconsumptive uses, such as instream flows for fish and water for people. They were not symbolic. They were legal, federally reserved, and foundational to our existence. Yet the BOR did not release water for the Nations because of the intense demand for water from the Klamath Reclamation Project for agriculture.

As to the ESA, coho salmon were listed on the Endangered Species List in 1997, and Lost River and shortnose sucker fish were listed in 1988. The ESA required the Klamath Reclamation Project to be operated without harming these listed species. In practice, this led to a bare-minimum flow for the River and low Lake levels. These low flows were the equivalent of life support for a human — hardly enough to support coho or suckers. Further, compliance with the ESA was hollow, and the BOR kept the Lake and the River even lower than ESA requirements. At the same time, the water contracts between farmers and the BOR called for water to irrigate more than 230,000 acres.

There were more water demands than water to fulfill them, even in wet years. The basin's water was overallocated, even without satisfaction of the tribal water rights. In an all-too-common unjust and illegal use of water, the federal government prioritized water for agriculture over tribal water rights and ESA needs, creating an intense battle for limited water that launched farmers and Indigenous nations into litigation beginning in the 1990s. The drought conditions in the summer of 2002 would stress this system of laws and management to a point of ecological disaster no one knew was possible even hours before it was upon us.

Unsuspecting, and ready to start my day at work, I sat down in the boat with my clipboard and pen to record data on the day's fish harvest. I was wearing rubber boots, a T-shirt, jeans, and my hand-knitted Yurok hat with the Yurok frog design in red and black. A must for any Yurok on the River. It was important that people knew who you were as a matter of claiming our territory and exercising our rights. A Yurok person on the River fishing was still an act of resistance and protest, even in 2002.

Merle revved the boat's engine and we pulled away from the dock. We headed west toward Rek-woi, gaining speed as we went along. I sat in the front of the boat, the estuary in front of me. I could see the wide, flat water sprawling west to the ocean, the sandbar, and the mouth. It was bigger than life. I felt content here, like this was where I was supposed to be: on big water cradled between the ridges lining the riverbank. The land had been spread wide by the water, unusual for this area's thick, green, wooded mountainous terrain. It was one of the few spots where the land opened up wide enough to see a few miles in every direction. The River ran from the east to the ocean, and the ridges lined the River on the south and north. The vast, wide openness, the colliding of land, River, ocean, and sky, made it feel like the whole world started here. Like all life could begin and live right here.

Fog rolled in from the west, originating from some unknown place. In Yurok geography, the deep west, as far as one can see in the ocean, is salmon's home. The fog continued past the sandbar, then rolled slowly up the ridge south of the River, obscuring the giant redwoods. The clouds were scattered, exposing a bright blue sky behind them while making room for the sun to shine on the other parts of the River.

As we approached the mouth of the River, the sound of the waves pounding the sandbar roared louder than the boat's motor. The sandbar separated the River from the ocean, a transition zone. The water moves from River to ocean, and ocean to River. It salinates and desalinates. The sandbar seemed an arbitrary divide, yet so powerful and important. Entire ecosystems were defined by this line of sand. As I looked beyond the line to the ocean, the power and magnitude of water before me made it seem like the water was never-ending and there would always be enough.

We entered a fish camp at the north-side river of the bank of the estuary, and Merle killed the engine. A gust of wind blew in from the ocean. I flattened the paper flapping like a bird's wing on my clipboard and readied my pen before climbing out of the boat.

Two men were fishing on the bank of the River.

"Hey, guys, how you doing?" I asked.

It was bad manners to start the conversation with "How many fish you catch?" even though finding an answer to that question was the reason for my visit.

"Hi. We're all right," said a fisherman in his fifties. He was short and stocky, with wide shoulders, built like a fire hydrant. His long, stringy hair snuck out of his Yurok beanie, pooling finally at his shoulders. "The salmon ain't moving for shit. Dam water is hotter than a horse's ass today and smells the same. It's an unusual color, too, a brighter green. What the hell is wrong with the water?"

"The bureau gave it to the farmers, we think," said Merle, his mind still on the BOR. We had heard rumors that US Vice President Cheney had been in Klamath Falls, the headquarters of the Klamath Reclamation Project, to meet with the Klamath irrigators to talk about water rights. In 2001, the BOR reduced the agricultural water allocation to provide water for coho salmon, as was required by the Endangered Species Act. The irrigation community was outraged that their contractual water delivery requirements could be reduced to comply with federal law. They appealed to the highest-level political office, calling on Vice President Cheney and the Secretary of the Interior, Gale Norton, determined it wouldn't happen again. The Vice President responded, assuring them they'd get their water the following year.

The Yurok Nation, while not given notice of these meetings, had foreseen the forthcoming political backlash from the water curtailments in 2001. Throughout the spring and early summer of 2002, the Nation anticipated the agricultural community would lobby hard for a full water allocation. In response, the Nation appealed to the federal agencies charged with co-managing Klamath water flows and salmon, stating that the hot water temperatures, drought conditions, and large returning salmon runs created conditions perfect for widespread fish disease. A full allocation of water for agriculture at the top of the River would result in insufficient flows for salmon in the lower River, increasing the likelihood and severity of a fish kill caused by disease.

"They gave more water to farmers. Well, what the hell for? A goddamn potato ain't worth more than this here fishery," said the fisherman.

"I know. Don't know what's going on," Merle continued. "You guys catch anything today?"

"We caught a couple. They're over in that cooler. You can check 'em out, if you want."

I walked over to the cooler, opened it, and grabbed the salmon on the top. I scraped a few scales off its back and put them in a small envelope to take back to the fisheries lab, where they'd be analyzed for their age and origin. I measured the fish and noted its species, then put it back in the cooler. I repeated this process for all four fish in the cooler, while Merle sat with the fishermen watching their net.

We were wrapping up when a large jet boat filled with tribal fishermen pulled up to the camp. They motioned toward us with alarming urgency.

"The salmon are dying upriver!" they yelled. "They are dying!"

"What do you mean, they're dying?" I asked.

"The salmon are coming out of the water, gasping for air, going under again, and then, dying, coming belly-up. From the glen all the way up to Blue Creek river, miles five to twenty, they're all coming up dead. I never seen anything like it."

We jumped in the boat and raced back to the dock. Mike Belchik, an esteemed biologist for the Yurok, was waiting for us. "We need to call Chairwoman Sue Masten," Merle cried. "The salmon are dying."

"We already called her. I went upriver an hour ago with Barry McCovey," Mike said of a Yurok tribal member who was a known rising-star biologist, "and saw a few dead salmon. But we need to head upriver to check it out again." Mike had been designated as the lead investigative biologist to determine what was killing the salmon and would spend most of his time on the River during the catastrophe. He was a tall non-Indian fisheries biologist whose heart and dedication to the Yurok Nation and its fishery were bigger than the estuary.

Mike climbed in the boat, and we headed upriver toward the glen. The sun had reached over the eastern ridge of the mountains and was beating down brightly on the water. The glare caused us to squint our eyes, and the heat warmed us, even as the wind whipped through the boat. The farther upriver we went, the lower the water levels became, exposing parts of the River we'd never seen before. The water was so low in parts we could see the River bottom, and we almost felt a need to avert our eyes out of respect for the River. I became worried it wasn't safe to travel in the boat. Merle knew this River better than most and used his cautious nature to navigate the troubled waters without complication.

We scanned the River bar and water for dead salmon. As we continued farther upriver, the water's color began to change from a deep blue to a bright green, and a substance that looked like moss floated maliciously. Ten minutes into our mission, we crossed under the Highway 101 bridge and then saw them: several dead adult salmon. Their one and a half to three foot-long corpses were floating morbidly on the surface of the water. Their bellies and dorsal and lower fins were exposed to the air, and their heads and tails were down in the water. Their bellies were so bloated their guts spilled out and their gills, a gray and white color, were rotten. Their lifeless, mangled bodies flowed effortlessly in the current, moving downriver in a death procession.

"Merle, right there! Slow down!" I yelled, pointing to the water.

Merle idled the engine, and we drifted toward the salmon. The air was sullied with the scent of their rotting corpses. There was hardly any water in the River and it was bright green.

The poison from Iron Gate Dam in the water, toxic blue-green algae, had reached downriver.

《《

"It smells like death," Mike said, "some kind of organic decomposing. I don't smell or see any chemicals, so it's not a chemical spill. It seems to be only salmon dying." There were no smaller fish, like trout, or larger fish, like sturgeon, dead. On the banks, the birds still flew and there were no visible dead animals. Only the salmon were dying.

"Should we pick the salmon up?" Merle asked, peering down into the electric-green water.

"How we gonna pick them up?" I asked incredulously. "Their gills and bellies are rotting, and the water looks toxic."

The fish next to the boat were dead, their mouths clenched open and eyes clouded over. The sides of their bellies were wounded, the skin brown, red, and gray where it appeared to have burned and then rotted. My stomach turned, followed by my heart. Their gills were not their usually bright pink and instead were light gray with white spots. I was paralyzed and in shock by the sight. I felt extreme panic, devastation, and confusion. These were the fierce River beasts that I had battled for me and my family's survival. I knew them as aggressive fighters who could break human bones with a whack of their tail or move their bodies back and forth to jump out of fishing boats. Now, they had succumbed to something so powerful it killed them en masse. What had killed them? How could we stop it?

Mike broke me out of my stupor. "This is serious, guys. Let's go up the River. There are probably more."

We turned a bend in the River near the glen. Merle pointed up the River.

"What is that? Do you see it?" He gunned the boat toward an eddy, where the water pulled in a circle and then shot out whatever it caught onto the riverbank. After which a five-hundred-foot straight stretch of River came into view.

"Oh my god," I murmured as we got closer.

"Stop the boat, Merle," Mike said somberly.

Before us, for the next half mile, were hundreds of dead salmon in the water and on the riverbank. Large salmon. Some were floating down the surface of the River and others got caught in the eddy, circling eerily. More had been pushed out of the eddy and were beginning to pile in layers along the riverbank, three to four salmon deep, their bodies distorted and tortured. Just like the first dead salmon we saw, here the salmon's gills, rotted and gray, swelled out from their heads. They were white and filled with small white dots, tiny organisms that had sucked out the blood and oxygen that would have normally flowed through a healthy gill. Their bellies had exploded from the inside out, like they had swallowed a bomb. Blood and guts poured into the River. What skin remained intact was a dark red, a stark contrast to its normal silvery chrome color, and gray from rotting. The water where the salmon pooled was covered with a bubbling film, toxic blue-green algae, and a gray sludge that moved with the carcasses.

We stood in the boat staring, slowly moving upriver. There were so many dead salmon in the water. We didn't want to run them over, but it was almost impossible not to. All three of us were silent, in shock.

"No one touch anything," Mike finally said. "This looks like ich, a fish disease. But in case it's something else, don't touch the fish."

"This is a massive fish kill. I don't know how else to describe it," Merle replied, staring out into the water.

"What is going on? How did this happen?"

"Why are they dying?"

"How do we stop it?"

We fumbled for words as our minds raced through a series of unspoken questions and fear of what could happen next. Nothing like this had ever happened before. I thought of all the fish stories and Yurok myths my family had told me. None of it made any sense. This River was made for salmon. It was September, when the salmon migrated up the River. How could the salmon be dying here?

"There has to be a biological explanation for this," Mike reasoned. "Some ecological reason. It's a drought year. The water has been low for a while, and it got lower recently. It's been hot, much hotter than normal."

"We've been catching a lot of fish over the last few days," Merle noted. "We have a big allocation this year. It must be a big run. I think the bulk of the run is in the River now."

"The water is so low it has been moving slow, almost stagnant. The water is hot too," I said.

"The flows at Iron Gate went down 41 percent to six hundred cubic feet per second two days ago. The bureau probably cut the water flows to the River to give more water to the farmers. The US Vice President was in Klamath Falls two weeks ago to visit the farmers," Mike said. "They must have reached a deal. They must have diverted the water. That would explain the low flows."

We started the boat back up and continued up the River. The size of the fish kill grew as we traveled. Just fifty yards ahead, in another eddy, the same scene: hundreds of salmon dead, their bodies mutilated. The farther we traveled, the more salmon we saw lining the banks of the River. The sun was baking them, turning rotting fish into rotten corpses. The smell was so concentrated and potent, I gagged.

"Here, put this over your nose," Merle said, handing me a cloth.

"Merle, let's stop at my dad's camp at Brooks Riffle and see if it's the same there."

"Sure," Merle said.

As we pulled around the last River corner before Brooks Riffle, two to three layers of dead fish lined the banks of the River for a five-hundred-yard stretch. They lay there mangled, battered, and bruised like a line of dead soldiers waiting to be buried. Yet the redwoods, alder, and willow trees all continued to stand tall. The mountains and the ridges towering over the River stood still. The birds still flew by overhead. The water still rolled toward the ocean, but it moved at a lethargic pace, quiet and solemn, as if in mourning.

If water has memory, it would remember this day. It would remember growing hotter, holding those salmon as they died, as they gasped for air, as the fish disease sucked the oxygen from the salmon and killed them. It would remember how it had failed the salmon, unable to provide them with sanctuary.

My dad's camp came into sight. Our family boat was docked next to Brooks Riffle, and on the River bar was a tent and a kitchen set up under a canopy. The gill nets were piled on the River bar next to the boat. There were no gill nets in the water. My dad and mom emerged from the back side of the tent carrying firewood, and my four siblings were scattered around the camp. They were packing up camp. They spotted us and set down the firewood next to the campfire. As we docked the boat on the River bar and all got out of the boat my dad called to us, "Why are the fish dying?"

We approached the campfire, and Mike said, "We don't know yet. What have you seen?"

"We had a net in the water last night. We caught a few, but they were in bad shape. Their gills were white, and their skin was red, like they got beat up. Then, this morning, we didn't fish because we saw several salmon jump out of the water, almost gasping for air, and then dive down again, only to reappear a few minutes later belly-up, dead. It was unreal."

"They are dead all through the River. It's like a war zone. No Indians are fishing but the white people are," I piped in.

"It's a massive fish kill. Reclamation must have given more water to the farmers and there is none left for the River, which would explain why the River water level is so low. I heard the toxic blue-green algae is especially bad this year at the reservoirs behind the dams," said Mike.

While there had been toxic blue-green algae in the River before, it appeared this year was particularly bad, especially because there wasn't water to dilute the poison and it was very hot, with increasing water temperatures and the spread of algae and other pollutants in the River. The River was stressed beyond conditions it had previously experienced.

The terror of drought was upon us. The poison from Iron Gate Dam was upon us.

"Goddamn government, always messing with us," Merle said. My mother, at the other side of the campfire, gave me a look, disapproving of Merle's choice of words.

"What are we gonna do? How do we stop it?" I said, looking at my dad for some reassurance.

"Nothing we can do. We should call the bureau, the president, the press, whoever will listen, and ask for water. These fish need water to flush out the toxins."

"Right," Mike said, as he jolted up and started moving toward the boat. "Let's go. We need to take pictures and get back into cell phone reception to make calls."

I turned to my parents. "You guys okay?"

"Yeah. We'll pack up and head downriver. No sense in catching more fish," Dad said.

I gave both my parents hugs. My father looked at me with concern in his eyes.

As Mike, Merle, and I pulled away, I watched Dad and two of my siblings gather the fishing gear. Dad lifted a heavy net and put it into the boat parked at the River bar below my parents' camp. My mom and my other two siblings started packing up the camp kitchen. How many times had they done these same tasks, after a perfect weekend of camping and fishing, returning home with beautiful, healthy salmon that would feed our family through the upcoming year? How many times had previous generations of my family done these same tasks at this same place? No previous generation had experienced a fish kill.

Back on the boat, my mind raced as I watched the dead salmon float on the surface of the water. In other spots, the water was so low one could see other sick salmon struggling to migrate upriver. The River and salmon were dying in front of our eyes. The River had existed and flowed for millennia and had taken care of every generation of my family. I recalled a Yurok myth. *When the Klamath River and salmon die, so will the Yurok people.* It seemed like this was the beginning of the end: the fishery, Yurok, the River people. I was witnessing the end of my people. This was ecocide. The killing of a natural resource a people are so dependent upon that its death leads to their demise.

I was devastated. It was a hopeless feeling. I felt marginalized, like no one cared. If they cared about the River, the salmon, and Yurok culture, water would have been provided. Instead, the needs of agriculture and hydropower were prioritized over us and nature. They took the water and killed the salmon. Now it felt like there was nothing we could do to stop the salmon from dying. It felt like watching your dearest family member tragically die before you without explanation.

While my family had fought for our rights to the land and fish, they'd never thought they'd have to fight for the water or the River's right to survive because it was unconscionable to harm the River's life force in my culture. It was clear now that my generation's fight would be to preserve the resources upon which the Nation's legal rights were exercised: the salmon, water, and the River. This meant we had to fight to save the salmon by restoring the River's health, because a fishing right is no good if there are no fish. We could not continue our fishing way of life on a dying River.

The World Renewal Ceremony had just ended. The prayer had been made, and the medicine and regalia were being packed away. With this tragedy downriver, we were eager to hear if the dance went well. I couldn't help but think of my grandmother's warning: if the medicine and ritual aren't done right, it can be fatal. Had it gone wrong?

Yet, perhaps the World Renewal Ceremony had worked. The fish kill signaled that the world was fatally out of balance. Maybe world renewal meant those fish had to die to show the world the delicate fragility of the natural world. Even Mother Nature has a breaking point, and if we push past it, the things we need to survive on earth will die. Then how will we survive? Maybe that was the agreement the Creator had made with the salmon. They would die to bring world renewal. Maybe the medicine of the ceremony was beginning to work. The world was just starting to renew, restoring balance by tearing apart power structures made to generate a profit, regardless of the impact on ecosystems and people.

The fish kill lasted just over a week, and we eventually learned the extent of the damage. It was the largest fish kill in American history. It's estimated between 34,000 and 78,000 adult chinook fall salmon died within the lower twenty miles on the Klamath River in the Yurok Reservation. The salmon were large, ranging from fifteen to thirty pounds. By the end of it, their bodies lined the banks of the River three or four layers deep, rotting in the hot sun. For weeks, the River was like a war zone; carcasses, rotting flesh, and the stench of death moved up and down the River.

The Nation alerted the media, but no one came. This made us feel more desperate. Chairwoman Masten decided if the world wouldn't come to us, we'd go to them. She sent a load of dead salmon carcasses to Washington, DC, addressed to the Secretary of the Interior, Gale Norton, and held a press conference on the steps of the Department of the Interior building, surrounded by more dead salmon.

The salmon died from ich (*Ichthyophthirius multifiliis*), a fish disease. Ich attacks gills, causing them to swell, which restricts oxygen flow from water to the blood in the gills, preventing respiration, stressing the fish, eventually causing death. Ich thrives in conditions that were present in 2002: low water levels, hot air and water temperatures, poor water quality infected with toxic blue-green algae, and high density of salmon. Salmon that year had no doubt followed O'-rey-gos's instruction and didn't try to migrate upriver, heeding her warning that the conditions there were poor. They stayed an unusually long time in the lower part of the River, which spread the highly contagious deadly disease. Most of the salmon run was killed. It was the first pandemic on the River.

This wasn't natural. It was a man-made disaster. It was later confirmed that Vice President Cheney had made good on his word to the irrigators. They got their water. As a result, the flows on the Klamath River fell to the second-lowest level on record. The warm, polluted water with toxic blue-green algae from behind the Iron Gate Dam spread the ich, which moved through one of the largest chinook salmon runs on the Klamath in decades.

A 2007 *Washington Post* article examining Cheney's role in the fish kill led to a congressional investigation of the same. It reported that Cheney, a few months after taking office in 2001, recognized the importance of securing votes from Republican farmers in Oregon, a state the Bush administration had lost by less than half of 1 percent in the 2000 presidential election. Opportunity knocked when the Klamath Water Users Association, comprising farmers from the Klamath Reclamation Project in Oregon, requested a full water delivery over the objections of federal fish biologists in 2002. The biologists had concluded that ESA-listed salmon needed more water to survive, and Cheney secured a National Academy of Sciences report overruling the conclusion. Then he sent the Secretary of the Interior, Gale Norton, to the Klamath Basin to open the irrigation headgate, sending the water to the farmers. The congressional investigation revealed that Cheney manipulated the science and midlevel federal government bureaucrats for political gain. Subsequent lawsuits confirmed that the water diversion was arbitrary and capricious and in violation of the Endangered Species Act.

Cheney's political maneuvering caused the fish kill and led to the collapse of the West Coast salmon fishing industry. Not only were Yurok fisheries closed in subsequent years, but commercial fishing in California and Oregon was cut by more than 90 percent in the following years, marking the largest commercial fishing closure in the history of the country. It's estimated that the accumulated damage of yearly fishery closures in California was between $500 million and $2 billion and caused a loss of between 2,300 and 5,000 jobs.

That day on the River, observing the worst of the fish kill, we didn't know it happened by the order of the Vice President of the United States. As we moved upriver, the hum of the boat breaking the silence, I thought about everything my family had been through. The invasion of colonizers in the 1800s, a failed treaty, a Supreme Court case confirming our rights to land and fish, the Salmon Wars, and the fight against the federal government defending those rights in the 1900s. We had survived what we thought was the worst of colonization; we had lived through California state and federal laws that put a price on our heads and made it illegal for us to fish and practice our traditions. I thought it was over. I thought we were safe.

I thought about my great-grandmother Geneva, who had lived through some of the most challenging times of colonization. She was born in 1904, was raised by her grandparents, survived boarding schools, family tragedies, the Salmon Wars, and yet remained strong and grounded in her culture and traditions. She passed away in 1986, but I knew her. I remembered her sweet smile and outreached hand asking me to give her a hug when I was a young girl. My mind grew still, and I faded away from the water, the boat, and the dead fish. Then it hit me. I felt a wave of electricity move through me like it was her. She traveled on the wind and whispered, "It's your turn. Go."

I immediately thought, *I need to go to law school to become a lawyer and prevent further destruction of my River and culture.* I would fulfill my duty to the Creator by becoming a lawyer. The fish kill was an act of ecocide against my people because we could not live without salmon. Whether the world renewal medicine was working or not, it was clear to me that the Nation would need lawyers to protect us, and if we had any luck, to heal us, our River, and our culture. In a clear stretch of River, I took a deep breath in. The air felt different. The world had changed. I had changed too. I was experiencing an existential threat to my people's and family's very existence, and I would not let it happen again.

PART II

How Yesterday Became Today

Geneva Mattz, Rek-woi, 1910s

CHAPTER 5
Indian Training

▲▲▲▲▲▲▲▲▲▲▲▲▲▲▲▲▲▲▲▲▲▲▲▲▲▲▲▲▲▲▲▲▲▲▲▲▲▲

1914

Yurok has a tradition of the women leading the Nation into war. The women go first to use words to resolve conflict. Only if a peace agreement cannot be reached do the men go into battle.

In conflict, ceremony, and family, men and women work together to live according to the first covenant between Yurok and the Creator. Each generation of my family trained in the instructions and accepted the responsibility to make sure anyone and everyone who came to Rek-woi followed the way, even after the colonizers arrived.

Our family tended the House of La'yeq and a fishing hole in the estuary below Rek-woi next to O'-rey-gos. The House of La'yeq was a Yurok redwood plank house that had been in my family since the beginning of time. The house has been there for so long, no creature could remember when it wasn't there. After the passage of many, many years, the earth had accepted it would be there forever and built an ecosystem around it to support the house rather than work against it. In aboriginal times, my family had kept water and food in watertight baskets made of willow, slept on reed mats with elk-hide blankets, and used rock, shell, and animal bones as utensils.

People called it the House of La'yeq because it was located next to the trail by the spring in Rek-woi. The redwood planks forming its walls and ceiling were seven to eight tall single boards from floor to ceiling. Together they formed a rectangular one-room house with two levels, with a slanting roof, a hole in the center of the roof above the fire pit in the middle of the house, and another circular hole large enough for an adult to climb through at the bottom of the south-facing wall for the door.

By the early 1980s, my family no longer lived in the house but maintained it well. I remember playing in the house as a young child. I liked to run around the edges of the house and explore the nooks and crannies of its four corners. Grandma would say, "No running in the house. This is a family house. Same rules apply." While it was hard to imagine my family members living in the one-room house with a dirt floor and wood walls without electricity or running water, the house made me feel safe because I knew countless generations of my family had lived under the roof with the smoke hole in the middle.

The House of La'yeq was a visible stronghold of my family and the Yurok people's legacy. It was one of the last redwood plank houses standing. The strength of its redwood plank walls and the way the earth supported the house sheltered us during the hardest period of my family history. In many ways, my great-grandmother was the same way because she lived through a challenging era yet remained strong and connected to Yurok culture.

Her generation transitioned from a Yurok aboriginal lifestyle to a modern one, which is very recent in the context of American Indian history. She was a bridge between the Yurok of yesterday and today, including for me, as she passed away when I was six. Her knowledge and presence inspired generations of Yurok people to fight the forces of colonization that continued to threaten our way of life in the twentieth and twenty-first centuries. She showed us how to go to war.

《《《

I recall a story about how my great-grandmother Geneva was to be trained as a medicine woman when her life took a dramatic turn.

It was 1914. My great-grandmother Geneva was ten years old.

"Geneva, wake up. It's almost time to go to Fanny's house. Today is your big day. You will start singing with my cousin Fanny the medicine woman. This could lead to something special, your birthright. Get ready," her grandmother, Susie Brooks, said in Yurok.[1]

Geneva dragged her feet. She was a petite, strong, smart girl, just like most of the women in her family, but she was a little scared to start singing with Fanny Flounder — her grandmother's cousin, who was a well-respected medicine woman and businesswoman. Fanny trained to be an Indian doctor at Gold Bluffs, thirty miles south of Rek-woi on the coast. To gain her power as an Indian doctor, Fanny had fasted for ten days to prove that she was willing to sacrifice for the power to be a good doctor and to clean her mind, body, and soul to prepare to communicate with the sacred. At the end of the fast, she stood and prayed next to certain rocks on the beach that were known to be spirits with the ability to grant people healing powers. She received her power and trained with another medicine woman to learn how to use her power.

Eight years earlier, Geneva's father, James Brooks, had died suddenly from a heart attack during the time period he was training to be a medicine man for the World Renewal Ceremonies. My family decided not to train anyone else. During this time Robert Spot asked them to train him, but they declined. With her father gone, Geneva and her siblings would have to work to maintain the family's status as a dance family by earning money. Decades after her father's death, the family wanted to continue the tradition of training medicine people to heal others. Fanny talked with Susie, and it was decided Geneva would sing with Fanny to see if she might become a medicine woman, a well-paid position in Yurok.

Yurok was a gender-egalitarian society, in part because both genders were needed to maintain balance on earth. Medicine people could be male or female, depending on the ceremony. To be a medicine woman was one of the highest honors in Yurok society. Medicine women were chosen by the Creator and head women, after which the candidate could begin their training. The medicine candidates were usually from dance families and had unique qualities of being exceptionally kind, good, insightful, smart, and pure of heart. Dance families had a high status and enough power and money to have accumulated sufficient wealth to host large intertribal dances and ceremonies. They could provide regalia to and feed all the dancers and their families. Medicine women or men presided over these dances and had the medicine and practices to heal the sick, creating a caste system, with dance families and medicine people at the top of it.

Geneva's mother, Martha Ruben Brooks Charles, was from Orleans, a village in Karuk Country up the River from Yurok, far away from Rek-woi. Her mother's people were a dance family that held the ceremonies at Katimiîn, about a hundred miles upriver from Rek-woi. Her mother had been bought with a full bride's price, allowing a full marriage. Yurok had a marriage system for full or half marriages. She would live with the groom's family and the children would belong to the groom's family. The bride's price was determined by the bride's family status and her skill set and beauty; the higher the status and skill set (such as basket making), the higher the price. If a groom's family was unable to pay a full price, a half marriage could be arranged, in which the bride would stay in her home village and the children could become a part of either family. It was a great honor to enter a full marriage. Families went to great lengths to arrange marriages between dance families and skilled people. (Martha was the last woman to be bought the Yurok way.) Geneva's father, James Brooks, was from Rek-woi. He also came from a dance family, which had the money to pay for Martha, who was healthy, young, beautiful, and from a good family. Her bride price was high. His parents showed her family respect by offering more than the full bride price. Her family agreed and was pleased with the match. Martha moved to Rek-woi.

"Here, have some breakfast. Your acorns and salmon are in this bowl. Make sure you eat it all. Today is a big day," her grandmother Susie said.

Her grandmother stoked the fire. The flames lit the inside of the house, waking up its four corners, drying up the morning dew. The day before, Geneva and her grandmother had gathered on the beach below Rek-woi. Geneva's job was to pick the seaweed while her grandmother gathered fish. Her grandmother had prayed to the Creator before they went to the beach that fish and other food would be provided. Answering her prayers, the large breaker waves from the ocean side of the beach would throw a fish onshore for her, or sometimes a little sturgeon, crab, or eel. She would put it in her burden basket, a woven basket the length of a woman's back made of strong sticks and roots of willow, hazel, and other trees with leather shoulder straps. These baskets were like modern-day backpacks, versatile and durable. She could load the basket and carry her catch home. Between this and Geneva's grandpa's successful hunting and fishing, there was enough food for the immediate family and for the elderly who couldn't hunt or fish anymore. Geneva's grandmother understood it was her responsibility to share with the elders so that everyone had enough. The Creator teaches, *I'll always provide for your needs, any kind of fish;*

in the hills you'll find greens, you'll find meat. So long as you don't quarrel about food and you always share. This is the way.

On the day Geneva was to begin her training, she asked Susie what she would do with Fanny.

"You will visit. She might teach you a song. You'll be fine. Nothing to worry about," Susie said comfortingly.

"Will she do medicine on me?" Geneva asked, referring to the healing process of medicine women mixing tinctures of sacred herbs and administering them to a patient while singing and dancing.

"Oh, sweetheart, only if you are lucky. She has good medicine. You'd be lucky if she did," said Susie.

Geneva loved and trusted her grandmother. After Geneva's father died, her mother married her *wherekler* — her father's unmarried next of kin. That was the Indian way: if a family paid a full bride price and the husband died, the wife had to marry the elder bachelor in the family. Geneva's mother married his cousin after James died. It is also the Yurok way for children of full marriages to stay with the husband's family because they paid for the wife. Accordingly, after Geneva's mom moved in with her new husband in Crescent City, Geneva and her siblings, one sister and two brothers, didn't want to leave her grandmother or Rek-woi, so she stayed. Her grandmother was happy to keep her and her siblings at home, consistent with tradition.

Geneva's great-grandmother's family were head people of the villages of Wechpues, Rek-woi, Pekwan, and Ore'q. Geneva was the steward of hundreds of acres of coastal lands from De Martins beach to Gold Bluff Beach, and had rights to first choice of the catch — whale and sea lions, including sea flippers, a Yurok delicacy, and much more. Her relatives Wa-Pa-Shaw and Sa-Sa-Mich had signed the treaty of 1851, an agreement with the US government that was supposed to have secured their family's rights to land, fish, and water. But the United States refused to sign the treaty. Somehow that meant the white people got the land, not Geneva.

Geneva's grandfather Billy Brooks was Yurok, too, from the village at Blue Creek, a short man with wide shoulders. In 1850, as a young child, Billy and his sister dared to visit one of the first white-man camps on the River, where he ate his first potato. "God but they tasted good," he reported back to his family. His adult Indian name was Las Awa, which meant in Yurok "the man that's married by the side of the road." He was named this because he married a high-class woman and took a name that reflected her position. When he applied for an allotment of land under the General Allotment Act, which divided tribal land and dispersed it to individual Indians, the federal Indian agent required applicants to take white names for the allotment papers. The Indian agent named him Billy Brooks. Billy and Susie had two allotments, one in Rek-woi in Billy's name, which included the House of La'yeq and land, and one upriver about six miles from Rek-woi by Brooks Riffle in Susie's, which was also named after him.

From the House of La'yeq on the allotment in Rek-woi, the ridgeline path started and went upriver, following the high ridgeline above the River. The path was an old Yurok footpath that had been used by the dance families only, as was Yurok custom. On main thoroughfares, there were two paths. One for the high families and another for others. Since more white people had moved to the village of Requa and were traveling on the footpath, it had been expanded to accommodate the modern way of traveling, by horse and buggy. At first, Billy had tried to enforce the rules: only members of Yurok dance families could use the path. Everyone else, including white people, had to use the path closer to the River. The white people didn't respect the restriction and used the ridgeline path.

Despite this transgression and transformation, Billy continued to steward the path through Rek-woi. He was constantly cutting and burning brush on the path that connected his home to the ridgeline path. He regularly burned the hillside to clear it of the blackberry bushes, stinging nettle, fennel, alder, and spruce saplings that would grow rampantly otherwise.

Billy was a smart, active, hardworking man. He knew how to exercise his responsibilities to the land, River, and species. He had been trained to live in a way that enabled his family and the environment to thrive. To provide food and shelter for his family, he fished, hunted, ranched, and tended his land, working with nature to make sure his take didn't negatively impact the species, ecosystem, or other people. He fished in the family fishing hole below O'-rey-gos and would dry, kipper, or cook the salmon. His property was well taken care of; the path leading to his fishing hole below the house in the estuary of the River was easy to travel. It wound back and forth up the hillside so that it was manageable to carry a few fish in a gunnysack from the fishing hole to the house. The path also led to the ocean, where the family could collect seaweed, mussels, and abalone, and driftwood for the fire. The sweat lodge was just below the house and toward the south, where he slept. It was common practice for the women and children to sleep in the house and the men of the village to sleep in the sweat lodge.

The population at Rek-woi had remained stable for some time now, despite the influx of white people to the area. The Senate's failure to ratify the treaty of 1851, however, had left the United States with an Indian problem. The Yurok people had legal title to land and resources the white people wanted, which the federal government resolved by creating the Yurok Reservation in 1855 by executive order. A series of subsequent executive orders designated a reservation a mile on either side of the Klamath River, from the Yurok villages of Rek-woi to just above Weitchpec, forty-five miles upriver from Rek-woi.

With the creation of the reservation, the Yurok people reserved their aboriginal rights within the area, including water, fishing, hunting, gathering, and sovereignty. Reservation status had deterred some white people from usurping Yurok rights, but not all. There had been battles with white people who had disregarded the federal reserve and aimed to take Indian resources by any means necessary. Those white people had killed Yuroks in unprovoked massacres up the River and at Rek-woi. By the 1910s, more than 90 percent of the Indigenous population in California had been slaughtered by the State of California, gold miners, and pioneers.[2] Only 10 percent remained, and a very small percentage of those remaining had been able to keep their homelands and waters. Susie's and Billy's families were considered lucky to have survived the massacres and to have held on to their landholdings and fishing holes. Still, Billy's grandparents didn't like to talk about it. He knew his family had lost people and that much of the family's historical Yurok wealth, position in society, and land had been stolen.

Billy and Susie had cause to worry that more would be taken. There were rumors on the reservation that the Indian agent was stealing children to send to a federal boarding school in Salem, Oregon. There was little if any communication with the children after they left the reservation, and many of them never returned. They feared Geneva would be taken.

For that reason, Billy joined Susie and Geneva for the trip to Fanny's. "Let's get going," Susie said. "Maybe Fanny will train you to be a medicine woman," she said to Geneva.

Later that day, settled in Fanny's redwood plank house, sitting next to the fire, Fanny spoke to Geneva in Yurok. She asked her what it meant to be a medicine woman.

"You heal people," Geneva said.

"Yes, good. I know the medicine to heal people. Often it starts with a song."

Fanny started to sing. Geneva listened. They visited for hours. On their way home, Geneva told her grandma she wanted to be a medicine woman just like Fanny when she grew up.

Sadly, Geneva's training would never be completed.

《《《

When Geneva, Susie, and Billy arrived back at the House of La'yeq, there were two white men wearing suits waiting for them in front of the old house. Billy recognized one of them as Judge Bowie from Crescent City.

"Geneva, go inside the house with the other kids and don't make any noise while these people are around," Billy instructed. They pulled up to the house and stopped the buggy next to the men.[3]

"Hello, Billy," said the judge.

"Hello," Billy replied.

Susie helped Geneva down from the buggy, while Billy secured the horse's reins on a post in front of the house. Susie nodded at the two men as she ushered Geneva into the house. Inside, Geneva's sister looked anxiously at Susie.

"Stay quiet. It'll be all right," Susie assured them.

Geneva joined her brothers sitting next to the fire, and Susie sat next to her. Billy showed the men into the house and offered them stools made of redwood and a spot next to the fire. Billy reached for kindling to put in the fire, stoked it a bit, and the cold air was replaced with a calm, warm flame, setting the tone for the discussion.

"Billy, this here man has come to talk to you. Now, you listen to what he has to say," said the judge, as he looked to the man and said, "You are here now; he will listen."

The other suited white man turned to Billy. "Now, Billy, you sold your timber on the top of the hill. I came to tell you that you can't set your net over in the River in the corner on this property here, where you always set your little net. You can't set your net there anymore because you're a white man now. You sold your property."

Billy's cheeks flamed red and his jaw clenched as he started breathing deeply, saying nothing.

"You sold your timber. You are a white man now," the man said. "That's what I came for — to tell you that," the man finished. The man meant that Billy had sold his rights to be an Indian by selling timber, implying that Billy no longer owned the land or had special rights to it based on his status as an Indian or land owner. He was on the same legal footing as a white man. Billy had fought hard to retain his and his family's rights to the land, water, and resources through colonization. Members of the last generation of his family had died trying. This man's message was deeply offensive and an act of aggressive colonization.

Billy stood up. The fire's flame lit his face, accenting the red in his cheeks and the deep brown color of his skin. He looked at his hands, still aching in the joints from last night's catch of salmon. His fingers had a few surface cuts from where the net had dug into his skin from the tension caused by lifting the heavy net full of fish.

"All right, Mr. White Man," he began. "You came to tell me what you wanted to tell me. Now, let me talk to you. From the time I was in the sweat house, a little boy just so big, when I was getting to be a teenager, I knew how to cross the River to go fishing on that side. I knew how to stand with the men and fish like a young boy. I was trained how to stand with the men on the fishing ground to fish on the shore. You don't quarrel. You don't fish and hook in front of another man. Every man has his place. If he sees a fish in front of him, he spears it — or if he hooks it — it's his. I was taught like that, to fish, I learned what to get so that I could survive if something happened to my folks. Every kind of a fish I was taught how to fish, and to hunt, and what to kill and what not to kill, so that they come back and nest the next year. That's the way I was taught to help provide for my family, as soon as I got big enough. And you come here and tell me that I can't fish anymore for my family. I have children to raise that we have to fish for. I have four children. My son died, and I have to raise his kids. And you, white man, come tell me what's been my life, all my life, I can't do anymore.... Now, you got anything else to say?"

Geneva sat still and silent in the corner. She could tell her grandpa was getting mad. She hadn't ever seen him mad; she was scared. She scooted closer to her grandmother.

Looking to the other man, Billy said, "Don't you bring another white man in my house who's gonna tell me how to live, Judge. I was trained to live the way I live. And you're not gonna tell me how to live." Billy stomped his foot and pointed to the door. "Now, you get the hell out of my house, and don't you ever come back here."

Geneva and her brothers had never heard their grandfather swear and giggled quietly at his indiscretion. Indians don't swear because there are no swear words in the Yurok language. Indians don't talk to one another like that. Grandpa had worked with white men in the woods and on the River. He had learned English, including swear words, from them, even though he never went to school.

"I'll fish as long as I live and as long as I can take care of my net or stand on the beach and fish. No white man's gonna tell me how to live. Now, get out of here as fast as you can and don't you ever come back to this ground again. Judge Bowie, don't you ever bring another white man here."

The men got up quickly and walked out fast, starting up the path. Billy turned and looked at his grandchildren, who had never heard him say anything mean. His eyes softened. They looked back at him, still in shock, not knowing whether to laugh or cry.

"Like heck I'm a white man," he spat. "Kids, get up, the fish are running. Let's go to the fishing hole."

Susie stood and turned to the kids. "Girls, listen up. Don't you mind those men. You are Yurok. The Creator made this River, this place, this village, for you. For you to live. You are from this dirt. The dirt right here." She touched the dirt floor of the house. "You remember the creation story and the footprints?"

Geneva's sister said, "Yes, Grandmother. I remember the footprints. Never take more than you need." There was a Yurok story that a holy man came through Rek-woi who said he was the Creator and reminded the people to live in balance with the natural world. He left footprints on the beach below Rek-woi and told the people the footprints would remain so long as the balance was maintained between humans and the natural world. (The footprints disappeared in the 1970s.)

"That's right. The Creator made this all for you, so you'll never want for anything. This River will support you and take care of you no matter what happens in your life. You will always have it. No matter what. In hard times, you come to the River and you pray. You go to O'-rey-gos and you pray. You go to O'-rey-gos's sister across the River, and you pray. You ask them for what you and the River need. O'-rey-gos and her sister will give you what you need. They are family too," Susie explained.

"Wait, the rocks are my family?" Geneva's sister questioned.

"Hush now, and listen. They are your family, and you must take care of them, just like we take care of each other. You must train to learn to live in a balance with it so that the fish, deer, elk, and acorns come back every year. That's what Grandpa was talking about. That's why the boys spend time with the men fishing — and, Geneva, that's why you come with me to gather. While men and women have different jobs, they are all important and necessary to maintain balance. You are all learning how the world works; you are in training.

"Never take more than you need to feed your family. You have to live in a good way. Fast to show your gratitude and to clean your mind and soul. Treat others well. Don't fight over fish or other things, and you'll always have enough, no matter what happens in your life. This is your River. Your place." Susie gently squeezed Geneva's hand. "The footprints in the sand down at the edge of the beach are there to show you that everything is okay. You are living right. If they go away, that's when you know you are in trouble."

"Your grandmother is right," Billy piped in. "I've never left this place, Rek-woi, and I never will. My grandparents lived here and so did their grandparents. My relatives even signed a paper making this land and River ours forever. No white man can take it away from us, not that judge, not anyone. Let's go."

The kids looked at their grandmother, who nodded the okay to follow Grandpa out the door of the house.

Geneva crawled out the front door, stood up, and looked before her. It was midday. The sun shone through low cloud cover that met the land on the tips of the trees on the ridge across the River. It was warm. The water below, in the River, flowed calmly. The sandbar stretched from O'-rey-gos and opened up on the south side to let the River into the ocean.

Geneva took it all in. Her heart swelled and she was filled with excitement. She'd never want for anything.

《《《

Sadly, this peace didn't last long. Shortly after she started her training with Fanny, Geneva was forcefully taken from her grandparents by a federal Indian agent and sent to the Chemawa Indian School, a boarding school in Salem, Oregon, run by the Department of the Interior, the Bureau of Indian Affairs, and the Catholic Church. She didn't want to go. The Indian agent forcefully gathered the children and shipped them 302 miles away from their homes. While she liked school, she grew homesick. She wasn't allowed to leave until she completed her studies. There she learned English, how to read and write, and basic math. She worked in the fields picking plums and berries. The Catholic nuns taught her to clean house so she could go work as a maid for a nice white lady, as the teachers would call them, because, from their perspective, that was the best future she could expect. Her life before Chemawa had prepared her for much more.

CHAPTER 6
A Bootlegger's Prayer

1987

I threw a small River rock into the big water in front of me. It landed
with a splash. I was seven years old, sitting on the sandy beach
between the Klamath estuary and the Pacific Ocean. The breaker
waves behind me roared, teasing that they'd get me by being so big
the water would rush to the other side of the beach to scoop me up.

In front of me, my dad was in a jet boat, tending his gill net, which
was set by frog rock, shaped like a frog crouching by the River as if
fishing, below the village of Rek-woi in the family's traditional fishing
hole in the estuary. He leaned over the boat to lift the net from the
water and pulled it until a plump silver salmon rose from the depths.
He pulled it into the boat with little effort.

I stood up to see if I could see him untangle the net from the
fish, but I was too small. It was the first commercial fishing season
the Nation had, because the federal moratorium on Yurok fishing
had finally been lifted. My mom, two sisters — one and five years
old — and I had come to the beach below Rek-woi to watch Dad
salmon fish. We set up camp with a cooler of food and drinks, a camp

stove, and chairs. We built a fire. I sat next to the water hoping he'd see me. While I was only seven, salmon fishing on the Klamath River was already a part of my identity. I don't remember the first time I saw a salmon because it had always been a part of my world. It was a common family activity to clean, smoke, can, and eat salmon. The salmon ran through our daily lives as much as they ran up the River.

Other boats and gill nets were surrounding Dad's net. The corks on the gill nets, set off the beach every hundred feet, looked like marshmallows tied on a string, bobbing up and down gently. Seagulls squawked, flying overhead, and seals patrolled the nets looking for a meal.

"Billy, fish on!" hollered a fisherman whose net was set next to Dad's.

Dad looked and saw where the fish was in the net, went to it, and relieved it from its binds.

"Dad, come pick me up. I want to help get those fish!" I hollered to my dad. He quickly drove over and picked me up. I jumped in the boat and sat down, not wanting to get in the way. This was serious business.

Dad started toward the net. "Here we go, Famous," said Dad as he saw a salmon hit the net. Then Dad transformed into another type of being. He moved swiftly from the driving console of the boat to the bow, scooped up the net with one hand, and used the other to grab a salmon out of the water. He shook the net and salmon, pulled the salmon tail out of the net, and then it slid out of the net to the bottom of the boat. This all happened within a matter of seconds.

"Wow, Dad. How did you do that!" I exclaimed.

He chuckled.

We sat by the net for a while in the boat waiting for the fish to hit. My mother, observing the pause in fish hitting the net, called to my dad, "Hon, dinner is ready."

We went back to camp on the beach and sat down at the campfire. Mom had prepared chili dogs. At that moment my great-uncle Marv, Uncle Ray's twin brother, who was fishing next to our camp, walked over.

"How are you doing?" said Dad.

"Looks like you caught some fish," said Uncle Marv.

"Just a few. Should get a few more tonight when the tide changes. Take a seat," my dad said, offering him a camp chair. "You hungry?"

My mom had learned to bring extra food because unexpected guests usually came to camp for dinner.

"Yes, thank you," he said. "This here fishery is hard to believe. About time we had a commercial season," said Uncle Marv.

"Finally."

"My whole life it seems like no one wants Indians to be Indians. First the state and then the feds said we couldn't fish. They criminalized our identity and way of life. We bootlegged salmon all those years," he explained.

"I did some bootlegging myself, not so long ago. I'll never forget one time I went north to sell fish. I made the transaction, had the cash in my pocket, when I heard a man say, 'Put your hands up.' I turned around and was surrounded by wardens. They took my cash but never gave me a ticket. I felt robbed," my dad shared.

"That's what I am talking about. Your uncle Emery Jr. and Ray had the same kind of trouble," Marv replied.

He took a bite of his chili dog and then proceeded to regale us with the story.

《《《

It was the 1940s. Geneva, now in her thirties and married with children, lived at the homeplace upriver about twelve miles from Rek-woi.

"Mom, I have to go. I have to take a load," declared Emery Jr., Geneva's son.[4] She was sitting on her couch in her living room as

Emery Jr. sat on the wood rocking chair beside her. Her young son, barely in his twenties, had seen hard times in his short years, and Geneva, in her forties, was empathetic.

"My boy, how can you take a load of salmon out to sell? There's a warden sitting right across the River watching and there's another game warden right below on the sandbar. They flash the light every half hour over the River. Why, they're just waiting for some young fellow that's bootlegging salmon. You'll be arrested and end up in jail." A 1933 California law prohibited Yurok fishing on the Klamath River within the Yurok Reservation. The law had criminalized Yurok culture and identity, and weaponized the law against us.

"Momma, you should see the salmon that's going up the River! They're huge and silver, beautiful. The kids are going back to school in September. They got to have school clothes. After my accident, I ain't got no other way to make money to buy them clothes or turn on the electricity at the house in town other than to sell salmon. I got to take a load out and sell it on the black market."

"How are you going to do it? You can't just take the gill net out fishing because they'll be looking for you. They'll catch you," said Geneva. "Well, if you are going bootlegging, then I am going to help the only way I know how. I'm going to go to the praying rock and you'll go with me. We will go pray together. We will go clean. We must do it perfectly or you will end up in jail."

"All right, then. We will go tomorrow afternoon," agreed Emery Jr.

《《《

Geneva was like an elegant royal River otter. She was brilliant, refined, and strategic. She was well mannered and kindhearted and never spoke poorly of anyone. She was petite, standing four foot ten with her high-heeled shoes on, and had soft brown skin, short legs, and wide shoulders. She was smart, politically, and business savvy.

She was unapologetically Indigenous, which was unusual for Indian people in the early twentieth century. Racism was rampant on the reservation and in border towns against our people. The federal government continued its campaign to assimilate Indigenous peoples into white Christian society. Many people understandably chose or were forced to abandon their traditional ways or disclaim their Indigenous heritage.

Instead, Geneva leaned into her culture and Yurok way of life because, in part, she was able to remain for most of her life in her homelands and waters. This enabled her to continue her unfaltering faith in the Creator and the Yurok worldview and lifestyle.

When she was released from boarding school at sixteen years old, the school nuns encouraged her to take a job as a maid in the city. She refused and returned to Rek-woi and her family. Within a year, she fell in love with Emery Mattz, the grandson of the last Tolowa headman from Smith River, about forty miles north of Rek-woi on the coastline. They met at a white-man dance in Rek-woi. He was strikingly handsome and taller than the rest of the boys, but he couldn't dance. Shortly after they met, he asked her to marry him. She thought to herself, *Do I have to marry him? He doesn't care to dance.* Geneva loved dancing and a partner with two left feet could be a problem. For the first time in her life, she prayed for an answer. The answer from the Creator was yes. They were married in 1920.

It turned out he was an excellent square dancer.

They moved to Geneva's family allotment land next to Brooks Riffle on the Klamath River about twelve River miles up from Rek-woi. (The family managed to keep the land through a period when the Bureau of Indian Affairs worked with logging companies to fraudulently take Indian land.) The land was far from any town, wooded with redwoods and evergreen trees that stretched up the steep hillside on the west side of the property, the forest ground covered with moss and ferns making the landscape green from forest floor to canopy. They cleared a small site for a cabin, orchard, garden, and farm animals just up from the River bar, far back enough to have privacy and be safe from normal flooding and the River's swells during winter and spring storms. There was a dirt path through the sandbar from the River bar to the cabin. It was just the right size to pull a small rowboat, a cart, or a wagon. They affectionately called it "the homeplace."

Geneva's training in domestic affairs at Chemawa, regardless of the purpose, had served her well. Her own house, a four-room cabin, was immaculate, always clean and organized. She spent her days cooking, cleaning, and tending to the kids. By the 1940s, she had nine children in two batches, six in the first, born between 1921 and 1935, and three more born in the 1940s, the last two twins, Marvin and Ray. She loved her family and took pride in taking care of them. She'd rise early in the morning to cook breakfast, collecting fresh eggs from the chicken coop, and occasionally bake biscuits. They'd never know hunger. The family had all they needed at the homeplace by Brooks Riffle.

The cabin was reached by boat. They didn't need much from town, so they hardly ever went. Only the kids went into town for school. Most of their supplies came from the River or land. They fished at Brooks Riffle, canned, dried, and smoked salmon, steelhead, sturgeon, and candlefish, or ate it fresh. They hunted deer and elk. They had a cow, pigs, and chickens and a beautiful garden with roses, big and full, just in front of the cabin. On warm summer afternoons, Geneva and Emery would sit in front of the house in the shade and look at the garden and the River.

〈〈〈

Geneva thought about her son and the prayer rock standing tall across the estuary from Rek-woi. It sat on the south bank of the River, near the mouth. It was a big rock, twice as tall as a man, and four times as wide. The last time she had seen it, the mist from the ocean waves covered its surface and moss grew up from the south side, covering it with a glossy green moss, the basalt rock black from the moisture.

Geneva prayed often because Yuroks believed the Creator would provide if you lived by the first covenant, as Geneva aspired to do. Her oldest son, Emery, was right. He didn't have any other options. Emery Jr. had worked for years in the woods as a logger. The logging companies would only hire Indians for the dangerous jobs. Emery was hired as a choker setter, requiring him to attach cables to logs for retrieval. His first injury on the job made one arm almost unusable and his second injury, caused by a fall, had damaged his head and brain. He had fallen, injuring his head severely at work. Now he could hardly work anymore, and the logging company fired him. He received a settlement payout that wouldn't be enough to support his family. He had to catch and sell salmon to earn the money. It was the only way.

This should not have been complicated or illegal, but things on the River had changed by the 1930s. There were more white people in Rek-woi, and there was a new town called Klamath just up the River, full of the same type of white people who sought profit from extracting what they considered resources from the River and forest.

Geneva knew her family had signed the treaty in 1851 with the US government reserving for the Yurok people an Indian reservation upon which to preserve their way of life. Geneva remembered her grandfather's stories about how they never understood the meaning of a treaty or a signature. They made a mark on paper anyway because the agents said that was required to stop the white people from killing them and to secure their land and fishing rights. It made no sense to anyone when, several years after the treaty signing, the Bureau of Indian Affairs agent announced that there was no treaty. Instead, the Yurok Reservation had been created by the president via executive order in 1855. While reservations created by executive orders are treated the same as treaties under the law, no one knew whether to be relieved that at least the River was still theirs or outraged that the reservation didn't include most of the land reserved in the treaty along the coast and the sacred High Country in the mountains east of the River. Even the small reservation didn't last long.

In the early 1900s, logging and fishing businesses were booming throughout Northern California, and Indian civil and property rights stood in the way of "progress." California had a solution. It claimed the Yurok Reservation was terminated by a federal act passed in 1892 that applied the General Allotment Act to the reservation. The General Allotment Act opened Indian reservations for land patents of tribal land to individual Indians and any "surplus" land to non-Indians. The 1892 act stated that the lands within the Klamath River Reservation would be subject to settlement, entry, and purchase according to the terms of the allotment act. The State of California interpreted the act to have terminated the Yurok Reservation, making the land and River within the former reservation state land and subject to state law.

In 1933, the state adopted a law prohibiting all Indian commercial and gillnet fishing on the lower Klamath River within the reservation, claiming the Klamath River, water, species, and any person on it were subject to state jurisdiction. As a result, the Indians, like Geneva and my family, had no special rights and were subject to state law. When it came to fishing, a state fishing permit would be required to pole fish, with catch limits of two to three fish per permit. The Indians would have to pay for the permit and keep it on them while on the River. Selling the fish and gillnet fishing were strictly prohibited, punishable by jail time and a hefty fine.

Geneva knew that wasn't right. They had "Indian rights" inherent to the Yurok people, which they reserved and vested in federal law by the executive orders creating the reservation. Those rights included the right to be on the Klamath River and enjoy the same lifeway as their ancestors. To fish, hunt, pray, speak, love, and be on the land, River, and ocean as their ancestors did — the family-owned land, great houses, and fishing holes where they had the power to control and use the property. She remembered her grandfather fishing from the family fishing hole in the estuary at a rock just below the House of La'yeq in Rek-woi. Billy had put his initials on the rock to mark his fishing hole, and from this rock had fished the great runs of salmon, steelhead, candlefish, sturgeon, and others that had fed every generation of his family. They ate fish for almost every meal, and Billy sold fish for money or traded for the things he couldn't make.

These were inalienable rights given by the Creator to my Nation and family to hold forever in the creation story and first covenant. They came from the Creator with instructions about how to exercise those rights sustainably. This was the source of our inherent sovereignty, not the US or state governments or any other sovereign. It predated the US government, the Spanish, the Russians, and any other sovereign that had come through Yurok Country. We existed on earth to exercise those sacred rights; this was our responsibility.

The US had responsibilities to us too. After the reservation was created, the US declared Yurok people wards of the state and assumed administration of Indian affairs, including managing bank accounts, entering into leases, and sales of lands and resources. This created a trust responsibility to protect our interests. Here, the Department of Interior had the power and obligation to protect our fishing rights against state intrusion. Our rights were not state-based rights, they were federally reserved Indian rights protected by the US Constitution, the executive orders creating the reservation, and trust law. Yet, it did nothing. When her son came to her declaring he would fish, she knew it was his inherent right to fish and to sell those fish to support his family, just as his ancestors would have. Yet, the state had criminalized their Indian rights and way of life through the 1933 act, and had weaponized the law to arm state game wardens with the violent sword of racialized state violence and discrimination. To enforce the 1933 law, the state had hired wardens who were known to be hot-tempered lushes, anti-Indian marksmen who weren't afraid to use their weapons against the Indians. Yurok people lived a subsistence fishing lifestyle and would not survive without fishing. With no other choice, my family and many Yurok people only fished at night and were forced to sneak around the River to avoid the thuggish wardens. In the absence of federal protection, Geneva had no other choice than to help Emery Jr. not get caught the only way she knew how: through prayer.

"Son, we will try the Indian way. We'll try the praying. We must do it right, absolutely right, so it works. Before we go, we will have to fast to be clean. No more food for the rest of the day. No smoking or drinking, and you can't stay the night with your wife. You stay here tonight. When we pray, we have to believe with our whole being. Do you agree?"

Emery Jr. nodded in agreement. Fasting would cleanse their minds and bodies to allow their spirits to better communicate with the sacred on the prayer rock. It would also show the Creator they were willing to sacrifice something and work toward their prayer being answered.

"Good. We will go to the prayer rock to pray tomorrow morning. We will pray you catch salmon and sell them in town without getting caught by the state game wardens. We will pray you catch enough fish to turn on the lights at the house and buy your kids school clothes."

Geneva paused. She turned to look at him. He was a handsome man, in his twenties, smart and kind, yet, compromised by his injuries. She saw the worry in his eyes. "Son, this prayer is the best way

I know how to protect you and keep you safe from those wardens. Indian prayer has always kept our family safe on this River. We have powerful prayers. I know things are changing now because the white people may have pushed out the sacred from our lands and waters. If you get picked up with that fish after we pray, you don't have to believe Indian way anymore. We will know it doesn't work anymore. Indian way be gone forever," she repeated.

It wasn't the first time the family had bootlegged fish. They continued to sell fish, as they had always done, after the adoption of the state law prohibiting the sale of salmon. They had a market in San Francisco with a buyer from the Mafia who didn't mind working fast and loose above the law. Still, they didn't understand the new law — it was like one day, it was illegal to be Yurok on the Klamath River. The wardens had shown up and arrested a Yurok fisherman for fishing for salmon in his family's traditional fishing hole. No one understood how fishing in the same place your family had been fishing forever could be illegal. It was like making breathing illegal.

«««

The next day, the mist and fog had been burned off by the summer sun shining bright over Rek-woi and the River. The mouth of the River changed every few years when it moved north or south, reminding the family that change was okay, and to welcome it. The fishing hole stayed productive through these changes, also reminding the family that salmon would always support them, no matter what changes occurred.

Geneva and Emery Jr. reached the boat. Emery Jr. stabilized the boat, then reached for his mother's hand. She stepped into the boat from the dock and sat at the stern, looking up and out toward the estuary. The prayer rock sat patiently on the other side of the River. Between the prayer rock and them lay the estuary of the Klamath River. For the baby salmon, this area was the end of the River, as they had traveled down from the spawning grounds through the River's arteries to the estuary, building enough strength along the way to venture through the River mouth and into the unknown of the ocean to begin their lifelong journey. For the adult salmon, the estuary marked the beginning of the River, and the end of their journey toward upriver spawning grounds.

Today the water was calm. Only a bit of wind moved briskly up the River, coming off the ocean. It moved west, and they'd have to row downriver to avoid the wind carrying them too far upriver. The water glided silently at Geneva's feet. She looked up, squinting to take in O'-rey-gos's large stature, shaped in the form of a woman with a baby on her back, rising from the water like a true goddess. Geneva bowed her head and asked O'-rey-gos for her prayer to work and for safe passage across the estuary.

Emery Jr. untied the rowboat and started rowing south to the prayer rock. The ocean waves were quiet. There was another rowboat about a quarter mile up the River they could see. Otherwise, the River was empty, and they could enjoy the serenity of the moment.

"Mom, do you think this will work?" Emery Jr. asked as he looked nervously toward the prayer rock.

"Son, if you believe, it will work. Do you remember how to move the boat when we get halfway across the River?" inquired Geneva.

"I think so," Emery Jr. replied.

"Remember to face the front of the boat directly square to the prayer rock. Don't approach it from the side, or it will think you are sideways. Look at it when you row too. It needs to see your eyes. Tell it in your head that you are coming to it to ask for help. It will know if you fasted," explained Geneva.

Emery Jr. nodded, following his mother's lead. Two strong pulls of his ocean-side oar made the front of the boat directly square to the prayer rock. Emery Jr. faced the prayer rock, looking directly at it as he rowed toward it. As they got closer, they both could see an opening, a slight cave, where the water had worn away the rock, forming the perfect place for the boat to be docked.

Once the boat was still, Geneva stood and walked to the edge of the boat, took Emery Jr.'s hand, and took her first step onto the prayer rock's edge. She touched her hand to the rock's surface. It was cold, slimy, and wet. The rock seemed bigger up close, standing two times over her head. Most of it was hard black rock, a deep black that shone just as bright up close as it did from across the River. There was an occasional strip of white rock moving through the black like air. She traced one white thread with her eyes from the top of the rock to the bottom, where it met the water's edge and disappeared below the water's surface. She took a deep breath in. It was time for the prayer.

"Pray along with me," she instructed her son, pulling her angelica root from her pocket. It was a small piece of root, a little shorter than a spoon. When she prayed, she burned angelica root. When Geneva was a girl, her grandmother had shown her how to use it. "Before you start your prayer, burn the top part of the root. Start with the sides, like this," she'd instructed as she lit the sides of the top of the root with a stick from the pit fire on the floor of the House of La'yeq. "And then let the flame grow a bit, and then let it burn out, so a good amount of smoke flares. Then start your prayer, and let the smoke carry your prayers to the Creator."

At the rock with her son, Geneva lit her root just like her grandmother had shown her. The prayer rock blocked the ocean wind from the west, and the smoke from the top of the root began to rise in a small stream like the water had taken flight. Geneva settled into her breath. She closed her eyes briefly. The image of herself as a young girl on the beach next to the rock collecting seaweed with her grandmother flashed before her eyes, and she smiled. This pleasant memory was a blessing, releasing a flood of positive chemical reactions in her body and mind. She was clean enough from her fast to experience a rush of energy preparing her mind, body, and soul for a positive communication with the sacred.

She let the image pass and focused in on her son Emery Jr. She saw him fishing at Blue Creek. She saw the salmon swimming into his net. They were big and bright chrome. There were many of them. She began to speak softly.

"Creator, keep Emery Jr. safe, let him catch and sell salmon without trouble. He has no other way to make money after his accidents. He needs to take care of his kids and get them to school. Please provide a safe path for him and let him make enough money to turn the lights on and buy school clothes without getting caught and thrown in jail. Please. Thank you, Creator, for all our blessings."

She looked at Emery Jr. "Anything else?"

He shook his head.

"Okay, let's go."

She took his hand and got back into the boat. Her heart felt light, and it wasn't just because she hadn't eaten in twenty-four hours. The prayer was strong. She felt it. If the Indian way had anything left to it, they'd find out tomorrow.

《《《

The next day as the sun began to set, Emery Jr. packed up his fishing gear, including a thirty-foot-wide gill net, a fish-cleaning knife, a spoon, two anchors, a thermos of coffee, a jar of smoked salmon, and a bag of saltine crackers.

"I am going with ya," said Geneva, almost bolting out of the house. Geneva had taught her son to fish.

"Momma, it's too dangerous."

"You think this is my first time bootlegging, son? You know I have done this before and never this safe. This is the first time I prayed for it. I just know those two state wardens are out there waiting for a fellow like you to arrest," said Geneva.

Geneva had always been determined and articulate. Strong-willed. He searched her face for that look of *You better not tell me I can't because I am your mother, and I will do what is best for all of us.* Finding it in a slightly slanted squint in her right eye, he resigned himself to the arrangement. At least now he had a fishing partner.

Emery Sr., Geneva's husband, and Ray, her youngest son (Marvin's twin brother), helped carry the fishing gear to the boat that was docked upriver at Brooks Riffle, below the homeplace cabin. Ray was a sweet, competent child who loved spending time with his parents at the homeplace fishing. Geneva, who had arrived at the boat and was standing behind her two boys, smiled. "Smells like fish. Let's go."

"Okay, you know what to do," cautioned Emery Sr. "No lights. No sound. Don't use the motor. Set the net just below the mouth of Blue Creek. Have you been praying?"

"Yes, Pa," said Emery Jr.

"Good. You'll be fine, then." Emery Sr. looked willfully upriver toward Blue Creek. He wanted to go with his son. He couldn't risk it. If they were caught, he'd be thrown in jail. If the folks in town found out, he wouldn't be able to get work. He had a good reputation as a hard worker, reliable, dependable, and smart. Because of his reputation, he'd been able to secure work in the mills when other Indians couldn't. That would all be ruined if he was caught red-handed fishing on the River. He could lose his job and any chance for a new one. The family needed his income.

"Sweetheart, be careful," Emery Sr. said, helping Geneva into the boat.

"Ah, you old goat, I'll see ya in the morning. Love you," she teased with a look.

Geneva took her seat in the front of the boat, in between the two gill nets. Emery Jr., sitting in the middle of the boat, grabbed the oars and began rowing from shore.

"Can I go?" asked Ray.

Emery Jr. stopped rowing and looked at Geneva. She nodded. "Jump in," he said, and they rowed back to the shore to pick Ray up. While this was risky, Ray was already a good fisherman and would expedite the trip.

By now it was dark. From Brooks Riffle to Blue Creek was about five River miles. Conditions were ideal for fishing. Summer held on, not giving in to the fall's chill just yet. The water was smooth, a blanket on the riverbed, tousled only by the oars. Barely tapping the surface of the water, Emery Jr. propelled the boat upriver in an elegant glide. The dew hadn't set in yet, so the air was light, and they moved quickly with no wind to impede them, the boat creaking slightly with every stroke. Geneva raised an eyebrow, looking at Emery Jr., careful not to talk, as her voice could carry over the water. She had asked him to grease the oar rings. Any noise could alert the wardens. He frowned. He had forgotten the grease.

The moon hadn't risen above the jagged coastal range lining the River. Its shadow moved upward from the east, daring to bring light to the sky, presenting a silver lining in the direction they were headed. They followed it as a north star even though they needed little direction. They both had traveled this stretch of River their whole lives. They knew it well: every eddy, fishing hole, large rock, gathering spot, and trail.

They passed the halfway point between Brooks Riffle and Blue Creek, marked by two large redwood trees that grew directly up from the bank of the River, reaching so high they carried condors and eagles and prayers to the next world. Geneva looked up, thankful the trees were still standing even after the allotment era and the timber company logged every accessible redwood tree. She wasn't sure how these two had survived. Just a few decades ago the timber company had used the River to move the logs downriver to be hauled off to the mill. The redwood trees had been cut down, pulled into the River, and floated down to the mouth. At times it looked like the River had turned into a horizonal floating forest.

She had seen so much destruction of her River and riparian forests. First it was the mining, and then the canneries, taking so many salmon, more than she'd ever seen come out of the River. Then it was the timber companies, logging entire hillsides from top to bottom. She questioned the sense behind ruining so much for money, and at such a great cost to the environment. They had destroyed creeks and springs, prayer seats and hunting grounds, and taken animals' lives without using their remains. What kind of people allow that type of waste? It wasn't right. She was lost in thought when she heard it.

A low rumble. A quiet rumble. Her eyes widened; her body tensed; she looked at Emery Jr. on alert. He nodded, acknowledging he heard it too. She put her finger over her mouth, signaling to Ray to not talk. She motioned with two fingers to row toward the River bar to the left, to a group of willow trees with branches hanging over the River. Emery Jr., without noise, except for the slight squeal of the oar ring, quickly navigated the boat under the branches. They were stationed there, well hidden, with only the whites of their wide eyes showing. They listened. Only the wardens, who would be on the hunt to bust Indian fishing people, had motorboats. The low rumble could have been from a boat motor headed toward them. If they were caught with gill nets in the boat, they'd go to jail.

They listened more.

A low rumble again, from downriver. It sounded mechanical, like the humming of a small boat engine. Their spines straightened. Ray was scared. They all looked at one another in alarm.

Another low rumble. Emery Jr. surveyed the boat, making sure it was under the branches. Geneva said a silent prayer asking for protection. They held their breath.

Downstream, two River miles, two wardens were slowly making their way upriver, barely running the boat motor and not using a spotlight, stealthily trying to catch *those damn Indians* in action. They didn't know the River; they were new. They'd come up from the Bay Area after game warden training, instructed to patrol the River at night and immediately arrest any Indian with a fishing net or salmon close to or in the River. Armed with billy clubs, pistols, and bulletproof vests, they had something to prove and were confident they'd prove it. River conditions got in the way because it was wilder than they'd expected.

Tonight, the wardens ran into trouble again. They turned a corner and read the riffle wrong. They went over a shallow spot and the motor sucked up gravel and quit, with a spitting sound like it was purging. They sat in the boat, trying to start the motor. It caught the current and started floating downriver. The wardens gave up on the engine and rowed to the riverbank. Arriving on land, still trying to be quiet, they opened the motor hatch and extracted as much gravel as they could. They started to try to turn the motor over again. With each attempt, the engine emitted a low rumble. They tried three times. No luck. They pulled the boat farther up the riverbank and secured it with an anchor. They'd leave it there tonight and walk back to the truck that was parked along a logging road a few miles into the forest. Leaving the boat, they headed toward the truck into the dense forest.

Emery Jr. whispered to Geneva, "Do you hear it? I think it's gone."

Geneva shook her head. She motioned to go.

Emery Jr. quietly grabbed the oars, while Geneva lifted a branch over her head as the boat began to move out from the willow branches emerging from the River's reach. They continued to Blue Creek.

They reached the fishing hole downriver from the mouth of Blue Creek. The creek ran low this time of year, though its flow was perfect for fish passage, enough for the fish to move yet not too much so it would have to fight hard, expending limited energy. Emery Jr. started rowing backward, the net in the front of the boat, the rope tied to the rock, stretching out long, pulling the net into the water. Geneva stood poised above the net, throwing it out of the boat into the water, setting it just right. Ray sat in the middle of the boat, watching them both.

They looked at the net. Only two corks above water. A close look was required to notice they were attached to a net. The net was set well.

Emery Jr. took a breath, and the wood cork bobbed. *Fish on.* Emery Jr. grabbed the cork line and worked methodically, moving his hands down the net, pulling the boat toward where the cork was bobbing up and down. Arriving there, he swiftly worked his way down the net, lifting it out of the water with a methodical motion: hand after hand, nylon net moving through his fingers, careful to not get tangled, moving lower and lower toward the end of the net. Then he saw it. A glowing silver slab, the shape of a crescent moon with a fat belly. Clear and bright, even as it rose from the water. His heart rate rose. His mother smiled. He still worked the net well even after his injury.

The salmon surfaced and he pulled it from the water into the boat. It landed with a thud, tangled in the net. Geneva silently thanked the fish for giving its life. Emery Jr. grabbed its head, separating its gills from the net, and then pulled the net down over the salmon's body. It shook its body, its tail flipping back and forth, fighting for its life. He freed it from the net, popped its gill, and laid it on the bed of the boat. Ray watched, in awe of his brother's precision and skill.

Another salmon hit. Emery Jr. smiled at Ray and Geneva. Perhaps the risk of fishing would be worth it. He'd been in dire straits about how he was going to take care of his family. He was lucky to have survived his injury, yet he'd felt hopeless and useless because after losing his job he couldn't find work to earn money for his family. He could farm, but there weren't any available jobs. The only thing left for him was bootleg fishing.

The night and conditions were proving to pay off. Salmon after salmon hit the net. By the time the moon had crossed the middle of the River and started to drop to the west toward the ocean, he had enough fish to sell to pay for the electricity bill for the year and buy school clothes.

Ray, while he had gone fishing before with his brother, had never spent the whole night fishing or caught that many salmon. He was hooked.

"I think that's enough, Mom," Emery Jr. said.

"Yes," she replied.

They rowed back downriver to the homeplace, the boat moving slow and close to the water, weighed down by a load of beautiful bright salmon. With every pull and push of the oar, Emery Jr. felt the pleasure of satisfaction move through his body. The closer he got to home, the closer he got to selling the fish, the more his confidence grew. Maybe the prayer had worked.

He relaxed a little bit. The fish were covered by an army tarp that belonged to his older brother, whose birth name was Arden but was called Jack, who had died on D-Day in World War II. Its thick green-brown material stiffly laid like a starched blanket covering the salmon. He could see a sliver of shine reflecting from the moon off the bottom corner of a salmon's tail. This made his heart rise. He quickly covered the fish tail, in case the wardens were hiding in the bush along the riparian grounds of the River looking for them.

They arrived at the homeplace just before dawn broke. The dark still covered them, working as a partner in their bootlegging scheme. Emery Sr.'s old truck waited for them at the River bar. Quickly and without noise, Emery Sr. got out of the front seat of the truck, and his daughter Lavina, a teenager, got out of the passenger seat. Geneva looked at Emery Sr. with piercing small black eyes communicating with a directed look, *What is she doing here? It's not safe!* Emery Sr. put up his arms as if to signal he had lost the battle with his daughter.

She smiled at her momma, saying, "Momma, I brought you two canteens of coffee, with cream! It's still hot!"

"Shh!" they all replied. Her enthusiasm faded as their response triggered her realization that they were all in danger. At any moment wardens could appear from the brush or the River with guns and arrest them all and take them to jail. They'd have to spend the night in jail and then pay fines with money they didn't have. It had happened many times before to other family and friends. She didn't say another word.

Instead, Lavina grabbed a fish from the boat and loaded it into the truck bed without a sound, following her family's lead, moving quickly and urgently. The fish were laid one by one in the truck bed on top of one another. No ice so there would be no water dripping from the truck bed. That was a sure sign of salmon bootleggers. They loaded more than fifty large salmon, until the last one was in the truck. It took only minutes. They placed redwood branches over the top of the salmon, four to five layers deep, to cover the load.

Emery Sr. and Jr. surveyed the load and the truck. No dripping water. No exposed salmon. The truck looked like they were bringing a load of redwood brush into town to sell. Emery Sr. nodded to Emery Jr. in approval. Geneva and Emery Jr. got in the truck. Geneva raised an eyebrow to Emery Sr. as she walked by, their hands brushing as they passed each other. It was a dance they'd done several times a day, connecting in passing, saying without words all that needed to be said.

By the time they hit the logging road, dawn had come, and it was light enough to see the road before them. Emery Jr. drove cautiously, his eyes peeled for anything out of the ordinary, particularly for signs of the wardens. The wardens patrolled the logging roads above the River looking for salmon bootleggers. They had caught people too.

She thought of this as they drove past the third of six bends in the logging road before they'd meet the highway. That's when she saw it. Emery Jr. did too as he braked slightly.

It was the wardens' truck. There, up ahead twenty-five feet on the side of the road, parked in the brush with its headlights still on, shining brightly through the morning sun over the road.

Emery Jr. slowed the truck and kept going. There were no places to turn off the road. There were no places to turn around.

"Mom, we have no option other than driving by," Emery Jr. said.

This was it. The moment. The test to determine if the prayer and medicine had worked. With all the white people here now, with all the new beliefs, the Christian ways, the lack of adherence to tradition, she worried there was no Indian way left. Was her way still here?

She closed her eyes and said a quick silent prayer asking for the Indian way to work.

They got closer to the wardens' truck. Close enough to see two wardens sitting in the cab of the truck asleep. The sound of the bootleggers' truck woke them up. They were tired from the late night on the River and the trek from the River to the truck. They had spent the night in the truck and were stiff, sore, and cold, and without food and water.

As the bootleggers' truck got closer, one warden recognized the passenger. Even though the wardens were new, they had been briefed by superiors about the Mattz family. He knew Geneva and her family lived upriver, and that she usually had warm coffee with cream when she traveled.

The warden said to his partner, "Hey, that's Geneva Mattz. Let's ask her if she has any coffee."

The partner nodded. They straightened up and got out of their truck. Stepping onto the gravel logging road, their bones hurt. They waved with a smile, signaling to the truck to stop, hopeful their warm approach would produce coffee or water or anything to soothe them.

Emery Jr. saw them wave but not their smiles. His heart began to race. He looked in the rearview mirror at the truck bed. The redwood branches bounced gingerly with each bump and showed no sign of disclosing the forbidden cargo.

"Mom, what do I do? They will see the salmon. They will arrest us."

Geneva took a deep breath. "It's okay, son," she said, looking at him confidently and calmly. "When you get close, stop the truck and keep it in drive. Let me do the talking."

Geneva and Emery's truck slowly stopped as it reached where the wardens were standing on the passenger side. Emery kept the truck in drive, ready to move if they needed to escape quickly.

They nodded with a slight smile.

Geneva rolled down the window.

"Hello, boys. How you all doing?"

"Hello, Mrs. Mattz."

"You all okay?" She observed them, noticing their dirty clothes, with dirt patches on the knees from tripping on the rugged trail from the River to the truck.

"Our boat broke down last night just above your place. We tried for a long time to get it going. It wouldn't turn over. We had to walk to the truck late last night. We slept in the truck last night. Just getting moving."

Emery Jr. glanced at Geneva, thinking the rumbling they heard last night was the wardens trying to start the boat. They had been so close to getting caught. If the boat had started, the wardens would have come upriver and caught Geneva and Emery fishing red-handed. They would have been taken to jail.

"Ah, I see. You boys need some coffee? We got a little extra."

The wardens sighed in relief and said, "Yes, ma'am."

She poured them each a cup, telling them to keep the mugs. They both took big sips; the warm, creamy liquid eased their discomfort and warmed their bellies. Their gratitude for a warm cup of coffee distracted them from what they'd come here to prove, and that they were talking to Indians.

"Sure is a good cup, Mrs. Mattz. Thank you," said the wardens.

She nodded in gratitude. "Good luck, boys. Be careful out here. It's not safe if you don't know these here woods."

"Where you headed, Mrs. Mattz?"

Emery Jr. moved uncomfortably in the driver's seat. He slowly put his foot directly over the gas pedal. He was prepared to hit the gas to escape if they asked to look at the load in the truck bed.

"Headed to town to sell some scrap wood and buy supplies. About out of coffee," she said with a wink.

They nodded. "Drive safe."

"Thank you, boys," Geneva said.

Emery Jr. waved and slowly pushed down on the gas pedal as they drove away.

They turned another corner on the tight mountain road. The wardens faded into a sea of green redwood trees and ferns. Geneva rolled up her window, exhaled, and laughed hard.

"Well, son, we fooled them boys!"

He looked at her, surprised by her exultation. He started to laugh hard too. They looked at each other and laughed harder.

"Nothing like your sweet cream coffee. Thank goodness Lavina packed two canteens."

"Why, yes, son! Thank goodness. Saved by the coffee and redwood load!" They laughed.

They had just stopped laughing, bellies sore from the exertion, when they turned the last bend and reached the highway. It would be smooth sailing from here to town. The fish would be sold. Emery Jr. would get his money.

The likelihood that the wardens' engine had died the night before and that Lavina had packed an extra canteen of coffee was not lost on Geneva. The Indian way had worked. There was still right in the world.

She looked at Emery Jr., his face glowing vibrantly as the late morning sun illuminated his profile.

"Son," she said, "it worked. The prayer worked."

"I know, Momma, I know. I'll never question the Indian way again."

CHAPTER 7

The Heart and Courage to Fight for It

1950s

The spring chinook salmon are the leaders of the salmon runs in the Klamath River. They enter the River in early spring when the dogwood tree flowers bloom, the first run of salmon to return home in the new year. Historically, they were the most plentiful salmon run in the Klamath. They are also strikingly beautiful, with bright silver scales and deep red meat. They have always been the family's favorite because they are the most delicious and nutritious.

Geneva shared stories about the spring salmon from when she was a girl. The first salmon ceremony would be held when they return in the spring and the chinook salmon enter the River. Downriver, families came to the mouth of the River to witness and celebrate the return of the salmon to the River. The families would gather for a week or so on the beach dividing the River and the ocean, setting up large camps with tents, kitchens, and fires. One family had the right to catch the first salmon. That family would fish at the very entrance to the River while the other families would watch, visit, cook food, sing songs, gamble, or play stick games, a popular Yurok sport.

When the family caught the first salmon, the entire beach would come alive, cheering, singing, jumping, and rejoicing for the salmon's return to Yurok Country. After the first salmon was caught, the other families could start fishing. This marked the beginning of the salmon-fishing season, after which different runs of coho and chinook salmon would be in Yurok Country until October. Geneva remembered her family fishing off their fishing rock next to O'-rey-gos during these first salmon ceremonies. There was plenty of salmon for each family, and everyone was happy. This was a joyous occasion that everyone looked forward to throughout the year.

The first salmon ceremony was a Yurok expression of freedom. Since time immemorial we have been a fishing people. The River is our lifeblood for many reasons, in part because it brings the salmon home, bringing a vital first food to the table that feeds our families and provides for our survival.

We were free to fish on our own terms. Even if salmon entered the River, no one would fish for salmon before the first salmon ceremony. Only the family with the first salmon rights harvested the first salmon, after which the other families would fish. This was a ceremonial regulation of the fishery that showed respect and honor to the salmon and regulated community behavior. It reinforced our reverence for the salmon and our duty to them by celebrating their return to the River. This was freedom.

A freedom lost.

〈〈〈

"Lavina, don't breathe," Emery Jr. whispered to his sister. He was eight years her senior, she in her early twenties, and Ray just over ten years old.

She held her breath, not daring to move. She lay under her late brother's thick green World War II army tarp between her brothers Emery Jr. and Ray on the River bar above Brooks Riffle at the home-place. They made their bodies as flat and still as possible. The River bar underneath them was cold, rocky, and sandy. The water moving over Brooks Riffle gently roared below them. It was pitch dark under the tarp. A stick poked Lavina in the back. She didn't dare move. Emery Jr. held her hand. She squeezed his hand. She worried her rapidly pounding heart would burst from her chest and move the tarp.

Moments earlier they had been fishing at Brooks Riffle, sitting in the boat tending the gill net, when they heard a motorboat coming up the River. The engine roar grew louder, and they saw a spotlight shine a few bends down the River. They knew the wardens were coming for them.

The wardens were after the Mattz family to keep them from fishing. The family found themselves in a justice system that viewed brown skin, braided hair, and fishing boots as probable cause. No one, including the Department of the Interior, thought to question whether the state had jurisdiction to regulate Indian fishing on an Indian reservation. It did not. Only Indigenous nations or the federal government has jurisdiction to regulate Indian fishing on Indian reservations. The state's actions were unlawful. The Department of the Interior should have intervened to protect the Yurok and Mattz family fishing rights, because it had a *trust responsibility* to protect federally reserved Indian rights. Yet, the Department did nothing. This was not just a bureaucratic failure. It was a betrayal.

Had the federal government exercised this responsibility to the Yurok people, the wardens would not have been on the River targeting the Mattz family, making them outlaws on their home waters.

Ten feet from Lavina, Ray, and Emery Jr., the River ran under a half-moon covered by scattered clouds. Its determined quiet flow to the ocean was disrupted only by the twenty-foot metal jet boat owned by the State of California. Two wardens manned the boat, looking for the Mattz family fishing.

"Just up around this bend, by Brooks Riffle. That's where they normally fish. I bet we'll get 'em this time," said one of the officers.

They turned the bend and looked up the River to Brooks Riffle. No sign of the Mattz family. No net in the water. No boat.

"Dang it."

"Well, hold on. Let's get a little closer."

The boat cleared the riffle and slowed down. They trolled slowly upriver. A warden holding the spotlight shone it on both sides of the River, surveying the riparian area around the Mattz homeplace. The spotlight illuminated the east hillside; brush, thick green vines, ferns, blackberry bushes, and willow and alder trees gave way to redwood trees that lined the ridge to the hillside like jewels on a crown. The light from the spotlight made the dew on the redwood tree branches sparkle. The wardens saw no evidence of fishing, no Indians, no gill nets, no boat. They flashed the light on the other side of the River, a bar of sand, rocks, and the occasional green bush. The River bar stretched wide along a straight stretch of the River, divided by an unpaved road to the Mattz homeplace cabin.

"Shine the light on that road on the River bar. Does it look like anyone has used it recently? Can you see tire marks?"

"I can't see shit. This here light is so dim." The warden shook the spotlight. The light flickered on and off, and did not increase in strength.

"Well, shoot. This thing is running out of batteries." The warden shone the light back on the River bar.

Lavina took one breath in, one breath out. She closed her eyes but could still see the light from the warden's spotlight pass over the green tarp a second time. She stopped breathing. Emery Jr. did the same. The light went over the tarp again. They could hear every word the wardens said from their boat on the water.

"See anything?" questioned a warden.

"No. You?"

"No, let's go."

They turned the boat around and headed downriver.

Emery Jr., Lavina, and Ray listened to the roar of the motorboat engine until it couldn't be heard anymore. Only then did they exhale and move.

"That was a close one," Emery Jr. said.

Lavina began to cry.

"It's okay, sister, we're okay."

She looked at Emery, reassured. She wiped her tears, as he pulled the tarp down. They stood up and stretched, stiff from holding still for so long. Their hearts pounding.

"I knew the warden would be looking for us here, after Ray and I were arrested. I knew they would keep looking for us at our fishing hole," Emery Jr. said.

Not long before, Ray and Emery Jr. had been arrested by the wardens for fishing at Brooks Riffle. Ray was thirteen years old when he was arrested for the first time for fishing. He and his brother had been handcuffed, their gear confiscated, and hauled to jail. Using the law as a tool of oppression rather than justice, the state aggressively enforced the state law prohibiting Yurok fishing. Violating this law, they kept fishing, just as they always had. The Mattz family and Yurok people had Indian rights based in federal law. From the Mattz family perspective, it was legal to fish and sell salmon because they had Indian rights from the Creator that had been reserved in federal law respecting the creation of the reservation by their ancestors. They were no bootleggers. They were exercising their inherent rights vested in federal law. Fishing was their way of life. They knew no other way to survive. Their survival had become dangerous, again.

《《《

Two California state game wardens sat in a 1950s Ford truck squinting to look through a pair of binoculars at the Klamath estuary. A heavy May rain shower made visibility difficult. It was night, the only time the Indians fished because they'd get arrested immediately in the daylight. The wardens were parked at the west end of the Requa Dock parking lot, hidden behind a felled alder tree. There were reports that Ray and Emery Jr. had been fishing at the mouth of the River. From the truck's location twenty or so feet above the water, the wardens could see the entire estuary. If Ray and Emery Jr. came again, they'd see them.

Ray and Emery Jr. had heard the spring chinook salmon were running hard at the mouth. They thought about the first salmon ceremony. But the night Emery Jr. and Ray quietly rowed downriver toward the family fishing rock in the estuary, there was no ceremony. By the 1950s, there hadn't been a first salmon ceremony for more than eighty years. Instead, Emery Jr. and Ray were like criminals in their own home waters, fishing under the protection of a pitch-black night, sneaking from one open stretch of the River to the next, rowing quietly with no light to avoid the wardens.

For several years, the wardens chased the Mattz brothers up and down the River. Most of the time they got away. The Mattz brothers could move up and down the River without a motor or a light because they knew the River and how to navigate it well. The state had to use a light to travel on the River. The brothers would see the light, hear the engine, and pick up their gill net and escape under the cover of the night sky.

That's how the wardens ended up at the Requa Dock on that rainy night.

Emery Jr. and Ray had thought the wardens were too soft to be out working on a stormy night like this one. With the salmon running, it seemed like the right time to fish for springers. Plus, they had grown tired of fishing like criminals. After a long summer of cat and mouse, Emery Jr. had grown tired and frustrated. If they were caught, Emery Jr. said, "the hell with it, let's go to jail if we gotta go to jail."

The Mattz brothers had a twelve-foot wood rowboat, loaded with a gill net, rope, and a large rock for an anchor. They had waited until the sun was gone in the west and the moon had not risen over the mountain ridge lining the River to the east. It was dark, cloudy, wet. They had rain gear and were still cold — the kind of cold that goes all the way to your bones. Luckily, the water in the estuary was calm.

They set a gill net quickly and stood on the family fishing rock watching it. Ray was old enough now to instinctively feel the satisfaction of this moment. This was where his family had always fished. Right here, in these waters, for the same run of salmon, from this very rock. Yet he also felt the tinge of darkness. Something was wrong, unjust. He and his family were the only people who couldn't fish on this River. He knew his family had Indian rights. He was deep in thought when a salmon hit the gill net.

"Ray, get that salmon," Emery Jr. said.

Ray swiftly jumped from the fishing rock to the boat, rowed to the gill net, and freed the spring salmon from its confines. The salmon landed in the boat and thrashed with its whole body. Even under a cloud-covered sky, the bright silver of its skin shone brightly on Ray's face. Another fish hit. Ray got it, and another.

Fish after fish hit the gill net. Ray ran the net up and down three times, pulling salmon into the boat. On the fourth time back toward the fishing rock he picked up Emery Jr., who took over rowing the boat while Ray worked the net. They moved methodically together, efficiently and smoothly.

The rain had stopped. The ocean breakers grew tired and calmed. They barely made a sound when they landed on the sandy estuary beach. Fifty yards away from the fishing rock, the two wardens had left their truck and were climbing over Windy Point. They reached the point, which protruded south to create a crescent-moon-shaped bay with Windy Point on one side and the fishing rock on the other.

Twenty yards away, they spotted the Mattz boys fishing. They didn't say a word. They knew if Emery Jr. and Ray heard them, they'd take off running or rowing. They moved quickly, crouched down over the point toward the River bar. Stealthily, they moved toward the fishing rock.

Emery Jr. and Ray were still taking fish out of the net and both were leaning over the west side of the boat away from Windy Point. Ray, with the net in his hand, was bent over the water.

"Don't move. You are both under arrest," said a loud voice behind Ray and Emery Jr.

They looked at each other.

"We mean it, Mattz boys. Emery, Ray, you boys are done fishing," said the second warden.

The Mattz boys heard the different voices and knew there were at least two wardens.

"You try to run, I'll shoot you both," said the first warden.

Holding each other's gaze, Ray and Emery Jr. let go of the net and slowly turned around.

"Now, put your hands up, both of you. Emery, you row that thing you call a boat to shore. Try anything, and I swear to God I'll shoot." No one else was on the River. There would be no witnesses, so this was not an empty threat.

Emery Jr. sat down and took hold of the oars. He thought about rowing with all his might straight out the mouth into the calm ocean and floating to San Francisco. Maybe there they'd let him fish under the same rules as everyone else. It was too dangerous. People died going out the mouth of the River. He thought about rowing up the River, but they'd never outrun the warden's gunshots. He started rowing toward the shore.

"Guess you boys got an ounce of smarts, although I would have liked shooting you, you dirty Indians," one warden said as they arrived at the shore.

A warden aggressively grabbed Ray out of the boat and shoved him down to the ground. The side of Ray's face hit a rock, cutting his face. He stood up with blood dripping down his left cheek.

Emery Jr. jumped out of the boat to help Ray, and the second warden clubbed him over the head. He fell to the ground. Ray went to help him, but a warden grabbed his arm and pulled him back, cuffing Ray's hands behind his back.

Emery Jr. came to, rolling over as the warden stood over him. They cuffed him and took the Mattz boys to jail in Crescent City.

《《《

Emery Jr. and Ray got out of jail the next night and went to the homeplace up the River. They were tired, bruised, and hungry. Ray's shoulder was sore from the wardens pulling his arms behind his back to handcuff him. His wrists were bruised from the cuffs being too tight. He had a black eye where the warden had smashed his head into the side of a rock on the ground. The wardens had done this on purpose to show the full force of the state's laws. Ray was a renegade who thought he was above the state. The state wanted to send a clear message that no one, not even Ray Mattz and his family, was above the law on this River and things had changed; the state now had control over the River. The Yuroks and the Mattz family had lost the war with the white settlers. The white people now claimed ownership over the River, the fish, and the land, and the Mattzes would have to follow state law. They'd make an example of Ray to show the other Yurok people what happened to anyone who broke the law.

Emery Jr. and Ray gathered at the dinner table in the kitchen with Geneva and Emery Sr. Geneva gave them a plate of eggs and biscuits. They all noticed but didn't say anything about what was absent from the plate. Had they not been arrested, the wardens confiscating their fish, there would have been a slab of salmon with over-medium eggs and warm biscuits, the yolks runny enough to soak into the fish. Today, there was no salmon. Ray was still thankful for a hot meal and to be home.

"What are we going to do?" Emery Jr. said.

"I don't know, son," his father replied.

"We will go to jail if we have to. But we can't keep doing this. Things have changed. Those wardens have grown worse over the years. They are hurting us now. Beating us up when they catch us. They know where we fish," Emery Jr. said.

"It's our rights, our Indian rights, Momma. It's like you told us, the Creator gave us this here River and the fish to use and protect. It's our rights to be here on the River. They can't keep kicking us off like this.

It ain't right, it ain't just. I'll do whatever we must to make sure we can keep fishing. I'll never stop trying; they can keep throwing me in jail. Our Indian way of life is still here," Emery Jr. declared.

Ray's bruises seemed to throb more as his brother spoke. Every word made his blood boil. The injustice of it all overwhelmed him, and he grew angry. "It's enough," he said. "We have to fight for our rights, our Indian rights," Ray declared.

«««

The next day, Emery Jr. left the homeplace to go back to his house to see his wife and children. His father took him on the boat across the River. He told Emery Jr. he loved him and was proud of him for being brave through the arrest and taking care of his little brother. Emery Jr. thanked him as he got out of the boat and started hiking up the path toward his sister's Volkswagen bus.

Emery Jr. drove down to the main highway and headed south and then east toward Weitchpec. From there, the road narrows to almost a single lane, winding on the side of a deep canyon, one hundred to two hundred yards above the River.

It was getting late, and the sun was close to setting over the west ridge of the River's canyon. The light grew soft, a gentle glow that suggested the sun was almost out of energy but would hang on just a little longer to get Emery home before dark. Emery Jr. grew tired but kept going because he was eager to get home. It had been a hard time. The arrest, the night in jail. He needed some space from it all and wanted to be home with his wife and kids. He grew more tired. The trauma of the last few days caught up with him. His eyes closed. His hands slid off the steering wheel and rested by his sides. His foot slid off the gas pedal.

The Volkswagen van went straight and then hit the canyon wall, propelling the car high enough in the air to clear the road, jump over the guardrail, and descend into the River canyon about two hundred yards below. It soared freely in the air, clearing the steep canyon walls, like a heron diving toward the River for a meal, swiftly, nose down, and without interruption. The car hit the ground just above the River. Emery Jr. was launched out of the car. The impact of his landing woke him, but he didn't understand where he was or what had happened. He was so tired. He couldn't feel his body. His eyes closed.

The next morning, Emery's wife called a neighbor, reporting that Emery Jr. had not made it home, and asked if the neighbor would go look for him. It was early morning; the road was still covered in dew. The neighbor turned a sharp curve and saw tire tracks that led toward the canyon wall. He pulled off to the side of the road and quickly started down the cliff. He found Emery Jr., unconscious, a few yards from the crashed car. The neighbor managed to get the paramedics to the scene.

The family rushed to the hospital. When they arrived, Emery Jr. was still alive but unconscious. He had broken his back, and half of his tongue had been either cut or bitten off. He had pneumonia. Geneva stayed by his hospital bed until he passed two days later.

She was temporarily paralyzed with shock. She had lost her father and four children, one in World War II, one to tuberculosis, one in a logging accident just months earlier, and now Emery Jr. Each time, she wondered why the Creator had taken those she loved most. She knew when they left her, they went to the Creator. Somehow that made her feel closer to the Creator and the source of all life; it empowered her to live more authentically and with conviction because at any moment another love of her life could pass on to the Creator.

The doctor told Geneva that Emery Jr. had done himself a favor by dying because he wouldn't have been able to walk or talk after his injuries.

This "favor" did not ease her pain, not even when, upon news of his passing, the state dropped the fishing charges against Emery Jr. and Ray.

CHAPTER 8

Court of the Conqueror

▲▲▲▲▲▲▲▲▲▲▲▲▲▲▲▲▲▲▲▲▲▲▲▲▲▲▲▲▲▲▲▲▲▲▲▲
▼▼▼▼▼▼▼▼▼▼▼▼▼▼▼▼▼▼▼▼▼▼▼▼▼▼▼▼▼▼▼▼▼▼▼▼

1969

Seven years after Emery Jr. died, on one late September afternoon, Geneva had a hankering for salmon heads and collars for dinner. Both are Yurok delicacies because of the tender, juicy, fatty meat. Geneva liked to bake the heads and collars with salt and pepper. First, she'd eat the salmon cheek, a medallion mound of dark meat that tasted like tender game meat. Then she'd eat the salmon collar. She loved its oily, soft, flaky meat.

"Ray, you go upriver to Brooks Riffle and catch me a few salmon. I want to cook salmon heads and collars for dinner tomorrow. Your nephews and sister Janet and Emery Jr.'s son are coming up from town today. You can take them," said Geneva to Ray.

The family had moved to the new house in Rek-woi because, sadly, a flood had washed out the cabin, orchard, garden, and animals at the homeplace two years after Emery Jr. died. The family had lost much in a few years. Making matters worse, Ray continued to be targeted by the state.

Ray was an excellent fisherman from a young age and even illegal prosecution could not keep him off the water. His life was the River. The River, salmon, and his family taught him to fish. He first learned to fish from Geneva and her sister. He started fishing on his own at nine years of age. Geneva had trained him in the instruction from her grandfather Billy Brooks, who had learned from his ancestors, who had learned from the Creator about how to fish; you don't fight over fish, you always share with others, and never take more than you need. This was consistent with the first covenant with the Yurok people because it resulted in a just and balanced distribution of a critical food resource.

Ray had intimate knowledge of the River and salmon because he spent most of his time observing them. His fishing was poetic because he had a way of working harmoniously with the River and salmon, moving artfully, setting his gill nets in the best holes on the River where the fish were, and harvesting them with ease. He deeply respected the subject of his pursuits and the River in which they lived. He understood the impact the salmon had on the River, water, and air. He could read the flow of the water to determine where the fish might take refuge or move through quickly. While he barely learned to read and write and didn't graduate high school, his intimate understanding of the Klamath River and its salmon made him an expert on the River. His extraordinary skills and gregarious personality made him well-liked and a leader in his community. He caught more salmon than most and shared with elders, helping to keep the community fed, even if it was under the cover of night while hiding from wardens.

But this drew the attention of non-Indigenous sport fishermen. The lower Klamath River salmon and steelhead fishery was world-class. It attracted sport and commercial fishermen to the River and they saw Ray and other Yurok fishing people as competition for salmon. Unlike Yurok fisher families, the newcomers were not trained in the ways of stewarding a fishery, sharing with others and self-regulating fishing practices to prevent overharvest. Instead, they felt the Yurok people and Ray specifically took what they considered "their fish." They wanted all the fish. Ray became a target of their racist campaign against Indian fishing. Sport and commercial fishermen harassed him, claiming he was killing off the Klamath salmon.

Perhaps it was at the direction of the sport fishermen that the wardens hunted Ray. He escaped their torment on most fishing excursions because he fished at night. But he was caught eighteen times and cited for fishing on the Klamath River within the Yurok Reservation by the time he was twenty-six years old. Each time, the wardens would confiscate all his fishing gear, give him a ticket, and take his gear to the local police station. Sometimes the wardens beat him just to prove a point — that they were in control, not him — one he never accepted. The fishing gear was expensive, and he was poor. He didn't have money to buy new gear. He'd have to wait to fish until he appeared in court, paid a fine, or sometimes spent a night in jail, before getting his fishing gear back. Then he'd go fishing again, undeterred by the hassle. He knew he was not an outlaw. He had Indian rights that he would exercise.

"Okay, Momma. I'll go tonight," he said, accepting that tonight could lead to his nineteenth arrest. Geneva was undeterred by the harassment and arrests too.

It was 1969. While the rest of the country was pushing the limits of the human experience at Woodstock, landing on the moon for the first time, and protesting for civil rights, the Mattz family continued to fight the forces of colonization and racism.

That evening, Ray took a few cousins, along with five gill nets and a boat, to Brooks Riffle to fish. They built a fire, set two nets, and left the other three nets on the River bar because two nets could catch plenty of fish. The leaves on the alder trees along the River were changing to shades of bright yellow and red. It was a nice fall evening, warm, with a light, cool breeze that reminded you winter was coming and the fish would be there for only so long, so best to catch them now — especially the big Blue Creek chinook salmon.

It was late September and the salmon that spawned in Blue Creek, a tributary of the Klamath River, were heading up the River. These salmon were typically huge, which made them particularly fun to catch because you never knew when you might catch a *hog*. Ray and his family watched the two gill nets from the River bar, standing around the fire with excitement and joy, hoping to catch big Blue Creek salmon.

When they heard a motorboat coming up the River, they knew it was the wardens and began to panic. It was nighttime and they were surprised the state was on the water.

"Ray, what do we do?" his nephew asked him.

Ray took stock: there was not enough time to pull the two nets, load up the three nets on the River bar, put out the fire, and hide himself and his family before the wardens arrived. Countless times he had fished with his family at the fishing rock at the mouth of the River below Rek-woi, at Brooks Riffle by the homeplace, on Blue Creek, and at other places along the River. He knew this River as well as anyone. But eighteen times the state had caught him, arrested him, beat him, took his fishing gear and boat, threw him in jail, and then made him pay to return his gear. He thought of Emery Jr. "I'll never stop fighting for my fishing rights," Emery Jr. had said right before he died. Ray thought, *I'll never stop either.* He knew what to do.

"It's okay, don't. Don't worry. Let them come," Ray said.

The wardens rounded the bend and drove up Brooks Riffle, the two nets in the water upriver from the riffle. The wardens pulled their boat up to the River bar. From the boat, they yelled, "Whose nets are those?"

No one said a word. There was a long silence.

"They are mine," Ray said. He was the youngest person there.

"All five of them?" the warden replied.

"Yes," Ray said. Claiming them all meant no one else would have to go to jail.

"All right, then, Ray. You're coming with us. I don't have to tell you, Indians can't fish here. You just can't get it through your thick head," said the warden.

Ray stood his ground.

The wardens got out of the boat, came to shore, cuffed Ray, and put him in the boat. The sun had just gone down, and it was getting dark and foggy.

"We can't drive down the River in the dark and fog," whispered one warden to the other. They paused for a while, contemplating what to do. They were six River miles from the Requa Dock where they'd launched the boat.

There was a long pause.

"Will one of you drive us down to the Requa Dock?" asked a warden.

"What?" said his sister Janet. "You just arrested my brother, confiscated our nets, and are taking him to jail, and you want us to drive you home? Unreal."

The wardens said nothing. There was a long pause.

"Fine, we will take you down, when we are ready," Jack, his nephew said. Ray nodded in agreement. The wardens had no choice but to wait. Ray was the only person in trouble; the rest of them weren't. So they waited.

Ray and his family had planned to fish late and had everything they needed for a long night, including a pint of whiskey and an Indian drum (a square drum made of wood and deer hide). Now that the fishing was over, they all sat down at the fire and passed around the whiskey. The wardens let Ray join because they were at the mercy of the family to get downriver, and they sat in the boat and waited.

"Here, Uncle. You will need this to get through the night." They handed Ray the flask, and he took a long pull.

They paused awhile. The bonfire was vibrant yellow, white, and orange, and it crackled as it burned. Their family had sat around a fire like this, in this very spot, since forever. Rarely like this, prosecuted like criminals, one of them arrested just for being on their own land and water.

"Well, right now, right here, we will be on our land, and we will have a good time. You guys remember Grandpa Brooks's fishing song? Hand me the drum."

They handed Ray the drum and started singing an Indian song, with Ray drumming. It was a rhythmic, repetitive chant that grew stronger and stronger through the three times it was sung. The night was quiet, and the family's voices projected off the wall of the eastern ridge to the hills surrounding the River, making it larger than life. The River joined in, singing in concert with its flow's steady roar.

Song after song, they sang and drummed. Old Indian songs, the powerful ones. They sang to save their way of life, their ancient rights, and to protect their cousin from what was to follow.

The wardens had never heard Indian songs. They had never been on the River this late, and they had never been with this many Indians before. They didn't believe in Indian ways and they knew nothing of them. They felt the power in those songs, but it crept into their hearts as fear — fear of the unknown and the potential of a power that was older and stronger than they'd ever felt before or anything they'd ever known. They were frightened, but they had no choice but to sit in the boat and wait. They held their hands close to their guns, resting their fingers on their holsters.

When Ray and his family had their fill, they loaded up the boats and drove downriver to the dock at Requa. The wardens took all five nets and Ray to jail.

《《《

A few weeks later, Ray and the family appeared in the superior court in Willow Creek for his fishing charges from that night. They could not afford legal counsel, so they went without. Ray wore a pair of blue jeans ironed with a crease down the middle of each pant leg, a collared blue button-down shirt, and black leather shoes — the same clothes he had worn to his brother's funeral. His mother had ironed his shirt and jeans. She believed you should always look your best and keep your clothes cleaned and ironed. That way, no one would know you were poor. Ray sat at the defendant's table facing the bench where the judge sat. He looked good, respectable. Maybe that would help with the judge.

"Now, Ray," said the judge, commencing the proceedings, "we have been through this before," noting the prior eighteen fishing arrests in Ray's record.

Ray observed the courtroom setting. It was sterile, the fluorescent lights hanging on the low ceiling devoid of the warmth and depth of the sunlight on the River. There were no windows. The table he sat at, and the one next to it for the plaintiffs, where the state's lawyer and a game warden he had never seen before sat, were made of a thin plywood with brown plastic edging. The chair he sat in was made of black plastic. The judge who looked down at him was bald, with teeth as yellow as the fluorescent lights. There was no life here. Everything in the room was artificial, fake. He felt trapped and began to panic. He remembered the county jail cells where he had spent too many nights. They felt the same way, a trap full of artificial things. They were dead places blocked off from anything, cages of concrete.

"This is the nineteenth time you have appeared in my court for fishing violations. It's clear you have no intention of following the law. I am willing to dismiss the charges and return your gill net and gear if you pay the court $1." Ray and the judge had a rapport at this point. Ray had paid the fine the eighteen times he had been previously charged with violating the state law prohibiting Yuroks from gillnet fishing on the Klamath. The judge expected payment.

Ray thought of Emery Jr.'s last words. Ray simmered with the kind of rage that overwhelms your nervous system and then passes and leaves you exhausted. He found himself numb, yet confident in his anger and grief. Emery's life would not be lost in vain. His family's Indian rights would not be lost in vain. Nor did he want to keep being arrested and beaten up. Nor was he willing to give up his fishery to the non-Indians.

For most of his life, tension had been growing on the River. He appreciated now that the balance had been disrupted because the people were fighting over the fishery. It was his duty to restore the balance by asserting his Indian rights to ensure his people could continue their fishing way of life while others fished too.

He knew what to do. He stood up, looked the judge in the eye, pounded his fist, and said, "Your Honor. I have fishing rights. They are my Indian rights, and I am going to prove it. I will not pay you $1. Not here, not ever. I am taking my case as far as I have to." He pounded his fist on the table to break the artificial stagnant air surrounding him, making space for life to enter the room.

Behind him, sitting in the front-row bench of the courtroom gallery seating, his mother sat up a little taller. Her eyes beamed with pride as she heard her son speak.

"All right, then. It's done. You are, once again, convicted of violating California Fish and Game Code Sections 12300, 8664, 8686, and 8630."

Ray turned to his mother. His eyes searched hers for approval. She smiled. "You did good, son. We will fight this. It is time." She patted him on the back.

《《《

Six hours south of the family's home village of Rek-woi, in Berkeley, California, California Indian Legal Services (CILS) had just opened its first office. CILS was founded to provide pro bono legal representation to tribal governments and individuals to assert and protect Indian rights and quickly expanded to launch the Native American Rights Fund (NARF), the largest and oldest legal defense fund for Indigenous nations and peoples. The office had both nonnative and native attorneys, some of whom were the first generation of Native American attorneys, like Abby Abinanti, the first Indian woman to be admitted to practice law in California, and John Echohawk. They had started their legal education at the recently founded Pre-Law Summer Institute for American Indians and Alaska Natives (PLSI), housed by the University of New Mexico School of Law. There they'd learned the fundamentals of US law but also an emerging body of federal Indian law. They were also engrossed in the civil rights movement and thought deeply about how the values of the movement — equality and justice for all people in America — applied to Native American people and treaty rights. They had observed that while the rights of Indian nations secured in treaties were the supreme law of the land, entitled to prioritization and protection over other rights, treaty rights were not upheld. Moreover, states frequently attempted to infringe on Indian rights and enforce state law on Indian reservations, illegally intruding into tribal sovereignty and jurisdiction.

Word of Ray Mattz's wrongful conviction, multiple previous arrests, and intrusion into Ray's Indian rights by the state traveled quickly south to the CILS office. He had been charged with violating a state law that prohibited *only* Yurok people from fishing on the Yurok Reservation. CILS was interested in representing Ray because his case had national implications for whether state law applied on Indian reservations and the process required to disestablish an Indian reservation. CILS arranged to represent Ray pro bono. The free expert representation meant the family for the first time had access to lawyers.

"Those lawyers aren't wearing socks! What kind of lawyer doesn't wear socks to a work meeting?" Ray's sister, Janet, observed. The family gathered by the window looking out toward the driveway. Parked about twenty feet away from the house was a worn Volkswagen van, three men standing next to it. They were holding briefcases and wearing faded jeans and collared shirts; two of them were not wearing socks.

Ray welcomed everyone to the house and started the first meeting, explaining, "I've been arrested nineteen times just for fishing on my home waters. It started when I was thirteen. I am only twenty-seven now. Each time, the wardens sneak up on me, give me a ticket, and take my fishing gear. They beat me up. I had put a lot of money into that gear. I have to fish at night just to try to not get caught. And it's dangerous. My family and I have to eat, and we need salmon to survive. We have Indian rights to fish. We will do whatever it takes to fight for those rights and this here River. Whatever it takes."

One lawyer confirmed that the family did have Indian rights. He said, "We call them federally reserved Indian rights that your ancestors reserved in the creation of the Yurok Reservation. Indian nations were sovereign nations before the United States came here. In the creation of Indian reservations, nations reserved their inherent sovereignty and legal rights on the reservation. What that means for you and your family is that your ancestors reserved your right to fish free from state regulation on the lower Klamath River when the reservation was created. Nothing has taken that away from you. We will prove that in court.

"Now," he continued, "California is going to argue that you don't have any of those rights because your reservation had been terminated by an act in 1892. If we can prove that nothing, including the 1892 act, has terminated your reservation, then the state won't have the authority to regulate your fishing. Only the Nation Yurok or the feds can. The state law won't apply to you, and they won't be able to arrest you for fishing anymore."

Ray looked at his mother, saying, "Then, that's what we gotta do."

"Ray, what the state has done to you and your family is not right. It's not fair or just. It's not constitutional. You've been unfairly targeted by state law enforcement and prosecuted. We won't let them push you around anymore. If anything else happens, you call us immediately."

Ray exhaled. It was now or never. He didn't know much about these young, white, no-sock-wearing attorneys, but he looked them in the eyes. He could tell their hearts were in it.

《《《

Ray and his attorney team were at the forefront of asserting Indian legal rights in court. Up until the late 1960s, Indian people and nations had minimal access to lawyers, and the federal government had been actively terminating Indian rights and assimilating Indian people. As a result, the body of Indian law remained largely dormant. That was about to change. Ray's case, and those that followed, sparked a legal revival of ancient aboriginal rights reserved by the Indigenous nations in treaties and executive orders, vesting them in federal law.

It took only a few months from Ray's nineteenth arrest on the River for his lawyers to develop legal arguments to defend him and appear in a California superior court in *Mattz v. Arnett,* in which

Uncle Ray was the defendant against the State of California. There, Uncle Ray's lawyers argued that Brooks Riffle, where Ray had been arrested, was Indian country because it had been reserved through an executive order as an Indian reservation for the Yurok people in 1855, and nothing had terminated the reservation. Accordingly, the Nation or the federal government had jurisdiction, not California, to regulate his fishing, and state law didn't apply to him. The state argued that the lower Klamath River reservation had been terminated by an 1892 act, opening the reservation for allotment and settlement. Accordingly, it was no longer Indian country under federal or tribal control. Further, an exemption to the prohibition on gillnetting by Indians on a reservation did not apply because the lower Klamath was not Indian country. Instead, it was state land and the state had jurisdiction over the land, water, and people there, including Ray.

During the hearing, Geneva bravely testified that her family had fished with gill nets without state interference until the 1940s.[5] During her girlhood, in the early years of the century, most of the Indians on the lower twenty miles of the River made their living by commercial fishing. Salmon was a staple of her family's diet, and Ray could only catch sufficient fish for his family's needs by means of gill nets. The family used every part of the fish; the meat was dried, kippered, cooked, and canned. The backbones were dried, and the organs were cooked and fed to the dogs.

After the hearing, one of the wardens whispered to Geneva, "Anytime you want to go fishing, we'll stay the hell out of that area. Just go. Let us know you are going. You folks don't waste fish."[6] Then the warden laughed, snickering in his perceived position of power to grant access to the River. Geneva didn't think it was very funny. Her family didn't need his permission.

My family lost in superior court. They were shocked that an 1892 act had terminated the Nation's title to land and their rights to it, legally ending the Nation's inherent sovereignty that the Creator had given their ancestors. The same rights that the federal government had recognized in the creation of the reservation in 1855 were now invalid. How could Congress take away the rights of American citizens without notice or compensation? This meant that not only were their fishing rights at stake, so were their rights to the land and the Nation's ability to exercise sovereignty over its territory and people. This raised the stakes. If this decision remained, the Yurok people would have no land left. They would have no rights to fish, hunt, or gather. They could be removed from the lands and the water. This could be the final act of conquering the Yurok people.

Ray's lawyers were disappointed but not surprised by the loss. State courts often misinterpret the interplay between state and federal law on Indian reservations, tending to unjustly prioritize state rights over Indian rights based on federal law in contradiction of the Supremacy Clause of the US Constitution. Pushing back, strategies often include a plan to move through state courts and appeal to the US Supreme Court. Following this course, the Mattz family appealed to the California Court of Appeals, which affirmed the lower court decision that the Yurok Reservation had been terminated and the state law applied. Uncle Ray appealed to the California Supreme Court to hear the case, but it denied the petition for a hearing.

My family did not give up. They appealed to what they were told was the highest court in the land, the US Supreme Court, which agreed to hear the case. They had one more shot.

Ray kept fishing during the two years he waited for the Supreme Court to decide his fate and the fate of his people. The family continued living at the village site in Rek-woi and fishing at the traditional fishing holes at Brooks Riffle. They followed the annual cycle of life, fishing for salmon during spring, summer, and fall, and growing vegetables in the summer. They hunted and gathered acorns in the fall and lived quietly through the winter. They found the idea of a court in Washington, DC, determining what rights they had to continue their way of life in their homelands to be absurd. They had inalienable rights to be on their home waters and lands, fishing and hunting — rights that were given to the family by the Creator. This new sovereign, the US government, had no authority to sever those rights. Yet the family understood that whatever the court decided would impact their ability, and that of future generations, to live a Yurok way of life.

On June 11, 1973, Geneva's phone at the house in Rek-woi rang. Ray, who was sitting on the couch closest to the phone, picked it up.

"Ray, it's your lawyers. We got news." Geneva and Ray gathered around the phone receiver. "Ray, you won. The Supreme Court held the reservation is still Indian country. It is still Yurok land. The state can't regulate your fishing. Only the Yurok Nation or the federal government can. You were right, we were right, the whole time! The Supreme Court confirmed you have Indian rights."

Moments before, the Supreme Court had released its opinion. US Supreme Court Justice Harry Blackmun, who had a practice of picking one Indian law case each term and completing extensive historical research to inform the case, had chosen the Mattz case as his pet case and wrote the decision for a unanimous court. The opinion began by acknowledging that from a young child Ray had fished "regularly, as his grandfather did before him," with nets at Brooks Riffle. The opinion continued artfully describing the federal government's legislative and administrative attempts to reserve and then unsuccessfully terminate the reservation, which seemed to fail in part because the Indians, including the Mattz family, never left their homelands and kept fishing in the Klamath River.

The opinion quoted a government report from 1885 that stated, "No place can be found so well adapted to these Indians, and to which they themselves are so well adapted, as this very spot.... No territory offers more to these Indians and very little territory offers less to the white man. The issue of their removal seems to disappear."

Justice Blackmun's thoughtful historical research and review of the lower court record revealed that the Mattz family had never left their lands or water or abandoned their fishing way of life, and there was no evidence supporting clear congressional intent to terminate the reservation in the nineteenth and twentieth centuries.

"We conclude that the Klamath River Reservation was not terminated by the Act of June 17, 1892, and that the land within the boundaries of the reservation is still Indian country. The judgment of the Court of Appeals is reversed."

Ray and the Family's resistance to state law by continuing to practice their fishing way of life was a major factor in the court's analysis upholding their rights. Geneva couldn't quite hear the lawyer's words over the phone. She watched Ray's face closely, looking for insight into the decision, as his eyes began to well with tears.

"Well?" Geneva said, not knowing how to interpret his reaction.

Ray looked up and said through his tears, "We won, Momma. We won."

CHAPTER 9
Indian Fishing Ban

▲▲▲
▼▼▼

1978

The US Supreme Court sent Ray's case back to state court in California to determine the existence of Ray's and the Nation's fishing rights and the applicability of California law to Indian fishing on the Yurok Reservation. In 1975, the Supreme Court of California held that the Nation did have federally reserved fishing rights on the lower Klamath River Reservation (the Yurok Reservation). It held that the state may not regulate fishing by Ray or other Indians because the federal government has jurisdiction. This, coupled with the US Supreme Court case, confirmed Yurok sovereignty within the reservation, ownership of land, and rights to fish on the Yurok Reservation.

This should have been the end of the Yurok war with the United States. One phone call initiated another round.

Shortly after the 1975 court case, officials from the State of California called the US Secretary of the Interior, Cecil Andrus, the leader of the federal agency charged with managing Indian affairs.

California stated in clear terms that if the federal government didn't regulate Yurok fishing on the Klamath River and stop Ray Mattz, they would.

In response to California's call, Secretary Andrus directed his staff to push through regulations in 1977 that recognized the Yurok right to commercial and subsistence fish but limited the commercial sale to a meager five salmon. They justified the limitation by claiming that the tribal fishery was in peril and that returning salmon stocks were declining. Regulations were necessary to "protect the Indian fishery resource."

Despite the restrictions on Indian fishing, local nonnative sport fishermen and commercial offshore fishermen were outraged that the Indians were allowed to fish at all. Prior to the adoption of the regulation, there were rumors among the non-Indian sport and commercial fishing industries that Ray Mattz was solely responsible for harvesting the majority of Klamath salmon that entered the River. Meanwhile, Ray and the other Indian fishing families were furious the feds had restricted their fishing after they had just won in the Supreme Court. Yet here they were, fighting the feds for fishing rights on the same River that the highest courts of the United States and California held they could fish. How could this be?

At the time, the Yurok Nation had no organized government and had been represented by a neighboring Nation, the Hoopa Valley Nation. In the late 1970s, the Yurok and Hoopa Nations were in vicious litigation over administration resources, and the two separate Nations refused to be governed by one Indigenous council. This left the federal government to manage the fishery.

The Secretary of the Interior, Cecil Andrus, accompanied by the assistant secretary of Indian affairs and the Secret Service, came to the reservation to meet with the Nation to evaluate the growing tensions over the Klamath River fishery between the California sport fishermen and the Nation.

"I have come here to protect your fishery," stated Secretary Andrus. "The returning salmon stocks are lower than expected. We want to make sure your harvest doesn't harm the salmon runs for future generations."

The crowd of Yurok people murmured. They didn't trust federal officials, yet they were excited that the Secretary of the Interior had come to the reservation to meet with them. They felt his presence meant the federal government valued protecting their recently secured, hard-won fishing rights. The federal government had a trust responsibility to the Indian fishing people to protect their rights. They believed that meant the federal government would help them.

"How will you protect our fishery? We have been fighting for our rights for two centuries. We finally won them. We know how to protect our fishery. We've been doing it since way before your kind was here," said a tribal member.

"Well now, you people don't have a tribal government. You ain't got no way to regulate it. You need laws, regulations, and a way to enforce them. We will help you with all those things," said the Secretary.

The crowd murmured.

"We have our own way of fishing here," another tribal member spoke up. "We don't need your laws and regulations or your courts."

The Nation had managed the fishery since time immemorial through complex aboriginal law and religious practices that included restrictions on when and how a person could fish. It was prohibited to take salmon before the first salmon ceremony. Once fishing began, restrictions ensured no one took more than was needed. Fishing holes were owned by families that had the power to exclude, use, and regulate fishing. They enforced these rules through payment for violations. This system had worked for generations, even though it was never written down.

After the meeting, the people went outside toward the fish pit, a gravel pit that looked like a long jump pit, with fish cooking on redwood sticks around its edges and an alderwood fire in the middle. The Secretary and his entourage walked toward the men cooking the salmon over the fish pit.

"We cooked this salmon in your honor. Thank you for visiting us," said one of the cooks. The other cooks smiled and shook the Secretary's hand.

Ray knew better. He saw straight through the bureaucratic talk and political theater. He walked up to Secretary Andrus and aggressively thrust a pointed finger into the Secretary's chest. "You are going to cut off our fishing," he said. The Secret Service agents quickly moved in between Ray and the Secretary and reached for their guns before Ray finished his first sentence, but he wouldn't be stopped, as they tried to separate them. "How dare you come here, eat our fish, and then leave and cut us off? At least have the dignity to tell it to our faces. You'll never keep me off this River. The only way I'll ever allow it is if I am floating downriver wrapped in a gill net."

As Ray tried to punch the Secretary, the other tribal people shoved him. He fell to the ground, tripping over an unstable leg that had been injured by a gunshot wound inflicted by his wife during a drunken argument a few years prior. When Ray hit the ground, the Secretary gave the signal that he was safe and said, looking down at Ray, "We have to protect your fishery." He nodded, and the Secret Service agents picked Ray up from the ground to escort him away.

The following morning, the Secretary of the Interior left the reservation in a convoy of black federal sedans. They drove south on

Highway 101, crossing the Klamath River just as Ray and three of his buddies drifted with three gill nets under the bridge.

«««

The Secretary arrived back in Washington, DC, and directed his staff to adopt new regulations that allowed commercial and subsistence fishing but limited the time of day, net size, and location. This version of the regulations lasted only weeks.

On August 28, 1978, just before the bulk of the fall chinook salmon run was expected to enter the estuary of the Klamath River, the federal government put a moratorium on all Indian fishing in the lower Klamath River, *a complete ban on Indian fishing*. Now *no* fishing was allowed. There was no hardship clause or appeal process. "Conservation problems" was stated as the basis for the regulation. Just as the state had done in 1933, now the federal government had criminalized our identity and way of life.

While the notice of the regulation in the federal register stated that California was considering a similar ban on offshore commercial fishing, California never issued offshore commercial fishing restrictions. In fact, it expanded fishing operations in 1978. That year offshore trolling fishing in Oregon and California caught more than 9.7 million pounds of salmon, and Oregon issued new offshore commercial fishing licenses to an additional 355 boats, increasing the number of operating licenses to 3,750.[7] Commercial offshore fishermen in Oregon and California made more than $6 million on salmon sales in 1978. Offshore fishing by white fishermen of Klamath salmon stocks accounted for 88 percent of the total take of Klamath salmon.[8] Commercial offshore catches from Klamath River stocks doubled from approximately 56,000 in 1971 to 107,000 in 1979.[9]

The 1978 state fisheries management plan stated that managers would consider offshore salmon fishing restrictions in 1979, which would include exceptions for boats with licenses issued in 1977 and a "hardship" appeals process to mitigate economic harm.[10] No restrictions were adopted in 1979.[11]

Meanwhile, between 1978 and 1979, spawner escapement levels — the amount of salmon allowed to spawn — of fall chinook Klamath salmon declined by 47 percent.[12]

Indians were the only group prohibited from fishing. It was clear to the Mattz family and other Yurok fishing families that the federal and state governments, as well as the non-Indian sport and commercial offshore fishermen, were willing to prohibit Indian fishing to maximize the non-Indian harvest and would deplete the fishery for their own financial gain. They had not been taught instructions on how to fish nor how to live in balance with the natural world.

«««

"Momma, I knew it. I knew he was going to cut off our fishing," said Ray.

"How can they do this after we won our rights in the highest court?" questioned Geneva.

Ray and Geneva sat at the family dining table at the Rek-woi house with several other family members. Everyone was still. The pressure was heavy. They thought for a while.

"It's our traditional fishing hole. They are trying to kick us out of our traditional fishing hole. The Creator gave us the right to fish there. We can't let anyone keep us from it," said Geneva. "We have to keep fishing," she said. The family did what it had to do to survive: they kept fishing during the moratorium. Within weeks, in response, the federal government dispatched a fully armed SWAT team of federal marshals to enforce the moratorium to the reservation. One day, they rolled onto the reservation in a convoy of government trucks loaded with guns, gear, supplies, and boats they put in the water at the Requa Dock. The federal occupation of the Yurok Reservation had begun.

140

CHAPTER 10

Warrantless Raids

◄◄◄◄◄◄◄◄◄◄◄◄◄◄◄◄◄◄◄◄◄◄◄◄◄◄◄◄◄◄◄◄◄

1978

A ll right, all you little fuckers, hit the floor!" yelled an officer holding a big rifle pointed at Ray's sons, Randy and David, who were
ten and eleven years old, respectively.[13] Five other federal officers stood
behind him, filling the doorway of the children's bedroom in the back
of the house. The officers had gotten into the boys' bedroom through
the back door of Ray's new trailer in Crescent City, twenty miles north
of Rek-woi. They were dressed in black uniforms and armed with large
rifles, batons, and knives hanging from their belts.

Raymond launched himself out of bed, ran into the next room, and
called his mother, Geneva, at the house in Rek-woi. It was one o'clock
in the morning.

"Mom, help me. They are invading, help!" Ray said frantically into
the receiver.

Geneva immediately went into panic mode. "Ray, is that you?
Where are you, son?"

No answer. Ray had dropped the receiver and run down the hall
toward his sons' bedroom.

"What the hell's going on? Get outta my house!" Ray shouted, holding his hands in the air. His long hair was wild and his black eyes were piercing in their intensity as he scanned the living room for a weapon while sizing up the federal officers. He felt his wife's presence behind him. They called her "Big Di" for a reason. While she was only five seven or five eight, she had a large frame. Her bones were structured like an elk, elegant and sturdy, with long legs and a wide torso. Her presence reassured him. She had always been loyal to him through all his fishing arrests and bootlegging salmon even if they had argued at times.

"On your knees now," an agent demanded. Ray knelt on his living room floor. He was wearing only boxer shorts. The officers brought Gloria, their daughter, into the room.

"You too," the agent directed Big Di. She knelt in her nightgown.

"Where is your warrant? I want to see it," Ray said.

"Don't worry about it. We're getting it," responded an officer.

"What do you mean you are *getting* it?" demanded Ray and Big Di.

"We are getting it," the officers kept saying.

The agents were already going through the house, moving aggressively. They tore through the house, starting in the living room, thrashing the furniture and clearing out the closet. When they found nothing, they moved to the kitchen. They searched every cupboard, the fridge, and under the sink in the economically sized kitchen. The contents were tossed to the floor, glasses broken, plates shattered.

"What are you looking for?" Big Di asked.

"A load of fish," they responded.

"Well, I'm sure I probably got it in my closet or someplace, if what you want is a load of fish!" Big Di said, beginning to crack in the violent absurdity of the situation. It would be almost impossible to hide a load of salmon in a bedroom closet or kitchen cupboard. The smell alone would give it away, and a load would never fit in such a small space.

They headed toward the bedrooms.

"Please don't hurt the children," Big Di pleaded.

The agent stomped to the kids' bedroom door. "Go to your mother," he instructed. They moved as fast as they could to their mother, who was still on her knees on the living room floor. The three children circled her, crouched down to the floor, grabbed her sturdy legs, and held tight for dear life. She wrapped them in her wide arms.

The agents continued through the house, the two small bedrooms and the bathroom. They were done in minutes and found no evidence of fish.

They gathered back in the living room. Ray was still on his knees, hands behind his back. His head was held high. His jaw was clenched. His eyes were bright and fiery with anger. "You ain't got no right to be here. Why the hell you here? Where is your warrant?"

"You know why, Mattz. It's illegal to sell fish. We know you've been selling fish. We seen you down at the River fishing. You know there is a moratorium on your kind of fishing. You can't be down there. It's against the law."

"That's my Indian right. We won in the highest court of the land. You or no other white man can tell me otherwise. Everyone else can fish. It ain't right. It ain't just."

"Indians ain't got no rights. You lost the war." The agent smirked, referring to the war between the white people and Indians. "We're taking you and your wife to jail. Get off your knees," he instructed as he pulled out his handcuffs. The agent cuffed Ray and Big Di. The cuffs cut tightly against Ray's red-hot skin.

"Now, let's go," said the agent.

Two other agents took Ray and Big Di by the arm and started leading them to the front door.

"My kids, man. My kids. What are they supposed to do? They're too young to be left by themselves," Ray said to the agent holding his arm.

They kept pushing Ray forward.

Big Di called back to her children, "There's food in the freezer. We will be back as soon as we can. Don't you worry about us," she instructed as she was shoved out her front door. The children hadn't moved, paralyzed in the trauma of the night. They were still huddled in the same position they were in when they held on to her legs, but now they were alone.

That was the first raid. Over the course of a few months, there was a second, a third, and a fourth. By the fourth raid, the agents told the children, "You know the drill," as they searched the house and then took their parents to jail. The kids stayed at their house, made themselves breakfast from frozen food, and got themselves ready for school on their own, despite any laws preventing kids from being left alone. They did, indeed, "know the drill."

The officers never found any evidence of illegal fish sales. They never had a valid warrant either. When the federal occupation started, Ray had stopped bootlegging salmon because he was too hot. The federal government occupied the Yurok Reservation to enforce the moratorium by what felt like to the Yurok people any means necessary, including violence and violating constitutional rights, just to prevent Yurok people from fishing. Ray was already a prime target of the occupation because of his Supreme Court case, and he was a proven successful leader. He was smart, articulate, and willing to fight. He was intense and brave. He would put his life on the line for his fishing rights.

His friends and family respected him, not just because he was a warrior but also because he was the best fisherman of his generation. He could smell fish in the water. He could read the water to tell where the fish were moving and where they'd be. He could set his gill net perfectly so that the tide and current would move the fish right into his net. He could barely read or write, but he had every tool a Yurok man needed to be a leader in aboriginal times. He would have been the headman of our family. He would have continued the long legacy of our family hosting the World Renewal Ceremonies and Brush Dances in Rek-woi. He would have been a rich man in aboriginal times.

Instead, he lived in a colonized world that didn't recognize his or his family's inherent rights. They had taken his family's land, water, timber, and fish and were destroying them. It wasn't just salmon; it was other fish too. All the species were becoming more and more scarce.

Like Geneva, Ray struggled to understand how a culture could so grossly exploit resources. And he knew in his heart the Creator had passed down to his family inalienable rights to the land, water, and resources. He knew it was wrong for the federal government to silo Indian people as the only group prohibited to fish on the River. He didn't know much about the US Constitution or the Bill of Rights, but he thought they said all men are created equal and that the pursuit of the Nation was to be a united nation with liberty and justice for all. He didn't understand why that didn't apply to him and his family.

The offshore fishermen were fishing. The recreational fishermen were fishing. But not the Yuroks. It wasn't right. It wasn't just. He thought he had solved the issue with the Supreme Court case. The lawyers said that if they could prove the land was still an Indian reservation, he could fish how he wanted on the River. He'd trusted them. So, why were the feds back?

He couldn't sleep at night with the thought that the agents were on his doorstep, in his backyard, just waiting to attack. Making matters worse, he had no way of protecting his family.

The raids at his house were the last straw.

The raids took him to a deeper level of distress and trauma. Drinking was something that helped Ray take his mind off how bad it was on the River. It distracted him from the injustice. He could tolerate more after a few drinks. If a Supreme Court victory didn't protect him and his family, what would? So he drank until he didn't remember, and he stayed that way for days.

CHAPTER 11

The Salmon Wars

▲▲▲

1978

Weeks into the occupation, Geneva looked down at the beach at the mouth of the River from the large window in the family dining room. The light of the beach bonfire danced in her eyes as she watched the birthday party her family and others were attending. Families, women, children, and men, came from up and down the River. They had a net in the water to catch salmon for the party, and she smiled to herself, pleased they were enjoying themselves. It had been so dangerous with the federal occupation, but this seemed to be a moment of reprieve in which they could get back to their fishing way of life.

As Geneva settled into bed with Emery Sr., her grandson, who was staying with them, burst into their bedroom. "Gram, your whole hillside is plum full of sheriffs, park men, and the sheriff patrol. They're all down there!"

A parade of flashes of yellow light and bright car lights was moving down the road past the house and toward the bonfire. Then she heard the jet boat motors, loud enough that she knew there were several boats also heading toward the beach. The partygoers saw the hillside light up with hundreds of lights, enough for them to see the outlines of more than a hundred bodies marching down the hill toward them. They didn't see the jet boats until they were upon them. They were surrounded and terrified. The law enforcement mob approached the party from land and sea, M16s and rifles wrapped around their shoulders, pounding their clubs against their hands.

The Yurok people at the party gathered closely around the fire as the law enforcement mob spread out, surrounding them, pounding their billy clubs, *smack, smack, smack.* The people grew frightened, yet they remained peaceful.

An elder, hearing the rhythm in the *smack, smack, smack,* picked up the Indian drum next to him and began drumming… *boom, boom, boom*…and then he started singing an old Indian song. He looked beyond the mob toward O'-rey-gos, who watched from the north side of the beach, just a few hundred yards away. He sang louder. The Indian people joined him, singing loudly with all their hearts. They held hands, some soiled themselves in fear. They were horrified about what was to happen next.

One officer abruptly grabbed my Auntie Diane around the neck, throwing her to the ground. She scrambled up quickly, looked him straight in the eye, and said, "I will kill you if you ever grab me like that again." The law enforcement agent, for the first time, looked her in the eye. She was small and fierce, and full of fear and rage. He looked around at the people holding hands in peace and solidarity. He questioned why he was there, and what the law enforcement mob was doing. These were peaceful people fishing. He walked away like a dog with his tail between his legs. Another officer stated that the reports they received were wrong and directed the law enforcement mob to leave.

When the officers departed, several Yurok people on the beach threw up from the fright. Others cried. Geneva watched from the house and saw the law enforcement mob moving toward her home.

She gathered up her granddaughter, Sue, and Emery, telling her grandson to stay inside. Sue had recently returned from San Francisco to help the family secure a fishing allocation, but then the moratorium was issued, and she found herself in the Salmon Wars rather than in negotiations.

Outside, Geneva and Emery confronted the officers as they approached the house.

"You aren't allowed on our property. Who gave you permission to come running down here like that? Scaring us people with all your guns?" Geneva demanded firmly.

"We can do anything we want to," said a deputy.

"Oh no, you can't," replied Geneva, still wearing her nightgown and robe, standing a foot shorter than the deputy.

The officers grabbed Emery Sr. In his late seventies, Emery was still strong from a life of farmwork but was elderly.

"He's coming with us," they said, and twisted his arm backward and crossways, cuffing him and spraining his arm.

Seeing this happen, Emery Sr.'s faithful dog ran toward the deputy, barking aggressively to protect his owner. Another officer grabbed the dog and put a gun to its head. "Call it off, or I will shoot." Geneva nodded, and the dog backed down.

Emery Sr. looked at his wife of fifty-five years. In that moment, he saw every time his family had been arrested for fishing on the River. He thought of Emery Jr. and his dream of fishing. He thought of Sue, standing beside him, home now to fight for them with words. His head slightly lowered, his eyes looked up at Geneva, intense with anger yet flooded with a calm bravery. He assured her with just one look. As was his way, he calmly said, "It's okay. They will take me to jail in town."

Sue, full of rage, yelled, "You ain't done nothing wrong. Why are they taking you, Grandpa?"

"Never mind. Just send someone behind the cop car to bail me out."

Sue looked at Geneva, seeking guidance on whether to attack or stand down. Geneva nodded. "Sue, take the car. Follow them closely."

Emery gave Sue a silent glower, urging her to knock it off.

The rest of the night worked methodically. The federal marshals loaded him into an unmarked patrol truck borrowed from the state fish and game department and took him to jail in town. Sue followed in the truck with Auntie Diane. They bailed him out of jail after several hours of waiting and took him to the hospital to address his sprained arm. They arrived back in Rek-woi at the family house before dawn, exhausted, with Emery's full arm in a sling.

The experience had changed Geneva. In the flash of Emery's glance, her husband held tightly by the federal marshal and handcuffs, she had realized this was war.

The first time white men with guns came to her house, she was just a child. Her grandpa Brooks had told those men to go away, that he would always fish and be on this land and water because the Creator had given this area to his ancestors. It was all made for them. They had left, and Geneva and her family had kept fishing. That was almost fifty years ago. Then, after all the fishing-related arrests, she had guided the family through a court case that went all the way to the Supreme Court. In the highest court in the land, they had won: the Yurok Reservation was still Indian country, and her family could still fish. They'd thought that was the end of it because they had won the family's rights in the highest court in the land. Yet here they were again: white men with guns enforcing an order to keep her and her family off the River and from fishing.

While Emery and her granddaughters were still sitting at the jailhouse, Geneva decided that she'd fight this invasion. She'd join the

Salmon Wars. Even though she was in her seventies, she still had energy. Her battles had made her wise. Her scars made her strong. Geneva found strength in knowing she had beat these men and the forces they represented twice now, and this time would be the same. She would win. She would kick them off her River, using the same techniques and strategies she had always used: her Yurok medicine and prayers.

Her method of battle was to protest on the River by doing a fish-in. She'd go down to the water when the time was right, set her gill net, and refuse to let the federal marshals take her in.

Geneva called her relatives from up and down the River, telling them about the law enforcement mob, the guns, the arrests, battered bodies, and broken spirits.

Call after call she repeated, "These people aim to scare us off the River. We can't let them, not now, not ever. I plan to do a fish-in. I'm taking my boat and gill net down to the fishing hole, and I will fish. The federal occupation must end, and I'd like you to be there, if it gets violent," she said to relative after relative.

Everyone she talked to agreed.

They'd be there.

«‹‹

Geneva had known pain before and had not broken. It made her fierce. Losing her father as a child and then four of her nine children before her sixtieth birthday had caused a chronic pain that she eased with prayer and living in balance. Five times over, the Creator reached deep in her heart, pulled it out, and held it right in front of her face. Now, in her seventies, on a boat in the middle of the Klamath River estuary, she was about to be surrounded by federal marshals

150

in full riot gear. As they got closer, the bright sun hit their metallic machine guns hanging from their shoulders, causing a sharp glare off the water. She knew the federal marshals would not break her.

"Mom, here they come," her daughter Lavina said. She wore big Jackie O–style sunglasses to block the glare from the sun, a light-colored kerchief around her hair, and jeans and a sweater with striped sleeves. "I'm going to grab the net."

Geneva and Lavina had set their gill net in the family fishing hole in the estuary knowing the federal marshals would try to take it to keep them from fishing. They would resist by holding on to the net, engaging in a tug-of-war with armed federal marshals. The point was to show the federal marshals that nothing, not even machine guns and jet boats, would stop the Yurok people from fishing. "They will try to take it. Be careful," Geneva warned her daughter.

Geneva and Lavina had carefully planned this fish-in to protest the occupation just by fishing. The moratorium prohibited them from fishing, so the mere act of fishing was an act of protest. Family members living off the reservation had returned home to protect their family, shocked by the reports of violence and harassment at the hands of the federal marshals. My dad was there, too, and he and his cousins brought machine guns and kept them in their trucks and car trunks just in case. News of the occupation of the reservation had spread and Indigenous peoples came from around the country offering their protection. Some brought more guns but were told to hide them in the mountains. Ray would give word if they were needed. A camp had been established on the River bar below Rek-woi, where about sixty people stood ready to help Geneva and Lavina.

Even in fishing clothes, Lavina was beautiful. She had delicate facial features with soft edges, full lips, and bright, inquisitive dark eyes. She, too, had known pain and faced it bravely, leaving her abusive husband to return to the reservation just a few years before.

Lavina was not the protesting type. She was a doer, but she tended to put what she had toward her five children, not toward protesting against the law. Perhaps that was what had led her to this moment: Lavina's children were fishing people. Her son, Bill (my dad), was one of the best fishermen of his generation. He had spent summers at the homeplace learning from Ray and other family members to fish, hunt, and know the River. He had bootlegged salmon up and down the Pacific Coast for years. He had returned to the reservation to fight when the occupation began. His siblings joined him. It was their livelihood. This was their traditional fishing hole.

Yes, for my children, she thought as she grabbed the net from the water and positioned herself securely on the front boat seat. Preparing for battle, her heart pumping with adrenaline, she faced the net and the River bar to the north.

"Here they come, Mom."

Geneva looked upriver to the east. She could see three large aluminum jet boats carrying the federal marshals. They were huge, moving fast, and coming straight toward them. The jet boats' engines roared, charging at full speed. The sound overpowered the estuary's normal buzz of bird calls, crashing waves, and sea lion barks.

Geneva secured her footing on her small wooden rowboat's baseboards, adjusting her rain boots to maximize grip and stability. She straightened her back and inhaled, her petite stature rising and expanding with the movement. She was calling in her power.

As the federal jet boats got closer, racing toward them to kick them off the River and take their fishing net, figures started coming into view.

"Mom, I think there are eight men in that boat," said Lavina. "They look big."

"Don't let your eyes play tricks on you. They are just men. They put their pants on one leg at a time just like us," Geneva said.

She squinted her eyes to take in the boat and its occupants. They wore black uniforms with riot gear and had bulletproof vests on their chests. Semiautomatic weapons hung from their shoulders. Large black helmets with clear plastic face masks covered their faces. Some of these men had been law enforcement agents at the Selma, Alabama, protest years before. They were trained to dismantle civil arrest using any means necessary.

Never mind their size or armor. There was no turning back now.

The spray of water from the front of the feds' jet boat splashed onto the lenses of Lavina's sunglasses, just as the metal jet boat rammed into Geneva and Lavina's rowboat. The aggressive impact rocked the wooden boat, causing the wood to splinter, and a wave rushed over the boat's edge. Water pooled in the boat. Lavina and Geneva moved with the impact, holding tightly to the edges of the boat. Lavina secured herself, still holding on to the net. The family onshore

shouted in protest at this aggression and to encourage them to stand their ground.

"You ain't supposed to be fishing. Get this here gill net out the water now," said the large federal marshal standing at the bow of the jet boat. His black combat boot, covered in gray river bar sand, was perched on the rim of the boat, his leg hiked up. He looked larger than life in his black law enforcement uniform, his face hidden underneath his helmet and face shield. Geneva could not see his eyes. His gun in hand was ready for use, a semiautomatic weapon, some kind of machine gun. It was an ideal size to be carried long distances, yet powerful enough to kill several people at one time. The other agents had guns too. "Don't make me tell you again," he warned them.

Lavina watched him carefully, the absurdity of the presence of the marshal's gun overtaking her. Why was it necessary? These law enforcement agents faced two women fishing who were unarmed, forty-three and seventy-four years old, both barely five feet tall and less than 130 pounds, who sat in an unmotorized small wooden rowboat. Sure, they were protesting, and the north bank of the River was lined with sixty people there to support them, but there were no other boats on the water around them. She thought, *This isn't right. There is no reason that gun should be here. There is no reason he should be here. This is my place.* She was not scared. She held tighter to the cork line of the net.

"Come on, girls, knock this off. We don't want anyone to get hurt," said another officer who was standing behind the man on the jet boat bow.

"Your momma wears combat boots," Lavina yelled loudly. The growing crowd on the north riverbank, just twenty feet away, roared with laughter. In Yurok, there are no swear words because it's unhealthy to have such bad will in your heart, and insulting a mother is a cultural taboo, a most serious offense. In 1970s Yurok culture, claiming a mother wore combat boots was as offensive as a sentence full of four-letter words. Lavina did so here without hesitation.

The man standing in the jet boat stomped his combat boot on the top of the bow, rocking the boat, and the other federal marshals swayed. He yelled back, "Give me that net!" squatting down and lowering his hands into the River to aggressively tug the net out of the water.

Lavina held the other end, pulling against the marshal's will. Her hands were strong from years of gillnet fishing and working as a waitress in a Chinese restaurant. The muscles in her hands were developed and agile, used to holding tightly to cork lines, gill nets, and plates full of General Tso's chicken. She also knew how to leverage the weight of her small frame against the boat to secure the fishing net, and when she did, her tight grip and low positioning in the boat made her a contender against the Herculean federal marshal.

The tug-of-war continued. The net moved toward the federal boat, one end of the net rising. Lavina tugged harder, and the gill net went in the other direction, toward her and her mother.

"You damn Indian! Let the goddamn net go," her armed opponent yelled.

He was close enough to her now that she could read the letters on his uniform across his chest. "Department of the Interior" it warned in yellow thread. How ironic, this was the same federal department that had a trust responsibility, a fiduciary duty to her and her family to protect their legal rights, including their right to fish, which her family had secured in federal law in the creation of the reservation 120 years ago and had just reaffirmed in the Supreme Court. Instead, its agents were violently trying to deprive her of her rights. She pulled harder on the net.

Growing more frustrated that he could not overpower this small woman, the federal marshal pulled harder on the gill net, letting go of his gun and grabbing the net with both hands. The gill net rose out of the water about ten feet and abruptly ended. The nylon netting should have been forty feet deep but had been cut short. Where the net should have been, there was, instead, light-colored cloth tied to the end of the net every two feet. As the net was pulled tighter, the cloth spread.

"It's bloomers. Underwear. They tied underwear to the net," someone said from the crowd, which burst into a roar of hard belly laughter.

The crowd's ravenous laughter was the final offense. The federal marshal looked Lavina straight in her face and pulled on the gill net as hard as he could. "You let go of this goddamn net, you dirty squaw!" he yelled loudly, making sure everyone on the boats and shore heard him. The powerful tug on the net launched Lavina forward off her feet, and her head hit the side of the boat on her way down. Still holding on tight to the gill net, she bounced off the side of the boat, and her body landed with a hard thud on the bottom of the boat. The federal marshal on the other end of the net snarled and snickered. "You better stay down."

Geneva, shocked and worried, cried, "Lavina, are you okay?"

"I'm fine, Mom. I'm okay," Lavina said, a bit in shock from the impact.

They had discussed that this protest could get violent. They were willing to put themselves in harm's way if this was what was necessary to end the occupation. It was getting increasingly dangerous for Yurok people.

Lavina quickly got back on her feet again. She did not look at her mother. Instead, she went right back at the federal marshal. "How dare you! Now, you let go of the gill net, now!" she yelled.

The federal marshal bent down to grab more net. The granny panties hung on the bottom of the net, being pulled one by one into the federal boat as he pulled harder and harder, pulling the net away from Lavina. One pair of granny panties dragged over his black combat boot, the lace on the top catching the edge of his toe. He kicked his boot to get it off, swearing as he kicked. He looked at Geneva and Lavina with rage and pulled harder on the net.

They continued their tug-of-war. Pulling back and forth. Harder and harder. The crowd yelled obscenities, throwing River rocks at the federal boat that landed just shy of it, causing splashes that wet the federal marshals. The other marshals in the boat started yelling at the crowd to stop throwing rocks. An officer reached for his gun.

Ray, who was watching from the shore, got in his boat and was heading toward his mother and sister. The family had decided he would come to the protest and stay on the River bar because it would be too dangerous if he was on the boat. The federal marshals would surely take advantage of the opportunity to shoot, beat, or arrest him. Geneva told her daughter to let go of the net. She repeated the instruction as she saw Ray rowing toward them, coming from downriver, only fifty yards away.

"No, Mom, I will not let go of this net. They have no right to be here. This is my net, our River, our fish!" she said, more to the federal marshal than to her mother.

The marshal driving the boat revved the engine and smashed the jet boat into the Mattzes once again. This time, it did not crack, and Lavina and Geneva were thrown to the boat floor.

As Geneva stood to her feet, she saw the crowd on the River bar. They were yelling at the marshals, "Get off the River! You don't belong here! Pig! Coward!" and still throwing river rocks, as hard as they could at the marshals' boat. Some of the marshals were yelling back, threatening to shoot their guns.

Again, the marshals' jet boat engine revved and they rammed into Lavina and Geneva's wooden rowboat. When the metal of the jet hit the wood frame of the boat, the wooden frame cracked from the floor up the left side toward the oar ring. Geneva noticed the crack. No water came through, but she knew the boat would not hold for much longer.

Her son was getting closer too. A marshal in the boat, who had been yelling at the shore crowd, turned toward Ray's boat. Tapping the shoulder of the marshal standing next to him, he pointed and mouthed, "There he is." The marshal's eyes turned toward Ray.

"Momma, go ahead — sing. Go ahead, sing, Momma. Sing your song, and we'll see what they will do," said Lavina.

Geneva knew this was her moment. It was now or a violent battle would break out. She had to believe it would work. She had no other tools, and she didn't want anyone to get hurt.

She looked to the west, toward O'-rey-gos, and said a silent prayer asking for help. Then she looked east toward Fanny Flounder's house and recalled singing with Fanny. In an instant, all the days and nights singing with Fanny came back to her. Geneva recalled Fanny saying, "Above all else, you have to believe in your own medicine." She committed to believing in her own medicine.

Geneva stood up in the boat and raised her arms and hands. She took a deep breath and started singing. Her song was a prayer. Methodically, she sang an Indian song. She believed with every inch of her soul that this song was powerful and would help keep everyone safe and end the Salmon Wars. The song was a single melodic verse, repeated over and over. She quietly sang it one time through. In the heated scuffle that surrounded her, no one even noticed. She started again, this time a little louder. She focused intently on the federal occupation ending and her people fishing again. As she sang a third time, she raised her voice and envisioned the federal marshals leaving the reservation, traveling away in their trucks. She saw her family fishing at their fishing hole on the fishing rock in the estuary and at Brooks Riffle. She saw herself entering a smokehouse hanging salmon strips to smoke, can, and eat in the coming winter. She prayed for safety. She sang a fourth round. A fifth and a sixth.

She took a deep breath to start the seventh round, when she heard a birdcall. It was high-pitched and long, a deliberate screech coming from the east, from upriver. She kept singing. Something was happening. She heard another birdcall, this time from the west, from downriver toward the ocean. It was familiar and was becoming force-ful and louder and louder. She realized the call was coming from sev-eral birds, a flock, heading straight toward her. Then there was another type of birdcall, perhaps a kingfisher, which grew strong and closer as she sang. Then another birdcall; this one sounded like a pelican. She kept singing. She heard the blue heron join, the raven, and the crow, all singing with her. Then osprey and ren too. Soon their calls har-monized over her boat. She heard the cries of the *per-gish* — the eagle and the hawk. She kept singing and looked up.

Directly over her boat, there were hundreds of different kinds of birds circling. Diving down, flying high, circulating up and down and round and round.

She kept singing.

More and more birds seemed to come from all directions — yet out of nowhere — more birds than anyone had ever seen over the estuary. They flew over the boat, circling above Geneva, who remained stand-ing and singing in the boat.

The birds were squawking, crying, screeching, yelling, singing.

The crowd on the River bar went silent. Looking for an explana-tion, they saw Geneva standing, singing in the boat. They knew she was praying. They knew her well enough to know her strong prayer had called in the birds to help her.

The federal marshals noticed the birds too. They stopped yelling and stood still, watching the birds.

Ray saw them. He kept his steady pace rowing toward his mother and sister's boat. He understood very well what his mother had done. He reached their boat quietly and steadied himself to them.

Lavina, standing in the boat still holding the net, for the first time realized how much her hands hurt. She looked down at them. They still gripped the net. Yet they didn't look like her hands. They had grown bright red from squeezing the cork line so tight for so long. Her knuckles protruded from her skin, clenched in a fist. As she opened her palms, her wounds where the fishing line had penetrated her skin from the tug-of-war began to bleed. She could hear her mother singing. The rhythmic chant, her mother's gentle yet assertive voice strong and unwavering, carrying the song. The birds circling. Lavina was in awe. She felt empowered. She had seen her mother pray and sing many times but nothing like this before.

Geneva held this moment with her breath and song. Her whole life force was in unison with the army of birds above her. The air became stagnant as the people stopped moving and stared at the birds. She felt the energy change as the Creator worked through the birds to protect Geneva, her family, and the Yurok people. She felt the Creator, deep in her prayer, answer her. The birds were frantic and not afraid of the black-suited two-leggers with the foreign metal boat. The birds were airborne. That machine could not reach them.

They circled and cried, *Get off our River.*

They circled and cried, *You don't belong here, feds, go home.*

They circled and cried, *This place is for the Yuroks.*

Their powerful wings moved the air, pushing the marshals away, back to the east, toward the capital of the marshals' government. The birds took control of the situation, guided by Geneva's song. Every person on the River within sight of the birds stopped and stared, mesmerized. The birds continued to circle the large metal jet boat and small rowboat that floated in its shadow. Immediately below them, on the two boats they circled, the power shifted. Geneva now held the authority and ability to win this battle.

The federal marshals could not comprehend the reason for this supernatural behavior. They'd never seen anything like it. It scared them. What else did the Indians have planned? Would they be attacked? What would the birds do? Could the Indians also call on the bears or other animals? What horror was next?

The federal marshal holding the other side of the net loosened his grip. "Let's get out of here, man," he said. The driver nodded.

The federal marshal took a step back and placed both his combat boots on the floorboard of the jet boat, dropping the gill net. As they pulled away, the gill net floated back into the water; the underwear sank back into the water, the cloth spreading wide as the air moved out from under it like moth wings falling into the abyss. The wood corks bobbed up and down on the water in the air pushed by the birds' wings.

The driver of the federal jet boat pulled the boat back and quickly turned and accelerated, splashing Geneva and Lavina with the wake. They didn't notice. They were too busy watching the birds.

The federal marshals never returned to the River. Shortly after, they evacuated the reservation as mysteriously as they had arrived, without ceremony or announcement. The occupation had ended.

The Indian way had protected Geneva's family and her inherent rights again, even when the Supreme Court could not.

PART III
World Renewal

Amy and her siblings gillnet fishing at Brooks Riffle, Klamath River, 2023

CHAPTER 12

Pack the Medicine

2003

Since my family had signed the unratified treaty with the US government in 1851, we had been fighting for our fishing rights and sovereignty to protect our way of life. Even though our rights were the supreme law of the land, the federal government allowed a system to develop that took our land, rights, and children, criminalized our culture, identity, and religion, and policed our existence. My great-grandma Geneva had carried this burden of injustice with strength, continuing the tradition of Yurok women leading the way to resolve conflicts by guiding the family through a lifetime of injustice. We had finally secured our fishing rights by the end of the twentieth century, with our fight, in the Salmon Wars. Tragically, at nearly the same time the salmon runs, upon which those rights depended, dramatically declined in the beginning of the twenty-first century. My family's victories would be in vain if there were no salmon to catch in a perishing River. We had no future without our River and salmon.

After the fish kill, I graduated from college and applied to law school. By then, I had learned enough about my culture, and my sacred responsibilities to the River and the salmon, to feel a deep sense of accountability for their deaths. The tragedy stayed with me.

I carried the grief of that moment like a wound that wouldn't close. Tens of thousands of dead salmon lined my home waters like fallen ancestors. It wasn't just the death of fish, it was an act of ecocide against my people. The government had opened the irrigation canals, drained the River, and left the salmon to die. Our relatives, our lifeway, our future — left to rot under the sun. The fish kill was not a natural disaster. It was a man-made injustice. A legal failure. A moral crisis.

The fish kill also shattered my faith in the US government. I couldn't comprehend how a culture and government was knowingly willing to commit ecocide — through the largest fish kill in American history — for political or financial gain. America, it seemed, was willing to sacrifice ancient cultures and species to benefit a privileged few. Even more devastating was realizing how deeply racism continued to dictate land and water use in the twenty-first century.

It felt as though my family was still at war with the settlers and the US government. Generations had passed since the murderous raids against us, yet our country continued to systematically devalue my people's rights in order to benefit those with white skin — and worse, it was willing to commit ecocide against us for profit and politics.

Yet, while I lost faith in the US government, my grief strengthened my belief in the Yurok people, our government, and myself. We were driven by something far more profound and authentic than money or politics. The desire to live in harmony with nature and to honor our first covenant with the Creator — to protect our homelands, waters, and the species that sustain us. I knew the Creator and the natural world would empower and protect us as we fought to preserve our culture, because we have a reciprocal relationship: we take care of each other.

I sought to become a lawyer to learn to navigate the very system that was used against my family since the founding of the United States. I wanted justice. As a Yurok, I knew that real justice would not be punitive — it would be restorative, rooted in our relationship with the Creator, salmon, and River. It would listen to these relatives, and not criminalize us for refusing to let go of who were are. Further, I remained committed to becoming a lawyer not to climb ladders or join institutions, but to defend what the forces of colonization had long tried to erase: my people, the River, salmon, and our sovereignty, and the sacred bond between them. It would take more schooling, and I was ready.

I had plans to attend the Pre-Law Summer Institute, the same program some of the CILS lawyers attended decades before. I had to learn as much as I could about the Nation's legal rights, its history, and our beloved River and salmon, even if it was tragic.

By the early 1900s, only 10 percent of California Indian people had survived the genocide of the 1800s, and by the early 2000s, less than 10 percent of the Klamath salmon runs remained. Ninety percent of the Klamath salmon and Indigenous peoples had been extirpated in two centuries of colonization. It's difficult to determine when the salmon decline started, because data on salmon runs starts in 1978. It likely started in the 1850s during the gold rush, when the River was dredged for mining claims. Or in 1905, when the Klamath Reclamation Project was built, draining wetlands and destroying lakes in the upper basin. Or in 1911, when the first Klamath dam was built, or in 1964, when the last dam was built. Or logging throughout the 1800s and 1900s. What was clear, however, was that the legacy effects of development of the Klamath Basin were killing the River and salmon in the twenty-first century. Not only had the Yurok people been colonized, so had the River, and both were doing poorly.

In 1987, the Yurok Nation had its first commercial salmon fishing season, seven years after the end of the Salmon Wars. The Nation worked diligently with the federal government in the early 1980s to adopt fishing regulations that reflected the Nation's traditional fishing practices. It organized a traditional Indian fishermen's association to represent the Nation until a tribal government was formed. My auntie Sue Masten was elected as the chair to represent the association in negotiations with the offshore commercial fishing people to secure a portion of the harvestable Klamath salmon stocks for the Indian fishery. Relying on the Mattz cases and NARF case *US v. Washington* (reaffirming the treaty rights of Indigenous nations in Washington to co-manage and continue to harvest salmon and other fish consistent with various treaties between the US and the nations), Sue was able to secure not less than 50 percent of the Klamath salmon allocation for the Indian fishery. The case law from the Mattz family cases and an allocation agreement set the legal foundation for the Nation to finally exercise its federally reserved fishing rights.

I was seven years old during the first commercial fishing season. My mother and father had married at the end of the Salmon Wars. My dad sold his machine gun from the Salmon Wars in the church parking lot before their wedding. Together they had hoped to start a family and replace guns and violence with mouths to feed and salmon on the table. I was born shortly after. My mother understood that she was marrying into a salmon fishing family, and had gone with my father on "fish runs" to sell salmon on the black market, with me in tow. I often napped wrapped in a blanket on the backs of a load of salmon in a truck bed. The legalization of commercial fishing meant their future would be safer and more stable in a truck bed, free from the risk of arrest, and with more financial stability.

I remember being at the Requa Dock in my dad's Chevy two-toned pickup truck bundled up in a blanket, doors locked while my dad checked his gill net that was set in the estuary in front of the truck. I would watch him diligently, trying to learn and eager to see him pull a fish out of the net. On early mornings, sometimes, he'd let me sit in the boat. Then he coached me through untangling a salmon from the net. He'd sell his fish. We'd buy school clothes and pay bills. I learned early the value of the fishery and the role it had in our family. As soon as my siblings and I were old enough, we started commercial fishing with Dad. It was serious business. We were trained how to fish hard.

Good training, however, wasn't worth much if there were no fish to catch. By the early 2000s, before the fish kill, water quality on the Klamath had been chronically poor due to agricultural runoff from the Klamath Reclamation Project. The poor water quality increased water temperatures to almost lethal degrees for the fish and wildlife living in the River. Each summer, the toxic blue-green algae blooms started in the reservoirs behind the dams, spilled into the main stem, and floated to the mouth of the River, polluting the entire 263 miles of the River.

Making matters worse, there was hardly any water in the River because it was diverted for use on agricultural fields in the Klamath Reclamation Project. The only legal requirement for instream flows to the River were the minimum flows required for coho salmon, as they were listed in the Endangered Species Act. These flows were the bare minimum to keep the River alive and were only required to support the coho life cycle, not other species in the River. Further, the riparian habitat on the Klamath main stem and the tributaries was poor from mining and logging. The lack of water and the poor water quality, along with bad habitat, made the River almost uninhabitable by any creature, including salmon.

The federal government's mismanagement of the Klamath Reclamation Project amplified the collapse of the Klamath Basin ecosystem and its species by depriving the River of water necessary for basic biological function, perpetuating the degradation of the ecosystem's health by supporting harmful agricultural practices. The historical legacy of the development of the River, primarily the Klamath dams, and the federal government's mismanagement of the Klamath Reclamation project caused the 2002 fish kill.

In the years following, conditions worsened. O'-rey-gos questioned whether the salmon should come in the River at all and called for help to the other spirits who had made a deal with the Creator to steward the Klamath River: the Yurok people. We answered.

Following the fish kill, a new generation of Yurok people, me included, dedicated their lives to protecting the River by becoming community organizers, cultural practitioners, fishing people, tribal leaders, biologists, engineers, lawyers, social media experts, and much more. We had allies, as other people working for NGOs, state and federal governments, and private businesses were also traumatized by the fish kill and joined our cause.

The agreement between the Creator and salmon to sacrifice their lives to alert the humans to the impending end of the Klamath Basin was working. The humans were listening.

《《《

Two months before I started law school, my great-grandmother came back for me late one night to give me protection.

I was sleeping, worn out, on my parents' couch in the living room, when Geneva Mattz came to me in a dream. Together we went to an old place — one that was dark, warm, and confined by corners I could feel, though I couldn't see the walls. All I could see was her, and all I could feel was the hard surface below me. I found myself lying on my back on a flat raised surface. Perhaps it was a bed, maybe a redwood plank.

She was there. I knew exactly who she was, even though I was six years old when she passed, and I hadn't seen her in seventeen years. I wasn't afraid.

Everything had already been prepared. She started dancing around my body, moving up and down, softly, gently, gliding around both sides of the bed I lay on. I lay still, frozen in the awe of the moment and not wanting to disturb her. She held in her hands, close to her face, a small medicine basket, no bigger than a small bowl, made of willow and hazel. It was woven in the expertly precise old way, to perfection. Watertight so as not to waste a drop of the sacred tincture made of water and herbs it held.

She began to sing a medicine song as she moved around me. The tone was deep, rhythmic, and circular. I couldn't make out the words, as I had not learned to speak Yurok. My blood memory recognized the meaning of the words, the cadence, and her actions. Even I, without training, could feel this song. This was a medicine song and a strong one.

She sang it three times, moving the length of my body with each verse. She sang quietly, methodically. I lay motionless, completely aware, feeling this experience like I was awake. I was protected. There was no fear, just deep acceptance that this experience was a gift, a blessing.

Then, at the end of the third time through the song, she blew the medicine from the basket onto my body. I watched the lit shards of herbs fly from the basket, bouncing through the air. They hit my skin, and my skin tingled where the herbs landed, all over my body. I jolted. My heartbeat raced. My breath was quick. I woke up.

I looked down at my body. I was still on my parents' couch, wrapped in a blanket, lying stretched out, my great-grandmother's picture framed on the wall above me. *Geneva Mattz, Traditional Yurok*, it was noted on the bottom of the picture. *Indeed,* I thought.

I looked at her eyes. They seemed to say, *That just happened.* She had packed medicine for me. I didn't know she had learned to pack medicine — the sacred practice of administering Yurok medicine by combining medicine, song, and breath. She had started training with Fanny Flounder and was taken to boarding school before completing the work. Maybe she had finished her training in the afterlife.

I went back to my body. There were no herbs and no burns from the lit ends that had spread chills through me when they landed on me. My heart was still racing. I could still feel my legs and arms tingling from where the medicine had landed. I was okay. I was more than okay. I felt the power of new energy moving through me. It was there, embedded deep in the tissue, bones, and marrow of my body.

My great-grandmother Geneva had packed the medicine for me. I think she knew the Creator and the salmon had made a deal in which the salmon would die to spark an effort to renew the world. Perhaps, when the Creator received the prayer from the World Renewal Ceremony, it consulted the salmon, and they agreed the salmon would die to show the world the Klamath Basin and River were on the verge of ecological collapse and species extinction, and with any luck, this would trigger the humans to stop it by organizing a movement to heal the River. Perhaps my great-grandmother was in on the agreement and knew the humans would need extra help. She packed her medicine to share it with the next generation of her family.

I had her protection, and I carried her with me. I knew her memories, pain, and sorrow, her joy and her source of strength. Her strength had flowed down through worlds, through generations, in the song and herbs that danced from the medicine bowl into my body that night.

Geneva had come to give me the medicine to heal the River. She knew me, the Yurok people, the River, and the salmon would need everything we had to survive the next century.

CHAPTER 13

We Will Remove the Dams

▲▲▲▲▲▲▲▲▲▲▲▲▲▲▲▲▲▲▲▲▲▲▲▲▲▲▲▲▲▲▲▲▲▲
▼▼▼▼▼▼▼▼▼▼▼▼▼▼▼▼▼▼▼▼▼▼▼▼▼▼▼▼▼▼▼▼▼▼

2003

I call to order this meeting of the Yurok Tribal Council. Welcome, tribal members and council members. Can I have a motion to approve the agenda?" asked Chairwoman Sue Masten.

The motion was made and accepted.

"First agenda item is the 2003 Yurok fishery," she continued. "Dave, what's the status of the fishery? How are the returning salmon runs?" she asked Dave Hillemeier, the Yurok Tribal Fisheries Department director.

"Well, I'm sorry to report it's bad. Returning numbers are low," he replied.

In 1988, Congress passed the Hoopa-Yurok Settlement Act that separated the Yurok-Hoopa Reservations and distributed assets. Yurok organized a modern tribal government and adopted a constitution in 1993. In the ten years since its creation, the Yurok Tribal Fisheries Department had become the Nation's largest government department. The Nation employed the second highest number of fisheries biologists in the state of California, second to only the State of California itself. The department's primary purpose was to restore the Nation's salmon runs and ensure the Nation's salmon harvest was sustainable. In this way, the modern tribal government incorporated the first covenant into the Nation's present-day exercise of tribal sovereignty. The Nation used traditional and modern scientific knowledge to accomplish this task. Each year the Nation worked with the Pacific Fishery Management Council to estimate the size of the returning fall chinook salmon run, set an escapement level necessary to allow spawning, and then allocate the remaining part of the run for harvest. The Nation received 50 percent of the harvest, split with the offshore commercial fishing people. The amount of the Nation's catch is its harvest allocation. The Nation would divide the overall harvest into amounts for commercial, subsistence, and ceremonial purposes. Dave worked with the tribal council staff and members each year to secure the Nation's 50 percent and divide it into the three categories.

"The Nation's salmon allocation is small," he reported.

"What's impacting the returning runs?"

"They're suffering from the similar River conditions that caused the fish kill last year. Water quality is poor, levels are low, and temperatures are hot."

"What's causing this, Dave? What do the fish need?" she asked.

"Agriculture and the dams. We can't save the salmon without removing the dams and making agriculture at the top of the basin sustainable. The dams were built without fish passage, cause poor water quality and raise temperatures, block cold water springs, and the reservoirs behind them release methane, a greenhouse gas. The fish need cool, clean water."

The fish kill led to a systematic change to the Nation's strategy to preserve its way of life. Now that Yurok fishing rights had been secured, the Nation turned its focus to conservation of the salmon and the River.

The Yurok Nation launched a campaign to restore the Klamath River to fight for our survival. The Nation developed its strategy by asking one fundamental question: what do the fish need? It relied on elders' traditional stories and teachings, and fishing people who offered information and data. Marrying Western science with Yurok traditional knowledge and law, the Nation answered the question of what the fish needed: cold, clean water and access to good habitat. It relied on its capable team of fisheries biologists, lawyers, and policy analysts.

This was not a surprise. Yurok people knew this already, as we had worked hard to manage our natural resources in a way that sustained ecosystem balance and health. Now we had to clean up more than a century of imbalanced mismanagement and destruction of the River caused by colonization. We had to heal the entire River. This would require support from entities from throughout the entire basin. A critical part of Yurok's strategy was to build a coalition to support the River's revival.

Yurok and our neighboring sister Nation, the Karuk, call themselves "fix the world people" because our religion includes World Renewal Ceremonies and our worldview requires us to live in balance with the planet. The task of putting the River back together and rebalancing our own homelands after colonization would put our purpose of fixing the world to the ultimate test.

The Klamath dams had to be removed. PacifiCorp, a US subsidiary of ScottishPower, owned the dams within the Klamath River Hydroelectric Project and operated them according to a license from the Federal Energy Regulatory Commission (FERC). FERC is the federal commission that oversees hydroelectric dams in the United States. It's a quasi-judicial agency that has hearings with process and procedure and commissioners who preside over the hearings to issue orders. It also has staff that works on permitting and enforcement of

FERC orders. Orders can include the issuance of a license to operate a dam with specific terms and conditions.

On the Klamath, PacifiCorp owned four dams with a combined energy generation capacity of 169 megawatts. It had a FERC license to operate the dams. The fifty-year license would expire in 2006. A relicensing proceeding would be required to renew the license for another fifty years. The proceeding would be like a court case where PacifiCorp would request to renew the license without updating the dams to meet modern water quality standards or install fish passage, and the Yurok Nation, and our allies, would request dam removal.

This was our moment.

《《《

In 2003, I graduated from college and started at the Pre-Law Summer Institute for Native Americans and Alaska Natives (PLSI) at the University of New Mexico School of Law. It was an eight-week intensive simulation of the first semester of law school designed to prepare students. This was my introduction to the law.

I had only ever met my Nation's two lawyers, and I didn't know what they did for work. I had never read a court case or a legal brief. I had never been inside a law school. I was fascinated with the law because I was, naively, convinced that the law was the ticket to saving the salmon of my home waters and my culture. I was twenty-four years old. I also believed that most lawyers were rich and famous.

There were around twenty-five or so other Indigenous people in the institute that year, from all corners of Indian country. They were brilliant. Together we were introduced to the law of the conqueror, a legal system that was designed to justify the taking of our ancestors' life, liberty, and property, to give to white settlers under the guise of a Constitution and Bill of Rights that aimed to create one nation under God with liberty and justice for all — all except for the Indigenous peoples, who were the stewards of the stolen lands and resources the country was built upon, and the enslaved African people who then built the country.

There was solidarity in learning these laws with other Indigenous peoples. Many of us shared similar family histories: our ancestors had been subjected to genocide. Our land and resources had been stolen. Our families had been confined to reservations and our children stolen, then later sent to cities to assimilate. And our people were now just trying to recover from being at war with the US government for the last 150 to 400 years, depending upon whether they were from nations from the east or west. This collective historical experience led us to an interpretation of cases that I would later appreciate was uniquely Indigenous. We viewed the cases from the perspective of the loser — the Indigenous nations — rather than from the white patriarchal Christian perspective that is commonly uplifted in textbooks and law classes. Guided by mostly Indigenous law professors, we dove into torts, property, contracts, legal writing, and — my favorite — federal Indian law. We had classes during the day and, on most nights, reading assignments of more than a hundred pages of court cases and analysis.

In midsummer, in the federal Indian law class, we were assigned reading on Indian reservation diminishment cases, which would be discussed in the class the next day. Late one evening, I was grinding through the assignment when there it was in my Indian law textbook, my family name: Mattz. I perked up with interest, my energy reignited by the surprise and anticipation of what would come next.

The book continued: In 1973, in the landmark case *Mattz v. Arnett,* the Supreme Court held the Klamath River Indian Reservation was still Indian country and had not been terminated despite an act opening the reservation for non-Indian ownership.[14] Termination of an Indian reservation requires clear congressional intent, which was not present in the 1892 act. The court explained "[t]he Act did no more [in this respect] than open the way for non-Indian settlers to own land on the reservation in a manner which the Federal Government, acting as guardian and trustee for the Indians, regarded as beneficial to the development of its wards."[15] The book noted that the Supreme Court explained that Ray Mattz had fished at his family's traditional fishing hole at Brooks Riffle, which supported that the reservation had retained its "Indian Character" throughout history. The case set a high bar for determining whether an Indian reservation has been terminated.

When I was growing up, I had heard that Uncle Ray's case had established our fishing rights. I didn't appreciate that it had also reaffirmed that our reservation was still Indian country. This meant that the land within the Yurok Reservation was still ours. The Yurok people's interest in the land, and jurisdiction to regulate it and its people, within the reservation were still valid. The court heavily relied on the fact that my family had stayed on the River fishing to determine that it was still Indian country. My family's resistance and bootlegging through the 1930s to the 1970s had worked in our favor.

The next day in class, I shyly, and with a bit of pride, told one of the teacher's aides, Deb Haaland (who would become the first Native American Secretary of the Interior twenty years later) that *Mattz v. Arnett* was my family's case. Haaland had attended PLSI the year before. She was very interested and wanted to learn more about the family's experience. During class, she asked me if I wanted to share my thoughts about the case.

I was so nervous about being called on in class, and the case being my family's, that I stumbled over my words and said something like, "We just like to fish," which elicited laughter and understanding from my classmates. Most of the students liked to fish, hunt, or gather too. I still had doubts as to whether I was smart enough to earn a law degree. Uncle Ray could hardly read and most of his generation had only gotten through the eighth grade. I was only the second person in my family to graduate college. No one had a graduate degree.

I was in uncharted waters.

After class, I called Grandma to talk about the case.

"Grandma, hi! We covered *Mattz v. Arnett* in class today. I was called on in class to talk about it. I was so embarrassed," I said.

"Oh, honey, you must get used to that. What did you learn?" she asked.

"Uncle's case sets a high bar for taking away Indian land once it's a reservation," I explained.

"Wow. We fought for that because we wanted our fishing rights. Long time ago, we couldn't fish like we do now."

"I remember you talking about that when I was growing up. It seemed dangerous."

"Yes, it was," she said. "Here, let me add Uncle Ray. He's sitting next to me."

When he got on the phone, I told them I couldn't believe he'd gone all the way to the Supreme Court. He told me how the lawyers had told our family that if we could prove we owned the land, we'd get fishing rights. They told us we'd have to go to the highest court in the land but that we could win. And we had.

"Uncle, why did you do it?" I asked.

"I knew we had Indian rights," he replied.

CHAPTER 14

Grassroots Rising

▲▲▲▲▲▲▲▲▲▲▲▲▲▲▲▲▲▲▲▲▲▲▲▲▲▲▲▲▲▲▲
▼▼▼▼▼▼▼▼▼▼▼▼▼▼▼▼▼▼▼▼▼▼▼▼▼▼▼▼▼▼▼

2004

In 2004, the same year I started law school, PacifiCorp submitted a petition to relicense the Klamath River Hydroelectric Project with FERC. With the renewal of that license, the Klamath dams would be operational for another fifty-year term, until 2056, as the license expired in 2006. FERC precedent supported PacifiCorp's bid for relicensing, even in the face of the environmental harm the dams caused, including the 2002 fish kill and destruction of Indigenous rights. From PacifiCorp's perspective, such future harm could be mitigated through hatcheries and money for habitat restoration, corporate loopholes and runarounds, with no regard for the Indigenous people who lived on the River. Ronnie Pierce, a fierce Yurok woman who was instrumental to Yurok's fight, stated, "I read their god dammed application and I couldn't even tell if a salmon lived in the Klamath River." PacifiCorp didn't even consider dam removal as an option.

We had something to say about that.

《《《

During law school summers, I would return home to subsistence fish for salmon to stock up for the coming year. Throughout college and law school, I often paid my rent with smoked salmon and relied on my prized canned smoked salmon or frozen fillets during tough exams or when I missed home. It always kept me going.

On those summer fishing trips, I fished with my siblings — Steph, Ashley, Lavina, and Will. We'd set up camp below the Requa Inn in the Klamath estuary, owned by our auntie Janet and her family, and gillnet for salmon. Our parents would often join us. Dad acted as our coach, while Ashley and Lavina joked around — something they could get away with because, as Dad put it, we were a "well-oiled machine," working so seamlessly together.

During these trips, I noticed a shift among the fishing community. People were calling for dam removal as salmon runs steadily declined and they caught fewer fish. Sitting on the banks of the River, we would often daydream about blowing up the dams.

In response to PacifiCorp filing its license renewal petition, the Indigenous grassroots activists, most of them fishing people, launched a campaign to "bring the salmon home" by undamming the Heyl-keek 'We-roy, the Klamath River. The Indigenous people on the Klamath have a long history of community organizing to protect the River's interests. It usually started with phone calls, like those my great-grandmother made calling for help during the Salmon Wars, and led to the formation of associations, like the Traditional Indian Fisherman's Association that my auntie Sue represented in the 1970s and '80s and the modern tribal government. Now, a new generation of powerful Indigenous organizers and others followed in their elders' footsteps to organize many groups, like the Klamath Justice Coalition and rose to tribal leadership. While the tribal governments fought PacifiCorp in FERC, the grassroots organizers pressured PacifiCorp to persuade the court of public opinion that the Klamath dams had to be removed. They hoped the protests would generate media stories that would highlight their cause and the environmental and cultural destruction the dams caused.

A delegation of Indigenous peoples and their staff from the Yurok, Karuk, Hoopa, and Klamath Nations traveled to Scotland to protest at a shareholder meeting of ScottishPower, the parent company of PacifiCorp, to urge the company to stop the relicensing petition and instead remove the dams. The protesters hoped to pressure the company to support dam removal as the company had billed itself as environmentally responsible.

"Undam the Klamath! Bring the salmon home!" chanted a procession of Indigenous peoples from the Klamath outside the meeting doors. They would go to the ends of the earth for the fish.

The company officials claimed that removing the dams could backfire because the dams help improve downstream water quality, holding back farm pollution in the reservoirs behind the dams. They warned that fish moving upstream of the dams would face hazardous water conditions, including toxic blue-green algae and warm, polluted water.

While I worked my way through law school studying the fundamental subjects of US law, including contracts, property, constitutional law, environmental law, water law, and federal Indian law, the Klamath dams were acquired by Warren Buffett, the owner of Berkshire Hathaway. Now the Indigenous nations and Indigenous peoples that were some of the poorest in all of California would take on one of the richest men in the world.

The protests continued while I was in law school. While I studied for my last semester of exams and prepared to graduate, another delegation of Indigenous protesters traveled 1,800 miles, from the

Klamath River to Omaha, Nebraska, to protest at a shareholder meeting of Berkshire Hathaway. Warren Buffett would be there.

The flood of protesters was as wide as the downtown Omaha street they marched upon and a quarter city block long. They wore blue jeans, T-shirts, and bandannas, Indian hats and necklaces, and carried their babies in Indian baskets. The protesters carried signs that read:

DAMS = CULTURAL GENOCIDE

ECOCIDE IS CULTURAL GENOCIDE

REMOVE THE DAMS & HONOR OUR FUTURE

WARREN BUFFETT KILLS SALMON, JOBS, AND COMMUNITIES

"Undam the Klamath! Bring the salmon home!" they kept chanting, as the executives walked into the building.

"It's time now," said one of the protest leaders. Twenty-four protesters gathered and walked into the auditorium, as the rest of the protesters continued chanting outside. Their cries for justice faded as they walked down a long hallway with gray concrete walls and fluorescent lights that seemed to get smaller as they got closer to the auditorium door, like a passageway in *Alice in Wonderland*. Then, they opened the door to the auditorium, and it seemed larger than life — huge, with a stage up front and arena-style seating. The stage was set with a long rectangular strip of tables and chairs. In the seating area, there were microphones in the aisles. People were sitting and mulling in the public seating section. One group of the protesters sat next to a microphone and the other went to the second floor of the auditorium, as they waited for the meeting to start.

The lights dimmed in the auditorium, the stage lights brightened, and the executives took their seats at the conference table onstage. The protesters released a banner from the railing on the second floor. It made a *whoosh* sound as it rolled out, catching the attention of the entire auditorium. Everyone looked in the direction of the noise and saw a sign that read *Warren, Un-Dam the Klamath!*

The meeting was called to order. The protesters waited for the public comment portion of the meeting.

One by one, the protesters stepped up to the microphone. "Klamath dams are killing the Klamath River. Klamath dams are killing my salmon. We demand you remove the Klamath dams now!"

"Undam the Klamath, bring the salmon home," one chanted.

"The Klamath dams kill salmon. They kill tribal cultures. They kill the River. They must be removed now!"

"Thank you for your comments," directed an executive. "We have heard enough about Klamath dam removal. Please sit down if you want to comment about dam removal."

No one sat down. They stayed in line to make a public comment.

Another protester approached the microphone and began, "Why do you hate Indians and kill fish? Undam — " But before she could finish, security grabbed her arm to pull her from the microphone. Eleven protesters were behind her and rushed in to support her. More security officers swarmed in.

"It is our right to make a public comment. You can't stop us," yelled the woman into the microphone. A security officer pulled her arm behind her back and cuffed her. The other ten protesters stood back.

"All of you, follow me outside. That's enough," said the officer.

They took their first steps toward the door, chanting "Undam the Klamath! Bring the salmon home!" Meeting participants cussed and

spat at them as they were aggressively dragged out the door and continued their cries out onto the street, joining the other protesters. No
one was arrested.

The protesters attended several more shareholder meetings. During
one protest, Dana Rose, an Indigenous leader, brought a mason jar
full of rancid-smelling bright toxic blue-green algae water from the
Klamath dam reservoir. She made several shareholders smell it. Perhaps it was the smell, or the protesters' consistent presence and steady
demand for dam removal and justice, that ingrained the idea of dam
removal in the shareholders' minds, which slowly began to change.

〈〈〈

I was in my second year of law school in Colorado when the school
announced that an alum, the Secretary of the Interior, Gale Norton,
would give a lecture at the school. Norton was in the final years of her
term serving the Bush administration and was a part of the interior
leadership team that had diverted water from the Klamath, causing
the fish kill.

I emailed the Nation's attorneys, whom I had interned with, saying
that she was coming. Their response was: "Do you need help making
a protest sign?"

That's it! I realized. I needed to organize a protest. By now, I was
the president of the law school's Native American Law Students Association and immediately sent an email to the presidents of the student
unions asking for support to organize a protest of the secretary's visit.
I explained that for political gain, Norton and Vice President Cheney
had made the decision to divert water from the Klamath River over
the objection of the Nation's and fish scientists who warned it would
cause water levels to drop too low to support ecological health and
salmon. This caused the largest fish kill in American history on my

home waters. We had confirmed the participation of most of the student unions, when I received an email from the dean's office requesting a meeting with me.

Arriving in the dean's suite, I remember being taken by how fancy it was. While I had gotten into law school, I was still adjusting to the wealth that surrounded it. There were Western landscape paintings of buffalo, open plains, and Indians riding horses in loincloths, framed awards, and small iron statues of buffalo and elk. I sat on a leather couch.

"The dean will see you now," said the receptionist.

I walked into the dean's office. It was more of the same Western-style decor. There were several people standing in the room, including the dean and several associate deans from the student support office.

"Welcome, Amy. Take a seat," said the dean, who directed me to sit on a chair across from her desk, where she sat in an office chair. In my two years at the school, I had not met the dean nor been in her office, nor had I met the six or seven staff who stood surrounding us. We exchanged introductions and pleasantries, and then she got to it.

She said something along the lines of, "I understand you have organized a protest of Secretary Norton's visit. Please call it off."

I had anticipated this request and considered how I would respond. On the one hand, I didn't want to get kicked out of law school because that would defeat my long-term goal of providing legal representation to my Nation. On the other hand, the Secretary's visit presented an opportunity to fight back and attempt to hold accountable one of the government officials responsible for committing an act of ecocide against my people.

"I don't have the authority, as most of the other student unions are protesting. I don't have the authority to direct them," I said, choosing a diplomatic approach to take advantage of the opportunity to confront the Secretary of the Interior.

"Well, what if we gave you and a few student leaders a chance to meet Secretary Norton and ask her a question?"

"That would be wonderful."

"Can you call it off?"

"No."

She paused.

"Well, how about if you introduce Secretary Norton before her speech to the law school?"

"Sure. It would be my pleasure."

"Will you call it off?"

"No, I don't have authority over the other groups."

"Well, all right, then. I will let you and a few other student leaders meet with her before, and you can introduce her. Whatever the Secretary has done, she is an alum, and we want to welcome her here. I hope that you will choose to represent the school well," she said firmly.

I nodded and thanked the dean. I considered this outcome a victory. Not only would I have a private audience with the Secretary of the Interior; I would also introduce her in front of a large crowd. I felt a duty to my tribal community to speak up for the River and the salmon in this rare potentially influential moment. This dictated that I call her out for her role in the fish kill. At the same time, I also wanted to stay in law school and graduate, and an aggressive approach could get me suspended. I was twenty-four years old and still believed in my mother's guidance — "you can get more with sugar than you can with salt" — even when it came to law and politics. So, I would attempt a balanced approach of discussing the fish kill respectfully. I wanted to express the deep offense she had committed on my reservation while still being respectful and reflecting my legal and political knowledge of the fish kill. I spent the days between the meeting with the dean and the protest planning the protest with the other student unions. We discussed the environmentally harmful policies of the Bush administration and its prioritization of corporate America over the rights of the environment and Indigenous peoples.

On the day of the protest, I wore a bright red T-shirt that said, *Bush Kills Fish, 70,000 Salmon Dead on the Klamath River, Yurok Reservation.* I was ready for this moment, with a question and introduction prepared and the protest well organized. I walked into the small meeting with the Secretary and student leaders. We stood in a circle and each got to ask one question. When my turn came, the Secretary looked at me and read my T-shirt, and her eyes widened.

"Secretary, how do you reconcile the decision to divert an excessive amount of Klamath River water for agriculture that led to the largest fish kill in American history with the US government's trust responsibility to the Yurok Nation? In 2002, over seventy thousand salmon died on my reservation in the Klamath River. Your administration killed those fish."

I had decided to be factual and direct in my question. Naively I had expected her to thoughtfully answer my question. I wanted her to provide a logical reason for the fish kill. I wanted her answer to finally bring peace to my grief.

Her eyes were still wide. She had not expected a question about the fish kill.

"Well, the United States has obligations to multiple user groups. The fish kill was unfortunate."

And she moved to the next question.

She had given me a nonanswer, dodging the question. At this point, I was not sure she even knew about the fish kill.

I had one more chance. I would not miss.

The meeting ended and we proceeded down to the lecture hall for her talk.

When we arrived at the lecture hall, it was full of students, staff, and the public. The room was jam-packed with protest signs exclaiming slogans like *Gale, Gale, what about the whale?* And — my favorite — *Bush Kills Fish*. When she walked in, the protesters hollered and waved their signs up and down. I walked to the podium, and the room grew quiet.

I introduced myself in Yurok and then spoke in English. "I have the pleasure of introducing Gale Norton, the Secretary of the Interior. Secretary Norton is an alum of this law school. She is known on my reservation as one of the government officials responsible for committing an act of ecocide against my people by killing the salmon that my people depended upon." I paused, then turned my attention to her. An environmental student union member chanted, "Gale, Gale, what about the whale?" More students joined in, while others booed and pushed their protest signs up and down. The secretary looked down at her feet.

"Secretary, in your remarks, please address how the Bush administration justified its kill of over seventy thousand salmon on the Klamath River to support agriculture and power generation."

I stepped from the podium, and she stepped rigidly up to the microphone. She was robotic and polite, and again dodged the question, continuing on about something else. I don't remember what. I don't think the room remembered either. I do think they remembered the visual image of the dead salmon, and the signs *Gale, Gale, what about the Whale?* and *Bush and Norton Kill Fish.*

There was no good reason for the fish kill. It was just as it had seemed: politics. The federal government doesn't always follow the law and is rarely held accountable. Instead, politics, power, and money often control. If that was the case, I would learn to use these forces for good.

CHAPTER 15

Bring the Salmon Home

▲▲▲▲▲▲▲▲▲▲▲▲▲▲▲▲▲▲▲▲▲▲▲▲▲▲▲▲▲▲▲▲
▼▼▼▼▼▼▼▼▼▼▼▼▼▼▼▼▼▼▼▼▼▼▼▼▼▼▼▼▼▼▼▼

2008

Coalitions of Indian grassroots activists and tribal leaders from the Klamath River were the first to call for dam removal. Most people didn't take them seriously at first. Opponents made arguments like, "Dam removal at this scale has never been done." By 2008, many smaller dams had been removed with good results, and larger dam removal projects on the Elwha and Penobscot Rivers were underway, but there had never been a dam removal project as large as the Klamath project on this scale. Plus, opponents argued, the Klamath dams provided green energy and flood control and were operational, even if they provided only 1.3 percent of PacifiCorp's power production. PacifiCorp wanted to relicense the dams to keep them operational without updating the dams to allow fish passage or comply with modern law. They maintained their opposition to dam removal, claiming it was risky because the amount of sediment and its contents behind the four dams was unknown. It would negatively impact water quality and aquatic species.

Many people just frankly laughed at the idea of dam removal because it seemed to be so outlandish. They claimed dam removal was "a terrible experiment" that would sully water quality and amount to a death sentence for fish. A representative from the Klamath Water Users Association stated that dam removal wouldn't work because it is "a classic example of oversimplification and a whole lot of myth-making by the tribes and their allies." In America, we build dams; we do not take them out. This sentiment is based on an assumption built into almost every natural resource policy of the US government: ecosystems need to be developed to better support the country's human population. On the Klamath, the white culture believed the River better served Americans by being dammed for energy production and diverted for agriculture. Removing dams would be a digression of progress because the Country needed the infrastructure to produce energy, especially at a time when hydropower was considered a green energy source.

My aunt, Chairwoman Sue Masten, had called for allies to help remove the dams while still making agriculture sustainable in the basin. The Nation began to develop a coalition to support dam removal such as with the Karuk and Klamath Nations, the states of Oregon and California, the Pacific Coast Federation of Fishermen's Associations, and Trout Unlimited, American Rivers, and many more. We learned the fish kill had caused many others to dedicate their life's work to Klamath River restoration, not just us Yurok. We came to appreciate that the salmon had not died in vain. Instead, their sacrifice was like the canary in the coal mine, warning us all that ecological collapse would only continue if we didn't work in balance with nature. Not only had we heard the canary, so had the rest of the world. Our coalition grew stronger. The Creator's agreement with the salmon was working as planned and the world renewal medicine grew stronger.

The timing of the canary's call to action was perfect. In 2004, after PacifiCorp filed to relicense the Klamath Dams in FERC, things got serious. PacifiCorp wanted to relicense the dams. The states of Oregon and California wanted to serve the public interest by building economies and ecosystems through relicensing or dam removal. The nations knew dam removal was the only option to save their way of life.

The relicensing proceeding presented a path forward to dam removal. PacifiCorp requested its license be renewed with the same terms to operate the Klamath Dam until 2056. This meant that no fish passage or additional environmental protection would be required of them. The Yurok Nation advocated for dam removal, arguing that the dams were harming the Nation's federally reserved fishing rights, which had been established in the *Mattz* cases, by diminishing the number of salmon available for harvest. Our allies, the Karuk Nation, Trout Unlimited, American Rivers, Cal Trout, and many more NGOs, joined us arguing that the dams were harming the River's health by creating conditions that increased water temperature, exacerbated water pollution, prohibited the flow of natural sediment, and increased the rate of fish disease. FERC had a trust responsibility to Indian nations to protect their interests. Here, it would be *illegal* for FERC to relicense the dams with the old terms because it would violate the Nation's fishing and water rights. The Nation argued that the dams were so harmful to salmon that dam removal was the *only* option available consistent with the law.

While the federal salmon regulators at the National Marine Fisheries Service did not have the power to block the license or require PacifiCorp to remove the dams, they did need to ensure that if the dams were to be relicensed, they would have to comply with current laws, and be retrofitted with fish ladders. None of the Nations and Conservation groups believed the fish ladders would work well or improve water quality. The coalition continued to push for dam removal.

PacifiCorp challenged the NMFS fish passage requirements in an administrative "trial type hearing" in FERC, arguing that the habitat above the dams didn't justify passage. Oregon didn't participate. California's participation was minimal. A Klamath coalition was formed with four Nations, including the Yurok Nation, joined with conservation groups and the Pacific Coast Federation of Fishermen's Associations to defend the need for salmon to return to the upper basin. Because the science was so strong and the Klamath coalition's experts and lawyers worked closely together, we won on virtually every count.

The victory united these parties in a coalition led by the Nations to defend the River. We were growing stronger.

In 2007, the year I graduated law school, FERC concluded the environmental review of dam removal and took the first step to renew PacifiCorp's license to operate the dams. While I was studying for the bar exam, FERC released its final environmental impact statement (FEIS), which recommended renewing the license. The document was hundreds of pages long. I was drawn to review it as I knew it would control my future. I was also deep into bar review materials, preparing for a test that would also control my fate. If I passed the bar exam, I could begin working for the River, salmon, and my Nation. I kept my nose to the law review books.

It was likely that FERC would follow the recommendation in the FEIS to relicense the dams. The FEIS ultimately recommended issuing a new license that included maintaining the four dams with the additional measures for fish passage.[16] Under this new license, PacifiCorp could operate the Klamath Dams for another fifty years only if it reestablished fish passage. This was a death sentence for the River. While fish ladders or other fish mitigation measures may reestablish fish passage, they would not address the environmental harms the dams inflicted on the River, like polluting water and preventing natural sediment from flowing downriver. These conditions were causing fish diseases, like ich, which caused the 2002 salmon kill.

It was also troubling for PacifiCorp, which completed an economic analysis that revealed dam removal was cheaper than installing the fish ladders and complying with the other fish-related conditions created by NMFS. This was a significant development. As FERC was not likely to approve PacifiCorp's request to secure a new fifty-year license with the old antiquated terms, they were willing to consider dam removal. Suddenly, dam removal became a rational business decision; it would be cheaper to PacifiCorp ratepayers to remove the dams than to install the fish ladders and other measures. PacifiCorp agreed to negotiations with Yurok, Karuk, federal and state governments, the Klamath Water Users Association, and NGOs to evaluate alternatives to relicensing, including dam removal.

The Nation's legal rights, secured in the creation of the reservation, and then affirmed in the *Mattz* court cases, were a driving source of law that required additional fish protection measures that prompted the negotiations. The resistance of my ancestors formed the legal scaffolding that could lead to the protection of the River, salmon, and culture for future generations.

The Nation also worked to expand our coalition during these negotiations to generate support for dam removal, habitat restoration, and water for the River. Our leaders, like Troy Fletcher, Auntie Sue, Tommy O'Rourke, and others, made strategic and passionate speeches and built relationships with leaders from other groups. They leaned into the farmers, with whom we had been in an active water war for over twenty years. They led with empathy and understanding by learning about each other's way of life. They worked to teach people about balance and the role of humans to restore balance. This inspired others and motivated them to help restore the balance on the River. It turned our enemies into our allies.

In 2010, these negotiations resulted in the signing of two historic agreements: the Klamath Hydroelectric Settlement Agreement (KHSA) and the Klamath Basin Restoration Agreement (KBRA).

These were signed by the Yurok and Karuk Nations, Oregon, California, the United States, PacifiCorp, and NGOs, totaling forty-seven signatories. The agreements complemented each other by addressing the major factors that were causing the ecological, social, and economic collapse in the Klamath Basin. The KBRA included a water allocation agreement for water for farmers, Upper Klamath Lake, and the River. It also included funding for and authorization of authority for restoration projects. The KHSA included terms to facilitate removal of the four Klamath dams by 2020 by seeking congressional approval for dam removal. These novel agreements equally valued the rights of Indigenous peoples, nature, and business. We had found balance.

We finally had a path to world renewal.

CHAPTER 16

Team Fish Hog

2012

In 2012, I had just given birth to my first son, Brooks, named after Brooks Riffle, and I was living in Boulder, Colorado, working at the Native American Rights Fund (NARF). One day, my dad called me with exciting news.

"Amy, how are you feeling?" asked my dad over the phone.

"I'm good. Baby is doing well," I said exuberantly. It had only been eight weeks since my son was born. I was still recovering physically and mentally and reevaluating my life priorities as a new mother.

My dad reported that the salmon were running. It was time to come home if I wanted to catch a few. Through college and law school I had come to love these calls from my dad. I could always count on him to bring me back to the River just as his mother, Lavina (my grandmother), had done for him.

"The salmon run came in last night," he explained. "The kids knocked 'em. The bulk of the run could be right behind them."

I immediately felt the instinctual urge to catch Klamath salmon, no matter how far away I was from the River. I had passed the bar exam and been practicing law since 2007. My eight weeks of maternity leave had been the longest I had been away from my work. While I loved my work representing Indigenous nations across the country on water rights, Indian education, and other matters related to protecting tribal cultures. I didn't miss it; I was so in love with my new baby boy. Receiving the news that the fish were running triggered in me a genetic response as deep as my urge to care for my new baby. *The fish are running, and I must catch them to prepare for the winter.*

I have observed that many Yurok people have this same experience every spring and fall. It must be a form of genetic evolution from fishing for the same Klamath salmon runs since time immemorial that causes an internal reaction, leading us to the River and giving us new energy to stay up late and work hard fishing. My dad often commented that Yurok people have been fishing the same runs of salmon for so long we now carry one another's DNA. Perhaps it's the same DNA that propelled us both back to our home waters annually. I realized that exercising my fishing rights, by participating in the commercial and subsistence fishery there, was just as important as my legal work to protect those rights. Now, with the arrival of my new baby, I could do that with a family, just like every generation of my family before.

Following the fish kill in 2002, I devoted my professional life to preparing to represent the Yurok Nation. Before the fish kill, I thought I would become a singer. After my moment with my great-grandmother Geneva — when I received my guidance during the fish kill and after she had packed the medicine for me in a dream — I felt strongly that this work was my life's calling. I wanted justice through restoration of my river, homelands, and culture. I wanted to help however I could, to the best of my ability, which I believed, perhaps naively, was to become a lawyer for the Nation.

Fewer than 1 percent of lawyers in the United States are Native

Americans. Plus, I was a woman from a family and community of humble means. I'd never paid attention to my disadvantages. Instead, I focused my legal education on federal Indian and environmental law and was active in the Indian law community, which fueled my passion. My first job out of law school was with the Native American Rights Fund (NARF), the oldest and largest legal defense fund for nations, Indian people, and organizations. NARF started with CILS in the 1960s. While CILS was representing my family in California, NARF was representing Indian families in Washington State and across the country.

While Uncle Ray's case was moving through the courts, NARF attorneys David Getches, Charles Wilkinson, and John Echohawk filed *United States v. Washington,* the 1975 landmark case that established that the treaties between the United States and the Indigenous nations in Washington were still good law. Importantly, the treaties included an off-reservation fishing right in the usual and accustomed locations, in common with the people of the state, in exchange for ceding millions of acres of Indian land in Washington. The case was filed after the state of Washington limited Indian fishing in violation of the treaty rights. Indian fishing people, like Billy Frank, a Nisqually Indian, and many more, protested by hosting fish-ins. The state responded by sending law enforcement to break up the fish-ins, just like my family had done in the Salmon Wars. The result was violent arrests of the Indian people who were on the right side of the law but ended up on the wrong side of metal bars, in jail, bruised and battered by police brutality.

NARF got involved, filing the lawsuit asserting that the treaty rights entitled Indian people to fish in the usual and accustomed fishing locations of their ancestors. In *United States v. Washington,* the presiding judge, George Boldt, agreed with NARF, upholding the treaty fishing rights and setting aside not less than 50 percent of the harvest to the Indigenous nations. Judge Boldt was almost hanged because of the decision.[17] While my family didn't know it at the time, Indian people throughout the Pacific Northwest were fighting the same fight for fishing rights against state governments in the 1970s. Powerful Indian leaders, like Uncle Ray, Billy Frank, and many more, working with NARF and CILS, established fundamental tribal rights, ending illegal state intrusions into tribal sovereignty and violent battles between the states and Indian people over fishing rights that had started more than 150 years before, when the colonizers arrived.

Since then, NARF has been at the heart of almost every major Indian law case. Its legacy is the body of Indian law as we know it today. The attorneys of NARF have served Indian country well by empowering tribal leadership and curating the body of Indian law to fully advance tribal sovereignty.

I was surprised when NARF offered me a job because they set the gold standard for Indian law attorneys. I didn't expect such a good job offer. I was an Indigenous girl who had only ever met two lawyers before going to law school. Yet, I had interned with NARF as a summer associate and loved every minute of it. I was told I had fire in the belly, likely the same fire that had ignited my family's 170-year-long battle against the US government to protect our way of life. When I received the job offer, I eagerly accepted it.

At NARF I learned how to practice law. I cut my teeth on drafting tribal law ordinances, water rights cases, Indian education law and policy, tribal-state compact agreements, and much more. Learning the law and how to practice it empowered me because I came to understand "their laws" and how to use them to protect Indigenous peoples and resources. For generations, treaty rights and reserved Indian rights were systematically ignored as the United States built its wealth by exploiting natural resources and seizing Indigenous lands — often at the direct expense of Indigenous sovereignty and survival. This was not only a grave injustice — it was a violation of the US Constitution. Treaties are not symbolic; they are binding legal agreements, enshrined as the supreme law of the land. And yet, their neglect led to the destruction of ecosystems, the loss of culture, and the unraveling of Indigenous lifeways across this continent.

As I traveled through Indian Country and worked alongside different Indigenous nations, I saw firsthand both the resilience of our communities and the shared history of legal erasure, environmental harm, and broken promises. The rivers poisoned, the forests cleared, the fish vanished — not by accident, but by design. Families like mine had endured the same struggles time and again, fighting not only for survival but for recognition of rights that should have never been denied.

I came to believe that enforcing tribal law and upholding treaty rights is not just a legal obligation — it is a path to healing. It is how we protect our lands, restore our waters, and rebuild our nations. It is how we ensure environmental justice is not an afterthought, but a mandate rooted in sovereignty and survival.

I practiced law for five years at NARF before my first baby, Brooks, was born. In many ways, the birth of my first child was the beginning of my adult life. Tribal sovereignty starts at home; I would exercise my own by raising my babies, fishing, and fighting for our rights.

《《《

I arrived in Rek-woi with my two-month-old son, Brooks, and husband. I brought Brooks' Yurok baby basket for him to rest in on the River bar while I fished. This is how countless generations of Yurok families have fished with their families. In 2012, my family would continue that tradition.

The basket is made of willow sticks woven into a perfect protective, secure, and safe refuge for a baby, two and a half feet long and a foot or so wide. The baby lies in the middle, wrapped in a blanket and secured to the basket with deerskin straps that wrap over the baby's chest and legs; another long leather strap wraps around a mother's shoulders. The design of the basket has stayed the same since as long as anyone can remember because it safely secures the baby to the basket and soothes it by holding the baby in a swaddle. Every generation of Yurok families used these baskets to carry babies while gathering, fishing, hunting, and traveling.

When I arrived home, my four siblings, mom, and dad had already made camp below the Requa Inn, the beautiful historic inn owned by my aunt and uncle, Janet and Marty Wortman, and their children, Geneva Wiki and Thomas Wortman. The fish camp was set on a grassy flat below the inn next to the family's fishing hole. The flat sat about fifteen feet above the River bar, lined with blackberry bushes and alder and willow trees, with leaves still holding strong to the branch in early September. The camp consisted of four medium-size tents — three for sleeping and one for gear and supplies — along with a table with kitchen and food supplies, and a generator. The family truck, Big Red, a 1990s double-cab Chevy, was parked on the west side of the camp, full of gill nets wrapped in blue tarps, twelve- and fifteen-pound anchors, fishing rope, and several pairs of fishing waders in various conditions — though most were covered in fish blood and ripped at the knees, with the occasional cut from a fish-cleaning knife. The inside of the truck was packed with blankets, cases of bottled water and granola bars, and wrappers from Chester's Chicken (the only fast food in town at the tribal gas station about a mile from the camp).

My brother, Will, an energetic twenty-one-year-old, threw another Chester's Chicken sandwich wrapper through the open window of Big Red. "Score!" he hollered, as the wrapper landed on the torn leather truck seat. He looked up and saw me, Brooks, and my husband, Daniel, walking down to the flat.

"You made it, Ames, about time!" said Will.

"We made it! How are you doing, Will?"

He was wearing dark green waders and an old T-shirt that was covered in moss and fish blood. We stood downriver from him, and the wind carried his scent of Winter Fresh–scented Speed Stick deodorant, last night's fish blood and slime, and River water. The smell was familiar and comforting to me. I gave him a hug.

"You all catch a few last night? Looks like it," I observed.

"Yeah, we caught a few," he said with a twinkle in his eye. I could see silver salmon scales and bruises on his forearms. He was as happy as a kid in a candy store.

We walked down the flat to the path, down to the fishing hole through the thick green-leafed blackberry bushes and overhead canopy formed by the trees. The narrow path, enclosed with green brush and tree branches, had the effect of transporting you from one world to another: arriving at the bottom of the path, I was now at the family fishing hole in the heart of the Yurok commercial fishery.

The family had two gill nets already set from the small dock the family had built and installed on the River for the fishing season. The family drift boat, a twelve-foot metal boat, was tied to the dock. On the wood dock there was a large white plastic fish tote and lid with four fish-cleaning knives on the lid. Down and upriver, there were several nets set and fishing people tending them. My dad and sisters, Lavina (named after my grandmother Lavina), Ashley, and Steph, were out on the water tending the net in the "mothership," a 1975 jet sled that had increased in value as it aged; hardworking and reliable, it was a classic and one of the best in its class. Dad had seen its potential when he purchased it in the 1990s.

"Famous, hi!" said Dad, who was standing behind the steering podium of the mothership. My sisters were bent over the side of the boat, Lavina holding the net, working it down toward the bottom — Ashley, next to her, was looking for fish. In their twenties, they'd inherited the beauty of their mother and grandmother. They were like singing sirens who had learned to fish better than most men on the River, beautiful, strong, smart, and expert fisherwomen. They looked up and gave me a holler.

"The fish in the tote need cleaning. Get to work, sis," Ashley said. I smiled, waved, and nodded to let her know I was on it. I walked up the path again and found my mother at the portable folding table at fish camp.

"Hello, love," she said enthusiastically.

"Hi, Mom," I said, giving her a big hug.

She smiled and reached for Brooks. She hugged him tightly. She took Brooks while I got my fishing gear on — a pair of rain boots and torn and stained waders from Big Red. I went down to the dock and started cleaning fish. Leaning over a fifteen-pound salmon, backside down, holding it between my feet with knife in hand, I was so grateful and excited to participate in this commercial fishery. We intended to sell our fish to make money until the commercial allocation was exhausted; then we'd fish for subsistence purposes. It was one of the largest runs in decades and one of the few commercial fisheries we'd had since the fish kill in 2002, and by now, in 2012, Dad had curated an army of fishing people made of me, my siblings, and our mother. We were a machine; we were Team Fish Hog. The resolution of the fishing rights in the 1980s made it possible for them to raise us fishing and loving our River.

The Klamath agreements (KHSA and KBRA), the two historical agreements signed in 2010, ensured dam removal by 2020, water for the River, and habitat restoration. There was hope in the air that these agreements would result in recovery of the River and salmon runs, hope that traveled from the ocean all the way up the forty-five miles of the Klamath River within the Yurok Reservation.

"Fish on," Will hollered. I looked up from the fish I was cleaning on the dock. Sure enough, a few white Styrofoam corks secured to the cork line on the gill net pulled down into the water, signaling a fish was in the net.

I jumped in the boat with Will. Will pulled the boat next to the cork line. Crouching over the front of the boat, I grabbed the cork line and began to work down the net, pulling it up from the depths of the water. I could feel something heavy in the net. As I was pulling, Will said, "There's another one," as the cork forty feet down the net pulled deep into the water. Then another cork at the end of the net pulled down.

"Ames, there are a few fish in this net, hurry."

I picked up the pace. Spotting the salmon, I worked the net toward it. It was a bright silver color, still alive and thrashing around in the net, trying to escape. When the salmon got to the surface of the water, I took a deep breath and heaved the fish into the boat. I quickly untangled it from the net, starting with the head and tail. I freed the salmon and slid it behind me to the center of the boat. The next salmon was barely in the net, caught by a gill and the rest of its body was loose. Salmon caught this way require extra care to get in the boat because they can easily fall out of the net while still in the water. I pulled the net to just below the surface, wrapped the net around the salmon, and grabbed its tail, pulling it into the boat. There was another salmon right next to that one, and I pulled it in too.

"Will, fish on, River side of the second net!" hollered my dad from the family dock.

Will nodded. I signaled to him that all the fish were out of the net. I dropped the nylon thread of the gill net and we motored over to the other net. I grabbed the cork line of the second net and worked the net down to the fish, pulling it into the boat as well.

This pattern went on.

"Come pick us up! Amy is having all the fun!" my sisters said from the dock. I laughed. I *was* having a lot of fun. I loved fishing like this.

"Get in the drift boat and work the other net," said Dad.

They jumped in the boat and rowed to the net.

With my brother and I in the mothership and my sisters in the drift boat, my father watched from a camp chair on the family dock as my mother sat next to him. She was holding Brooks, who had nodded off in his baby basket. We worked together in tandem as a large salmon run moved up the River under a blanket of fog. It was beautiful.

We took those salmon with the confidence that the Klamath Basin Restoration Agreement and Klamath Hydroelectric Settlement Agreement would be implemented and the dams would come out by 2020.

This simple moment, on the River with my family, fishing a salmon run in this very spot on the River, is what my ancestors' Sa-Mich and Wa-Pa-Shaw had tried to reserve for my family two centuries before in the unratified treaty. They knew the right to fish was as important to us as breathing, and if future generations had any chance of survival, they must be able to fish on the Klamath River.

CHAPTER 17

On Behalf of the Yurok Nation

2014

Two years into being a mother, in 2014, I felt the need to restore balance between my personal and professional lives. My NARF job required travel and long hours, both of which I enjoyed while I was training to be a lawyer. Now that I had a son, I wanted to be present for his formative years. The Yurok Nation had an opening for a staff attorney in its in-house Office of the Tribal Attorney (OTA). At this point the Nation was one of the largest employers in the two counties the reservation occupied and was providing many government services to both tribal members and non-tribal-member reservation residents. It was also attempting to rebuild as a Nation by reclaiming jurisdiction over people and resources within the reservation. Legal strategy and representation were critical. The OTA was charged with leading this legal effort. I accepted a remote part-time position with the Nation. I worked from home in Boulder, Colorado, while caring for my toddler. Twelve years after the 2002 fish kill and receiving the direction from my great-grandmother Geneva, I joyfully began my career as a lawyer for the Yurok Nation. I was excited and remained strongly committed to the notion that my and the Nation's work together could serve justice by restoring our River, fishery, and culture. The fire in my belly burned stronger than ever. I was ready to get to work.

I worked with other OTA attorneys to empower the Yurok leadership with the legal and political knowledge they needed to make informed decisions. I honed my working knowledge of the Nation's legal rights and the regulatory and legal hurdles necessary to accomplish dam removal, and developed legal strategies to increase instream flows and restore habitat throughout the Klamath Basin. I worked with the tribal council to translate this information for tribal leaders, who could then use it to advance dam removal.

My work focused on implementation of the KHSA and KBRA by participating in large stakeholder meetings and completing the legal and technical work to support the Nation's position. I frequently worked with the Nation's scientists, many of whom I had met on the River fishing, such as Mike Belchik and Dave Hillemeier. It was fascinating to learn more about how River conditions impacted the salmon. For example, salmon move upriver when water is cool. We could compare how this biological knowledge supported ecological knowledge: no doubt O'-rey-gos could feel the cool water at her toes on the River bar and would signal the fish that conditions were right to travel upriver.

Most impressive during this time was to witness Yurok leadership, like my aunt Sue Masten, Troy Fletcher, and Tommy O'Rourke, negotiate issues related to the implementation of the KBRA and KHSA at stakeholder meetings. At this point in time, the primary issue was lobbying Congress to pass a bill to authorize funding and federal agency authority to implement the KBRA. The stakeholders included

PacifiCorp, the federal government, Oregon, California, the Karuk Nation, the Klamath Water Users Association (which represented the farmers in the Klamath Reclamation Project), and several NGOs that were attempting to develop and implement a lobbying strategy.

These meetings were my introduction and training in the Yurok way of doing business. I learned early on in life at grandma's house that the best way to learn is to listen and observe the behavior of elders. Children often attend community meetings, ceremonies, hunting, and fishing with family members, who teach them by words and action how to be. I used these techniques to learn how to represent the Yurok Nation. I participated in these meetings, listening and observing how Yurok leadership commanded the room. They had worked hard to develop personal relationships during the negotiations of the KBRA and KHSA with the leadership of the other entities. The investment had paid off by building empathy, trust, and understanding. Each took time to understand the other's way of life — for example, fishermen spent time with farmers learning farming or fishing practices; meals of salmon and potatoes from the Klamath were shared. In this way, the medicine from the World Renewal Ceremonies worked to turn historical enemies into allies. I observed how new allies used respectful language when speaking to each other and brainstormed about leveraging resources from each entity to maximize political power and influence in Congress. This was my first lesson in Yurok diplomacy.

Then, in 2016, I received a phone call that would change the trajectory of my life. Nine months earlier, I'd had my second son, Keane (a Yurok word for fisherman). I held the phone with my left hand, head tilted to secure it between my shoulder and ear as Keane snuggled into my right arm and hip.

"Chairman, hello. How are you?" I said into the receiver. I started to pace the kitchen floor in my home in Boulder, Colorado. The baby was more likely to stay quiet if I walked.

"Amy, how are you?" said the Chairman of the Yurok Nation, Tommy O'Rourke.

"Well, thank you."

"It's time to come home. We need you to be the Yurok Nation's general counsel."

When I received the Chairman's call, I had been working as a part-time remote attorney for the Nation, to allow me to take care of my two young children, who were three years old and nine months old, and my husband, Daniel Cordalis, was working full-time. Hearing the Chairman's words asking me to be Yurok's general counsel, I was thrilled yet worried about how working full-time would affect my family.

"The Klamath Basin Restoration Agreement died. We don't know what the heck is gonna happen with dam removal. Congress wouldn't pass the gosh-darn bill. They won't approve dam removal. We gotta do something. It is time you come home," explained the Chairman. Being asked to come home was not unusual for Yurok people; in some ways we all feel a gravitational pull back to our homelands. We rotate around our homelands the same way the sun and moon orbit each other.

The Klamath Agreement stakeholders, including PacifiCorp, farmers in the Klamath Water Users Association, the Yurok and Karuk Nations, Oregon and California, and NGOs, had formed a coalition to lobby Congress to pass a bill to authorize dam removal and funding for the agreement and provide federal agency authority to implement the agreements. It was a diverse coalition of business, nations, states, and farmers that held promise and power. Unfortunately, they were met by a resistant conservative Congress controlled by the Republican Party. The coalition believed it had a champion in Greg Walden, a top-level member of the Republican Party, whose district in Southern Oregon included the northern tip of the Klamath Basin and the Klamath Water Users Association, and the Klamath Nations, both supporters of the legislation and signatories to the KHSA. They were important members of the coalition. He had committed to support the bill. The Tea Party contingent of the Republican Party's conservative politics was gaining support in the House and adamantly opposed dam removal, claiming it was anti-American to remove infrastructure that generated power to electrify America. After years of trying, the coalition was unable to move a bill through Congress. The self-termination clause in the KBRA was triggered in 2016, six years after its adoption, killing this historic agreement.

While I was only in my early thirties, I had waited more than a decade for the Chairman's phone call. I had been working as a part-time attorney, and this meant I could lead my nation's legal affairs. This was my opportunity to fulfill my duty to the Creator to protect my homelands and waters, and more specifically, to work to prevent harm to my River and culture as I had vowed to do that day on the boat during the fish kill. I felt I had something to offer the Nation: experience and expertise gained by working alongside some of the Nation's best Indian law attorneys at NARF. He had my attention.

"Amy, only 3 to 5 percent of the salmon are left. We don't have any more time to save them. It's now or never," said the Chairman. I needed no more convincing.

I worked with the Yurok chairman to negotiate the terms of my employment. My family and I relocated to Yurok Country. I started as the Nation's general counsel a day after my second child turned one year old.

My job as general counsel was to run the Nation's legal affairs. Arriving back at the reservation, I was impressed by the Nation's historic effort to rebuild the Yurok Nation after a long, hard period of colonization. It had organized into California's largest Nation, with more than 6,300 members. It had formed a modern tribal government with a healthy budget and several departments to provide services to members, adopted a constitution and various ordinances, and regulated people and natural resources on the reservation and was working to get its land back and recover its fishery. I spent time with Chairman O'Rourke, tribal council members, and my family, and I attended almost every Yurok Tribal Council meeting, frequently traveling with Yurok Tribal Council members to meetings all over the country and to every corner of the Yurok Reservation. These meetings were often tedious, long, and hard, and took me away from my family. The hard work of those days taught me about inherent sovereignty in a way no law book or courtroom could.

The law defines *inherent sovereignty* as the ability to make laws and be governed by them. I had read the cases that established the legal definition of inherent sovereignty and applied it to the facts of a particular case. I had drafted legal arguments to protect tribal inherent sovereignty and drafted tribal ordinances asserting such sovereignty. This textual work was just the surface of inherent sovereignty. It runs much deeper.

Our exercise of making laws and governing ourselves reflected our cultural values, religion, and worldview. This meant that how the Nation exercised its inherent sovereignty was controlled by Yurok values; every tribal council action that was approved via motion, every legal position the Nation took, every project it implemented, was done according to the Nation's cultural values and done to advance the Yurok Nation and the first covenant with the Creator.

Also, the Nation's governing structure had been modeled on its traditional government structure and updated to formalize roles of the tribal council, tribal court, police, and departments. The Nation adopted its constitution, which delegated authority to each branch of government. The Indian way, what my great-grandmother Geneva had fought so hard to preserve, was still alive in the tribal government's exercise of sovereignty. When I asked my grandmother what inherent sovereignty means to her, she replied, "It's mine. You can't take it away, and you can't say anything about it." That about sums it up from the Yurok perspective.

Yurok people view nature differently than most Americans. Rather than working to tame nature or make money from it, our goal is to live in balance and work in partnership with it. We strive to restore nature by understanding it, anticipating its needs, speaking for it, and taking action to protect it. We steward the land, water, and species, and they seem to understand our kinship.

Frequently, when I traveled for meetings, during car rides through remote parts of the reservation, deep in the forests or near the River, there would be a sign — a bird, a downed tree, an elk, or a bear. These signs sent a message triggering a thought that led to an improved advocacy point or different strategy. These messages seemed to be sent from the Creator to help us. This became so apparent that often, when I struggled with developing a legal argument or reached a difficult point in a negotiation, I would take a walk next to the Klamath River to talk to it and pray, to see what it offered me. It never failed me. For example, my favorite practice was to pray for the right words to speak on behalf of the Nation. Often, in response to these prayers, I would see a bird, for example, a hawk, which is a symbol to fight. I would then lean into a legal position opposed by others. Or I would see a hummingbird, which is a symbol that strong medicine is at work, and I would know to trust the process, to use kind words as the right result was on its way.

To represent the Nation well, I needed to use my legal education and experience, and perhaps more importantly, I needed to use my knowledge of Yurok aboriginal law and culture. The more I could learn about the Yurok worldview, the better I would represent the

Nation. Success comes from working with the Indian way, empowering it, and letting it guide your work. The early days working as a lawyer for the Nation were as informative and important as any education I had received in university. My job was to protect and assert the Nation's legal rights to enable the Nation to develop as a modern Nation consistent with its culture in a post-colonized world. The health of the Klamath River was at the heart of this pursuit.

《《《

In 2016, I arrived home along with a mere 3 to 5 percent of the historic Klamath salmon runs. The River, salmon, and people were all the victims of genocide.

"Let's call the meeting to order," said Chairman O'Rourke. I sat at a table that formed a rectangle around the edge of the large meeting room at the Weitchpec Tribal Office. The tribal council members, and a few staff including me, sat at the tables.

"We got a hard meeting today. There ain't no salmon. Our salmon harvest allocation is six hundred salmon, which means we can't catch more than six hundred fish. That ain't enough for our 6,300 members to have a single serving. We got to decide what to do. If we are gonna close the fishery or not," said the Chairman. Closing the fishery would mean that the Yurok people would not be able to fish on the Klamath River for any purpose.

The other council members squirmed in their chairs. This was a difficult, heavy decision, with widespread implications for the Nation's culture, economy, and safety. If the fishery closed, many tribal members would not have enough food to eat or enough money to pay basic bills. This would create a chain reaction of stress, potentially leading to a rise in drug and alcohol abuse, police arrests, and then an increased need for government services the Nation provided.

"Dave, what do the fish need?" asked the Chairman.

"Nothing has changed on the River since the fish kill in 2002. In fact, it's gotten worse. There is a pandemic on the River. A new fish disease called *C. shasta* is killing the baby salmon. Between 2014 and 2015, the disease wiped out 80 to 90 percent of the outmigrating salmon runs."

"Why is it in the River?" asked a council member.

"*C. shasta* spreads viciously in warm polluted waters that run through riverbeds with little to no sediment because the worm it occupies can attach to bare riverbeds. *C. shasta* colonizes rivers with dams like the Klamath because the dams usually lead to poor quality and high water temperatures, and sediment that would naturally run down a River gets caught behind the dams. As a result, the riverbeds below the dams are bare, smooth surfaces. The *C. shasta* worms thrive in polluted waters, eating the nitrates and phosphorus, and attach to the bare riverbed. They emit spores, which attach to baby fish gills, infecting them with the fatal *C. shasta* disease. The disease is a compound killer because it reduces the genetic diversity of the Klamath salmon stocks year after year to almost extinction. Frankly, the Klamath salmon stocks are running out of genetic diversity to repopulate. They could go extinct in our lifetime," Dave explained.

I raised my hand, and the Chairman acknowledged me.

"To address these problems, we need the dams out, and we still need more water in the River. The Klamath Basin Restoration Agreement (KBRA) died, and it's not clear what will happen to the dam removal agreement. Negotiations to amend the agreement are going well to put dam removal back into the FERC process," I added.

"Well, let's do what we can in those negotiations. Is there a motion to close the commercial and subsistence fishery?" the Chairman called.

No one spoke.

Finally, a council member said, "I motion."

"Is there a second?"

"I second," said another council member.

The motion passed. For the first time in history, Yurok people would not fish for salmon for subsistence purposes.

Later that same year, the Yurok Tribal Council declared a suicide emergency on the reservation, as seven tribal members between the ages of sixteen and thirty-one committed suicide in an eighteen-month span. My sister Lavina was among them. It was clear our youth were as sick as our River. It was also clear our youth saw no future without salmon.[18]

《《《

In this dire moment — for my family, the Nation, River, and salmon — as the KBRA had terminated and the fish and the people were dying, I worked with the Yurok Tribal Council to develop a strategy to save ourselves rooted in the exercise of our inherent sovereignty and cultural values. I had trained for years for this moment. The complex grief I felt for the loss of my sister and witnessing the devastation of the fish kill didn't break me — it transformed into fearless, fierce purpose, because our survival depended upon our Nation's ability to save the River and bring the salmon home. There was no turning back. I wasn't alone — many others felt the same way.

We worked to recover our land, water, and species and the jurisdiction to manage them consistent with the first covenant and Yurok value of living in balance with the natural world. Our strategy was informed by our thousands of years of traditional knowledge.

To do this, we sought to recover our land within our aboriginal territory and reservation. The Yurok aboriginal territory includes 1.5 million acres in the far northwestern corner of what is now known as California. It stretches from the coast to the redwood forests east past the Klamath River toward the Klamath Siskiyou coastal mountain range. Our reservation includes only 56,320 acres, a mere 3.75 percent of our aboriginal territory, a mile on either side of the Klamath River from its mouth up forty-five miles to the confluence with the Trinity

River. By 2017, only 5 percent of the land within our reservation was in trust status (held in trust by the federal government for the benefit of the Nation). By 2017 we had lost 99.72 percent of our land to mostly private logging companies and the federal government as land within Redwood National Park, the Forest Service, and the Bureau of Land Management. We were surviving on a meager .28 percent of our lands. Timber companies, such as Green Diamond, logged and sprayed pesticides, destroying habitat and poisoning water supplies along with prohibiting tribal members from accessing the land. Tribal members were also limited in accessing, and often barred from using, sacred sites and cultural natural resources on federal land.

The Yurok Nation had already launched a land-back strategy that included a sixty-thousand-acre land acquisition from Green Diamond timber company within the Blue Creek watershed on the eastern side of the reservation. I worked with Daniel Cordalis (Navajo) and Cheyenne Sanders (Yurok) who were lawyers for the Nation on the complex land and financing deal. The purchase required several sources of funding from the federal government, new market tax credits, and private funders. It also included multiple entities, phased land transfers from one entity to the next, easements, and multiple land management plans. Even in the late 2010s, the land conservancy involved in the project had paternalistic views about returning the land to the Nation and required permanent easements on the land. I was surprised by the difficulty of recovering our homelands and how much the outside world questioned the Nation's ability to manage land for conservation purposes, even after their worldview had raped and pillaged the land and water. I appreciated the tremendous effort the Nation made to protect our resources and educate others about Yurok stewardship. Our tribal leadership had remarkable vision, patience, and a good plan. We were only limited by the lack of technical staff and funding. While this was just a beginning, it was meaningful, because once we owned the land, we could exercise our responsibility to it by restoring balance to ecosystems. We later realized this was the largest land-back project in California.

On the water, one of the first lawsuits I filed, with co-counsel from Earthjustice, was *Yurok v. BOR* to address the fish disease Ceratonova shasta (*C. shasta*) that had been killing baby salmon in the Klamath River. The Nation argued that the Bureau of Reclamation (BOR) had violated the Endangered Species Act (ESA) by causing "take," the statutory word for "killing" baby coho salmon, a threatened listed species, by operating the Klamath Reclamation Project in a way that had allowed *C. shasta* rates to skyrocket in 2014–16. We won, and the judge ordered the BOR to release more water from Upper Klamath Lake to flush out *C. shasta*, in the River. The BOR had been withholding water for agricultural deliveries. This case was key to starting the process to secure more instream flows to support the Klamath River's ecological health and salmon. It was still active as of 2025, almost ten years later, because the BOR has violated the ESA almost every year since in its operation of the Klamath Reclamation Project by failing to provide sufficient water for coho salmon and the River's basic ecological functions, in order to meet agricultural demands for water.

Coho salmon on the Klamath were on the ESA list in 1997. The ESA requires that National Marine Fisheries Service and US Fish and Wildlife Service analyze the impact of the Klamath Reclamation Project on coho salmon and develop measures in a biological opinion, such as minimum River flows, to prevent the project from killing salmon and implement the measures in the Klamath Reclamation Project Annual Plan. The Yurok Nation has been very active in working with the NMFS and US Fish and Wildlife Service to develop measures to protect salmon. It is forced to sue only when the federal government fails to follow its own measures, opinions, and plans and violates the law.

I also worked with my staff and the tribal council to declare in Yurok law personhood rights for the Klamath River in 2019. The Klamath was the first River in North America to have personhood rights. Legal personhood expands the legal rights of the River by treating it the same as a person for purposes of standing and legal protection. It has great potential to increase environmental protection by covering ecosystems as a whole rather than parts of the system. For example, the Clean Water Act can limit the amount of pollution in water, but it doesn't protect other aspects of River ecology. Already, in the United States, corporations have personhood rights. It follows that nature, like a River, should also have personhood rights to provide it with the highest level of protection under the law. If nature, such as a River, was granted personhood rights in federal law, the River would have a constitutional right under the Fourteenth Amendment to "exist, flourish, and naturally evolve." This is a much higher standard of legal protection than is offered to rivers, fish, or water now.

The law is merely a reflection of a society's values; we make legal behavior we want to promote and prohibit behavior we want to prevent. For the Yurok people, it was a natural progression to declare personhood rights for the Klamath River because it's consistent with our relationship with it. The Klamath River is our family member, as much as any grandma or auntie. Along with us, the River has been hurting since it was first colonized. We have a duty to steward the River and offer it the highest legal protection. We feel this way about the planet: earth is a relative, not a resource.

The Nation declared personhood rights for the Klamath through a tribal resolution and passed a tribal ordinance expanding the River's rights. The ordinance recognized the River's *right to naturally exist* by having adequate water supply to support ecosystems and to be free from pollutants and structures or actions that inhibit its ability to flow freely; a *right to naturally flourish* by having ceremonies performed to balance the world and benefit the health of the River, restore declining salmon and other species, maintain instream flows at naturally occurring levels, and maintain clean water and air; and a *right to naturally evolve* by changing, adopting, and performing new ecological functions over time.

The ordinance also declares the River as a cultural property for purposes of the US National Historic Preservation Act, the US National Environmental Policy Act, and the Native American Graves Protection and Repatriation Act. The ordinance declares the River's right to be restored. My dad had become a Yurok Tribal Court judge who would be in a role to enforce the ordinance.

Our most urgent work on the River was to amend the KHSA to keep dam removal moving. The parties to the KHSA scrambled to negotiate an amendment to keep it alive by transferring the dam removal approval process from Congress back to FERC. This would grant the stakeholders more control over the dam removal process because unlike Congress, FERC has set rules, processes, and procedures, including hearings, that force FERC to act. There were countless hours in conference rooms at hotels and at the headquarters of PacifiCorp, a subsidiary company of Berkshire Hathaway that operated the dams, negotiating the terms for an amendment. PacifiCorp was primarily concerned with liability from dam removal, as the amount of sediment and its makeup behind the dams was unclear, although it had been studied extensively. The trick was to address PacifiCorp's liability concerns while accomplishing dam removal.

I recall the strength of Yurok leadership in these negotiations. The voices of Chairman Tommy O'Rourke and Executive Director Troy Fletcher were strong and clear. The Nation would not settle for anything less than what was needed to heal the River, which was removal of the four dams by 2020. The coalition built by the Nation was tested by this ambitious goal. It would be the largest dam removal ever completed, and it would be done on a very quick timeline. We leaned into our partnerships with the state and NGOs. Further, these brave leaders relied on their attorney and scientist staff to develop creative solutions for fish and liability concerns, some of which they presented and negotiated into the KHSA. I was still nursing my second son, who was then fifteen months old, and I recall breast pumping in a black suit and heels in the PacifiCorp women's bathroom during breaks from negotiations for the $450 million dam removal deal to save my home waters and culture.

Our work paid off, and an amendment to the KHSA was finalized by the end of 2016. The amendment established a process by which PacifiCorp would transfer J.C. Boyle, Copco No. 1, Copco No. 2, and Iron Gate Dams to a dam removal entity called the Klamath River Renewal Corporation (KRRC), which would then seek approval to physically remove the dams under FERC's relicense procedures by 2020. The PacifiCorp and the KRRC would submit an application to transfer the license to the KRRC and then submit a second application to decommission the dams. The deal would be paid for by PacifiCorp customer surcharges, capped at $200 million, and $250 million from Proposition 1 water bonds. We had a path forward to dam removal that started with PacifiCorp and the KRRC filing a license transfer application at FERC to transfer the license to operate the dam from PacifiCorp to the KRRC.

All went according to plan, except for the timeline. The KHSA called for dam removal by December 31, 2020. FERC didn't act on the application in time, and the project fell behind schedule. Once again, the Klamath stakeholders launched a campaign for FERC to approve the license transfer application. With focus and dedication, the Nation, our allies, and I leaned heavily on FERC to educate their representatives about the importance of Klamath dam removal. The Nation regularly requested tribal-FERC consultations, referred to as government-to-government meetings, to teach FERC representatives about our way of life and the role of fishing and the River. At the meetings, the Nation presented legal arguments that dam removal was the only option that protected the Nation's legal rights and advanced the public interest. While FERC was trying, it historically had not worked closely with tribal governments nor adequately considered tribal legal rights in approving hydropower projects. FERC is subject to the federal tribal trust responsibility relationship that requires the agency to protect tribal rights and consult with Indigenous nations should a project impact tribal rights, like those established in Uncle Ray's Supreme Court case. During our consultations, tribal members and leaders would share passionate stories about the negative impacts of dams on their way of life.

"The dams are killing the River, salmon, and my way of life," tribal member Georgianna Gensaw passionately explained. "There are hardly any fish left. Our communities depend on the River for sustenance. No fish means no food," she continued.

"When I was little, I could swim in the River and catch fish. The River was my playground and my grocery store. Now, my kids can't swim in it and there are no fish for them to catch. I have to scold my kids if they try to get in the water because it's polluted and will hurt them," Yurok Tribal Council member Ryan Ray described.

Meanwhile, the Nation had government-to-government meetings and submitted written documents to the California State Water Resources Control Board and federal agencies to secure environmental and cultural permits, such as those required by the Clean Water Act, the National Historic Preservation Act, and the Endangered Species Act for FERC to approve the application.

Finally, in July 2020, FERC approved a partial transfer of the project, the first order required for dam removal. The order required PacifiCorp to stay on the license. FERC found that it would not be in the public interest for the entirety of the burden and liability of the surrender and dam removal, the uncertainties of final design and project execution, including public safety and cost overruns, to fall solely on the KRRC. It required PacifiCorp to remain on as a co-licensee to provide legal and technical support, as well as sufficient funding to finish dam removal.

PacifiCorp interpreted the requirement to stay on the license as inconsistent with the terms of the KHSA. PacifiCorp's primary concern was limiting its liability stemming from the facilities' removal, and remaining on the license meant it could be liable for impacts to the River and cost overruns in unknown amounts. This was a risk PacifiCorp did not want to bear.

CHAPTER 18

Blue Creek vs. Klamath Dams

2020

A my, we have an issue. We need you," said Yurok Nation Vice Chairman Frankie Myers, a skilled, intelligent negotiator who was a leader of the grassroots dam removal campaign turned tribal leader. I was on maternity leave with my third child, Tobiyahz (Navajo for born of water or child of water), when I received this phone call at my home outside the Yurok Reservation. I had been tracking the FERC order, and the behind-the-scenes politics, as Yurok's board member to the dam removal entity.

"I heard. Is it true? Is PacifiCorp threatening to back out of the dam removal deal?" I asked. After FERC issued its partial license transfer order, which required PacifiCorp to stay on the license through dam removal, the company threatened to pull out of the dam removal deal due to concerns about unlimited liability and cost overruns for dam removal.

"Perhaps. We need to get them to the River. We invited Warren

Buffett's top two executives, Bill Furman and Greg Able (Greg would take over for Warren Buffet a few years later) to Yurok Country to tour the River. We have a meeting scheduled next week at Blue Creek. Can you make it?"

It was July 2020. The Covid-19 pandemic brutally cloaked the world, and most people were still not traveling to avoid contracting the disease. I was surprised the executives had agreed to travel to Yurok Country and also appreciated the safety precautions of holding the meeting outside.

I looked at my six-week-old son, who was rolling on the floor on a blanket. I was out of shape and hardly sleeping. I worried about the risk of getting Covid from exposure to other people. But this was for the River and I remained deeply committed to the cause.

"Of course," I said. "Just let me know when. We need to prepare a term sheet to get the deal started. Tell me everything."

The Vice Chairman proceeded to update me on the details of PacifiCorp's reaction to the FERC order and the posture of the other parties. I prepared the term sheet the following day for tribal leadership's review.

The following week I went to the mouth of the River to attend the meeting. I dropped off my baby with my mother, whose house is just a quarter mile away from the mouth of the River at Rek-woi. It was a beautiful September day. The leaves were just starting to turn colors. The Rek-woi hillside above the estuary was splattered with yellow and green with the hint of red from the alder and willow trees and underbrush. These colors reflected off the calm waters of the estuary, where the fog had broken to let the sunshine through the trees onto the water. The ground was still wet from the morning dew, it wasn't hot enough yet to burn off. A distinct scent of fresh and salt water, mixed with moss and salmon scales, had me wishing I was going fishing rather than to a meeting.

Arriving at the Requa Dock, I spotted a group of about a dozen people. A few tribal council members, including Vice Chairman Myers, Yurok staff like Mike Belchik, Taralyn Ipiña, and more, and four middle-aged white guys dressed in button-down collared shirts, slacks, and hiking shoes, who were clearly the Berkshire Hathaway and PacifiCorp executives. They were standing next to the *River Otter,* the Nation's water taxi, which would take the group to Blue Creek up the River about twelve River miles. I had grown accustomed to the look and speech of PacifiCorp employees. They were always cordial yet slightly uncomfortable, like they had never spent time with Indians and weren't sure what was going to happen next.

Today, in this moment, we wanted them to feel comfortable so that they could feel the River and connect to it — to allow the River to speak for itself. To make them feel in their hearts and minds that the River needed to heal. A core Yurok point of diplomacy is letting the River speak for itself; it's the job of Yurok people to invite others to listen. We hoped the executives would accept our invitation. We loaded into the *River Otter* and one other private boat and started our journey upriver. I was in the private boat with two executives and a Yurok staff member. We had only gone about five hundred feet upriver when the boat broke down. The motor stopped and could not be fixed. While we made other arrangements to get upriver, the *River Otter* continued.

Fifteen minutes into their trip upriver, the River Otter turned a bend and spotted something familiar blocking the River.

Undam the Klamath: Close the Dam Deal! read a white banner that spread almost across the entire width of the River, blocking the *River Otter*'s passage. Several small boats full of Indian people at either side of the River were anchored in place holding the banner.

As the *River Otter* approached the sign, you could hear the Indian people chanting, "Undam the Klamath, bring the salmon home! Undam the Klamath, bring the salmon home!"

They pumped their clenched fists in the air with each chant. The *River Otter* was forced to stop in front of the sign. "We don't want any trouble," whispered the executive to Vice Chairman Myers, who nodded. One boat of protesters headed toward the *River Otter*. When it got within hearing range, Vice Chairman Myers said, "Hey, Annelia. How you doing?"

These were his colleagues from the Klamath Justice Coalition. They wore red bandannas tied around their heads, black *Undam the Klamath* shirts, jeans with holes, and old tennis shoes. Their long black hair was wild from the wind that had moved up from the ocean, and their cheeks were red from windburn.

"These folks are from the power company. They came to talk to us about dam removal. What would you like to say to them?"

The executives looked nervously at the Vice Chairman, expecting the protesters to unleash their wrath. Vice Chairman Myers kept his cool. He knew he was diffusing the tension by giving the protesters, whom he knew and trusted, an opportunity to speak directly to the executives. Their years of protests and dedication to the cause had earned them the right to this audience.

"Close the deal. Undam the Klamath. We will never stop protesting and advocating for dam removal. If you back out of this deal, we will just protest more. We will never go away. Close the deal!" Annelia said clearly and calmly, looking up at the executives as she stood in the bow of her small jet boat.

The executives nodded and thanked her for her comment. Then Annelia motioned to the others to lower the sign, and the *River Otter* continued up the River to Blue Creek.

《《《

My boat caught up to the *River Otter* just as it was docking at Blue Creek. As it has always been, Blue Creek was breathtaking. The size of a river in most areas, Blue Creek flows in crystal clear shades of blue, light and dark varieties that blend, reflecting off the creek's gravel bed, creating a beautiful mosaic of color. Miraculously, the water remains almost as clean and as cold as the Creator made it. It flows down from the Nation's High Country, our spiritual lands where we commune with the sacred, which includes parts of the first coastal mountain ridge surrounding the Klamath River. For millennia, geological movement and the water moving down the mountains have created the ideal canyon for the water to travel, down from those sacred lands to the Klamath River. At the mouth of Blue Creek, part of the water goes underground, cools, and then re-emerges as a cold-water refuge at a deep pool just below the creek's mouth. Blue Creek's water flows into the Klamath main stem like a breath of fresh air, spreading clean, cool water through the Klamath's polluted and clogged main arteries.

When I was growing up, my family often fished and camped at Blue Creek. My father loved it there, and it seemed the creek loved him back. One day, in his fifties, he was fishing at Blue Creek when he began experiencing signs of a heart attack. He called out to his fishing partner — his teenage son Will Bowers — and then slipped into the frigid-cold water. After fully submerging, he emerged feeling notice-ably better.

The next day, he went to see a doctor, who immediately rushed him into quadruple-bypass surgery. After the successful procedure, my dad shared his story with the doctor, who declared that Blue Creek had saved his life by "recharging" his system and stopping the heart attack when he fell into its frigid waters.

Not only does the creek have healing qualities for humans, it also creates a phenomenal habitat for all fish. Salmon, steelhead, and other fish congregate at the mouth of the Blue Creek and the deep pool like kids at a playground; they rest and play, jump and eat, in the comfort of a safe and fun place. It is a salmon and steelhead stronghold that provides fish the rest and energy they need to make it to the spawning grounds upriver.

Long before there were phrases like "cold-water refuge" or data to prove just how clean and pure Blue Creek's waters are, the Yurok people inherently knew Blue Creek was sacred. The Yurok name for the trail through Blue Creek translates to "stairway to heaven" because it goes from the Klamath River to the High Country, where people go to pray and make medicine. The Nation recently reacquired most of the Blue Creek watershed through the land-back strategy my office and I worked on. While the lower part of the watershed was in the Yurok Reservation, a lumber company acquired title to a few parcels of riparian lands and logged them through the 1950s to 1990s over the objections of the Nation. The rest of the Blue Creek watershed was under US Forest Service Management, which logged parts of it. This was done over the objections of the Nation and the Nation's lawsuits against the Forest Service to prevent the logging of our sacred sites.

In *Lyng v. Northwest Indian Cemetery Protective Association,* a First Amendment freedom of religion case, the Supreme Court held the First Amendment of the Constitution did not protect the religious freedoms of the Yurok people against the federal government logging and, essentially, destroying the Nation's sacred lands, because it was *after all the federal government's land,* as the opinion noted. The land and water, of course, and the duty to protect it, will always be ours, no matter what the Supreme Court has to say about it. The forest service still has these lands after the land-back project. We nurture and care for the Blue Creek watershed to the best of our ability under these constraints.

The landscape surrounding the mouth of Blue Creek, where the boats were docked and the meeting participants began to explore, reflected this history. Yet, the power of the creek was still very much alive. The water moving under the gravel bar where we gathered created an energy, making one feel like one was walking on water. The

River bar rocks and gravel moved underfoot, creating a connection between the underground water and the human body. And the air coming down from the High Country was crisp and warm as it moved through our lungs. The experience of connecting with the land and the air pulled our bodies and our minds to the task at hand, centering us together and creating connection with one another. Today that power, we hoped, would be our strongest advocacy tool.

The Nation had set up camp chairs and a tent by the side of Blue Creek. We all gathered. The Chairman and Vice Chairman of the Nation spoke, welcoming the Berkshire Hathaway and PacifiCorp executives, and called for dam removal. The executives nodded politely.

I spoke last. Standing up in front of the group, holding a microphone, I felt slightly uncomfortable. I was postpartum. The nicest pair of pants I could fit in were awkward, and I kept hoping I wouldn't lactate through my silk blouse.

These feelings passed when I looked out at the group and saw the faces of my people who had worked so hard for so long for dam removal. Chairman James and Vice Chairman Myers stood confidently next to the tent, nodding, ready for me to deliver Yurok's terms. I saw Taralyn Ipina, who had worked tirelessly for the Yurok tribal government. I saw Yurok council member Phillip Williams, a diehard fisherman, whom I'd first met in 2002 while commercial fishing at the estuary. And I saw Mike Belchik, who was the best scientist on the River, and many more. Their faces were intense with determination to save the deal. Their confidence and resolution empowered me, and I was at Blue Creek. All the power and medicine I needed to close this deal was surrounding me.

I had already prayed for the right words in this moment to come to me as was my usual practice before I spoke for the Yurok people, the River, and the salmon. I had also prayed with my baby in my arms, hoping his special connection to the Creator would be shared with me to make my words more powerful. I added a special silent prayer in a single breath before I spoke. Remembering my great-grandmother, I asked the Creator to make the Indian way work, for my words to work with the power of Blue Creek to protect the River and convince the executives to keep the deal to remove the dams.

I began:

"The Yurok people here are members of historic Yurok families that have lived on the River since time immemorial. For millennia we have exercised inherent sovereignty over our lands and waters.

"We live according to a complex system of laws that make sure we live in balance with the natural world — never taking more animals, creatures, or plants than we need to survive. We complete religious ceremonies to pray for world renewal to maintain the balance.

"We were never relocated when white people came. In the creation of the Yurok Reservation in 1855, our ancestors reserved our aboriginal rights to fish, hunt, gather, and to water and land. We reserved our inherent sovereignty. For almost one hundred years, the state of California and the federal government tried to take away our rights. We fought back, and always stayed on the land, water, and fished, and continued our way of life.

"The dams, which your company owns, make our River sick. So sick fish can't live in it. Those dams are killing our River, our fish, and our way of life. The dams are the current threat to our way of life and our existence.

"We haven't had a commercial fishery in ten years. Our people are living in poverty. Fishing is our only way out.

"At Yurok we believe that if the salmon cease to exist, so will Yurok people. The threat from your dams to us is existential. We have worked for fifteen years with you to remove these dams. While we have made progress, we aren't there yet. We can't wait any longer.

"We understand the company is not satisfied with the FERC order and is considering pulling away from Klamath dam removal. We brought you here today to begin discussions to keep you in the deal. What you need to understand is we will never stop fighting for dam removal. Every generation will keep up the fight. If you pull from this deal, we will launch a nationwide protest like the one on the Standing Rock Reservation fighting against the DAPL pipeline, and we won't stop until the dams are out of our River."

I walked to my seat and sat down, relieved I had made it through the speech without leaking breast milk through my blouse. I saw the Vice Chairman look at me with an expression that suggested I had forgotten something. Remembering, I quickly stood and started walking back toward the microphone.

"Oh, and I forgot the term sheet. To avoid a nationwide protest, dam removal must proceed, and quickly. Under the KHSA, those dams are supposed to be out now. We can't wait any longer. I have prepared a term sheet which lays out a few new ideas about how to cover the company's liability under the terms of the new FERC license transfer order. We'd like a response from the company by next week. I'll explain them in more detail now."

I proceeded to explain the terms. We negotiated for some time and paused when a bald eagle flew over the meeting, no doubt checking in. The company executives kept their cordial and uncomfortable demeanor without responding much to the terms. We concluded the meeting, exchanged closing formalities, loaded the boats, and went back down the River.

On the flight back to Portland in a corporate jet, an executive stated that the only way out was to remove the dams. His staff, calling from a private jet, consulted the company lawyers to determine if any of the Nation's terms were amenable. After twenty years of a local, Indigenous-led grassroots activism and legal strategy, they finally understood we would never stop fighting for dam removal, even if it took multiple generations.

The following Monday, my phone rang, and it was Warren Buffett's second-in-command, Bill Furman.

"Amy, I'd like to talk about removing the dams. It's time. Let's get to work. We need liability protection. I need a briefing on the KHSA. What can you tell me?"

Luckily, the baby was napping when I received this call. I made small talk while I told my husband he was on baby duty, walked into my home office, shut the door, took a seat, and gave the executive a briefing on the KHSA, including how the dam removal entity, the Klamath River Renewal Corporation, would assume most of the liability for dam removal and would be protected by a comprehensive insurance package that was similar to those offered to construction companies for massive construction projects. I explained that in many ways the dam removal project was similar to any large-scale energy construction project, just in reverse, because infrastructure would be removed using the same engineering principles and construction equipment, and liability protection. We agreed to schedule more calls. I coordinated with Yurok's leadership, including Vice Chairman Myers, and KRRC Executive Director Mark Bransom, and Richard Roos Collins, the KRRC's lawyer, to complete a series of briefings for the executive. We were told we had five days of his time — and only a senator, congressperson, or the president of the United States would pull him away. He was true to his word and actively participated in our briefings for five business days. During this time Vice Chairman Myers spoke with Bill almost daily.

We also called on close friends and colleagues such as Richard Whitman, Director of the Oregon Department of Environmental Quality, and the head of California's Department of Fish and Wildlife, Chuck Bonham, who brought in Governor Newsom to call Warren

Buffet. This would have been unimaginable in 2006, when California could barely participate in the FERC proceedings, let alone a generation back during the Salmon Wars. Or worse, three generations ago when the state's founding principle was extermination of my people. I realized I was the first generation of my family to have something other than a violent relationship with the state of California.

In November 2020, a few months after the meeting at Blue Creek, a memorandum of understanding (MOU) was entered into between the Yurok and Karuk Nations, the states of Oregon and California, and PacifiCorp. The MOU provided that the KRRC and PacifiCorp would not accept their co-license status. Instead they, along with the states of Oregon and California, would submit a new surrender application to the Federal Energy Regulatory Commission (FERC) for Oregon, California, and the KRRC to be co-licensees, and not PacifiCorp. PacifiCorp, Oregon, and California would pay an extra $15 million each for a total of $45 million for cost overruns. They would also equally share any cost overruns beyond the dam removal budget of $450 million from Proposition 1 water bonds and PacifiCorp customer surcharges. The Yurok term sheet was an informative document for the terms of the MOU. Berkshire Hathaway Chair Warren Buffett stated, "We appreciate and respect our tribal partners for their collaboration in forging an agreement that delivers an exceptional outcome for the River, as well as future generations. Working together from this historic moment, we can complete the project and remove these dams."[19]

When the campaign to undam the Klamath started in 2020, no one knew each other. Now, one of the most powerful men in the world was our ally. At least seven officials of the two states were personally involved. They united forces with us and Blue Creek. Blue Creek's beauty spoke for itself, moving us toward restoration through the fresh air, its clean water, and its gentle yet steady roar.

CHAPTER 19

It's About Dam Time

▲▲
▼▼

2022

After Blue Creek and the MOU signing, our coalition of the Yurok and Karuk Nations, NGOs, PacifiCorp, Oregon, and California were more aligned than ever toward the goal of dam removal, after almost twenty years of working alongside one another and with the dam removal entity, the Klamath River Renewal Corporation (KRRC). On November 17, 2020, several days after the MOU was signed, the KRRC and PacifiCorp submitted an amended license surrender application to the Federal Energy Regulatory Commission that updated the application to be consistent with the MOU, removing PacifiCorp from the license and adding the states of Oregon and California, and adding the $45 million to the project funds and the agreement that any extra overruns would be split between PacifiCorp and Oregon and California. This was the final step to approve dam removal. The stakes were high.

To approve the application, FERC required permits from several environmental and preservation laws, such as the Endangered Species Act, the Clean Water Act, and the National Historic Preservation Act, to name a few. This required coordination with state and federal agencies with responsibility for issuing the permits. Multiple weekly calls between PacifiCorp, tribal, state, federal, and NGO scientists, lawyers, and leaders were required to coordinate this historic effort. The Nation was at the heart of this work, encouraging the agencies to act promptly and consistently with the Nation's rights, and for the first time, the Nation and PacifiCorp's interests were aligned toward the goal of dam removal. We used tribal sovereignty and the power of corporate America to jump over what seemed to be every environmental and energy regulatory hurdle the US Congress had passed in the last fifty years.

Yet, even with this unlikely powerful alliance, the wheels of bureaucracy were turning slowly. The KHSA planned for dam removal to be completed by December 2020. The project would be delayed, as it would be impossible to complete the regulatory permitting process, for FERC to approve the amended license surrender order, and to remove the dams in 2020. It was unclear when this work would be completed. Delay costs money. Delay gave our opponents more time to fight against us. Delay put more pressure on the KHSA stakeholders.

Could our unlikely coalition withstand this tremendous burden?

I worked with the Yurok Tribal Council to use FERC tribal consultation requirements to gather information about the timing for FERC to act on the application and kept in close contact with PacifiCorp, state, and federal lawyers to develop permitting strategies and timelines. Tribal leaders developed strong relationships with PacifiCorp and Berkshire Hathaway executives to maintain close contact and coordination to support dam removal. Federal employees in various agencies reviewed the permitting requirements. Once again, state officials Chuck Bonham and Richard Whitman did heavy political lifting to keep the coalition together. This tremendous effort took hundreds of people working together.

Finally, two years later, FERC noticed it would act on the final license surrender application. On a late November day in 2022, my oldest son, Brooks, who was now eleven years old, my husband, and I took an Uber from my home in Arlington, Virginia (where I had moved in 2020, shortly after the meeting in Blue Creek), across the Potomac River into Washington, DC, to the FERC headquarters, located behind the US Capitol. FERC was scheduled to approve or deny dam removal at a hearing that afternoon by taking action on the KRRC, Oregon, and California's application to surrender the license to operate the Klamath River Hydroelectric Project (the Klamath dams). It was the last regulatory approval required to begin dam removal and the largest River restoration project in history. We had waited decades for this hearing. Barely able to sit still in the car seat, I felt the energy of every generation of my family that had fought for this moment. Five commissioners, none of whom had been to the Klamath River, were about to vote on the fate of the River, our Nation, and our way of life.

After Blue Creek, the Yurok Tribal Council asked me to focus my legal work on Klamath dam removal and restoration, concerned that Klamath dam removal was in jeopardy. With Molli Myers, the brilliant Karuk strategist and organizer, I cofounded and became the executive director of the Ridges to Riffles Indigenous Conservation Group (R2R), a nonprofit to represent Indigenous nations in the area of cultural natural resource protection. The work focused on Klamath dam removal, water rights, and habitat restoration throughout the entire Klamath Basin. Founding R2R increased the Nation's capacity by creating a separate entity with more operational flexibility and focus that could fundraise and organize to move power and money consistent with Yurok values and in advancement of its rights. For example, the Nation's legal advocacy was limited by the lack of funding to pay for lawyers. It's difficult to fundraise because only .4 percent of philanthropic funds go to Indigenous communities for several reasons, in part because those communities haven't had access to foundations.

While there are other NGOs doing important work on the Klamath, it was necessary to start a new organization run by Indigenous peoples, with our cultural values and ways of doing business. One example of this is making sure that Indigenous knowledge is included in science, law, and policy on the Klamath. The Indigenous nations of the Klamath Basin have existed there since time immemorial, providing them with ancient traditional knowledge about the basin that has historically been left out of analysis and decision-making. Further, running my own business was also important because I had three children and needed a flexible work schedule to raise my babies while working to heal my River. Tribal sovereignty starts at home.

By the time of the hearing, the Yurok Nation and our allies had done everything in their power to educate the FERC staff about the implications of Klamath dam removal. The KRRC, PacifiCorp, Oregon, California, Karuk, and the NGOs had diligently responded to requests for information, meetings, and briefings. We made it clear our lifeway and very existence depended on Klamath dam removal because the dams were severely harming the River and killing salmon. We backed these statements up with the best available science and traditional knowledge that supported our position. Wise and strong tribal leaders carried these messages from the River all the way to DC.

While we expected a successful vote, FERC is a quasi-judicial entity comprised of commissioners with voting rights and discretion to vote freely. FERC's institutional legacy is the damming of American rivers, creating hydropower to electrify the country, oftentimes to the detriment of tribal treaty rights and nature. Its precedent supports energy projects, not decreasing energy production through dam removal. Indeed, building dams in the United States is as fundamental to our national identity as is the Declaration of Independence: the equivalent of one dam has been built in America every day since the Declaration of Independence was signed. Since its inception, FERC has championed the regulatory approval required to build and operate hydroelectric projects. In the past, FERC authorized destruction of ancient Indigenous fishing spots and salmon habitat in violation of treaties to approve dam construction, as at Celilo Falls, upon which the Dalles Dam was built on the Columbia River, which was the largest inter-Indigenous fishing and trade spot in the western United States historically. Plus, it had only ever approved a few small dam removal projects; never had it approved a dam removal project on the scale of the Klamath. Further, the Klamath vote was risky because it would set a precedent for the United States that dam removal was an acceptable outcome, which could open the floodgates for dam removal projects across the country. I questioned whether America was ready for this next era.

This was countered by a few important developments. PacifiCorp had already replaced the power generated from Klamath Dams. The dams were legacy assets that required expensive updates. Further, the California and Oregon Public Utility Commissions determined that removing the dams according to the KHSA was in the best interest of the ratepayers because the costs to ratepayers were capped at $200 million and the cost of building fish ladders was at least double that. PacifiCorp agreed, supporting dam removal.

Many federal employees had worked diligently on the studies for the regulatory permits that clearly demonstrated the significant benefits of dam removal to the River, salmon and other aquatic species, and tribal cultures. Single digit percentages of the historical Klamath salmon runs were left and on the verge of extinction. Yurok tribal fisheries for commercial purposes had been closed for ten years, and subsistence fishing was severely limited, along with offshore commercial fisheries for Klamath salmon, for more than a decade, costing millions in lost revenue. Dam removal was the best option to rebuild the River, salmon, and fishing communities. Dam removal would provide access to more than four hundred miles of historic fish habitat and spawning grounds to rebuild salmon runs, improve water quality and lower water temperatures, reduce the likelihood of fish disease, and improve transport of natural sediments.

Collectively, this was a strong case that dam removal was in the public interest because the power had already been replaced, and dam removal was cheaper and better for the salmon, the River, and Indigenous peoples. Would this be enough to overcome the country's legacy of damming the West?

Entering the four-story white marble building, my family and I cleared security and spotted the familiar middle-aged white guys wearing collared shirts, sport coats, slacks, and, this time, leather dress shoes, in the hallway next to the FERC hearing room. It was the team of PacifiCorp executives and a KRRC lawyer who would attend the hearing. Admittedly, I was thrilled to see them and gave each of them an enthusiastic hug. To their credit, they had come through. They had supported dam removal because it was the best business decision. (It would have been more expensive for ratepayers to keep the dams in than to take them out.)

My family and I took our seats next to them in the FERC hearing room. My son and I were the only Yuroks or Indian people from the Klamath River in the room. The FERC hearing room was typical, with a semicircular table in the front of the room for the FERC commissioners and public seating in rows to the back of the room.

Back home, many were watching from Johnson's bar, a long stretch of open River bar on the mid-Klamath, via a large screen connected to the internet through a satellite connection set to the side of a large bonfire. Behind it, the River flowed calmly and slowly, as if to pause to watch the proceedings. It knew its fate was at stake.

"Madam Secretary," said FERC Chairman Richard Glick. "We are ready to begin...I want to comment on two of the Orders...on today's agenda...the Commission...is approving PacifiCorp's application to surrender its license for Lower Klamath Hydro Project for the removal of the project's lower dams."[20]

Did he just say "approving"? Sitting in the hearing room, twenty feet from the Chairman, I stared at him and hung on every word, my heart pounding.

"Some people might ask why in this time of great need for zero emissions and energy, why are the licensees agreeing to remove the dams?"[21] Chairman Glick continued.

I sat up a little straighter. *Does that mean they will approve it?* I sat on the edge of my seat. I squeezed my son's hand.

"Ouch, Mom," he said under his breath.

"Oh no, sorry," I whispered to him.

"First of all, it doesn't happen very often...and these projects have a significant impact on fish and wildlife...and a number of years back, I don't think the Commission actually spent time thinking about the impact of our decisions on Indigenous nations, and that is a very important element in today's Order. That is for the good...We still have a way to go, but we will make progress there,"[22] explained the Chairman.

I was levitating out of my seat at this point. This was headed in the right direction.

Commissioner Clements spoke next.

"I think part of serving the public interest includes recommitting to and upholding the principles of Tribal Sovereignty and Self-Determination...the Nations provided important consultative perspectives...the record created through this consultation as well as staff's strong environmental analysis...demonstrates significant long-term benefits for water, quality, critical fish species like salmon

and steelhead, as well as commercial fishing and recreational fishing...
the record presents overwhelming support for removal."[23]

Our consultations had worked. All those hours of research, writing, and briefing the Tribal Council on our legal arguments, and the
time spent in consultation with FERC staff explaining the impact of
the Klamath dams on our way of life, had worked. They had heard
us. The years of dedicated Yurok and Klamath River Indigenous
peoples pouring their hearts out and passionately and eloquently testifying at FERC hearings had worked.

"I now call for a vote to approve the agenda," said the hearing clerk.
This motion included approving Klamath Dam Removal.

Commissioner James Danly: "Yes."

Commissioner Allison Clements: "Yes."

Commissioner Mark Christie: "Yes."

Commissioner Willie Phillips: "Yes."

Chairman Richard Glick: "Yes."

It was done. Just like that. Klamath dam removal was approved.
Almost two hundred years of fighting to protect our fishing rights, and
almost twenty years of direct action to remove the Klamath River dams,
had culminated in this one single motion in FERC that happened so fast
we hardly knew it had happened. Except I found myself crying.

"Amy, it's done!" said the KRRC lawyer. He smiled and patted my
shoulder. I put my hand over my heart, turned to my son, and whispered the dams would be removed. This moment meant that he didn't
have to inherit this fight. He didn't have to fight for dam removal. He
could make another choice. At eleven years old, he didn't fully appreciate what he had just witnessed, and what it meant for his future. I
hope one day he will.

I sent a celebratory text to Mike Belchik, Vice Chairman Myers,
and his wife and R2R cofounder, Molli, who were at Johnson's River
bar. They had devoted their lives to dam removal. There, surrounded

by many of the Indigenous people who had worked on the Undam the Klamath campaign, everyone stood around the fire looking at the screen. The fire crackled; the River flowed. Bottles of champagne chilled in a cooler next to a truck.

Someone said, "It is approved? What happened?"

"I just saw them approve the agenda. Did that include Klamath dam removal?" said someone else.

Mike, looking at his phone, said, "It's approved!"

The group erupted with cheers.

"Ha, that happened so fast we missed it!" they joked.

〈〈〈

Back in DC we left the FERC hearing room, walked outside, and breathed in a new future: one the Yurok people had fought for with blood, sweat, and tears for generations. Now it was real. The Klamath River dams would come down. Our whole world was renewed.

I called my grandmother, who was at the family home in Rekwoi, from a Washington, DC, K Street law firm that my close friend worked at.

"They approved dam removal! The dams are coming down!" I said quickly and enthusiastically to Grandma.

"Who did what? They are taking down dams, where?" Grandma said.

"The Klamath dams, the federal government approved dam removal. They are finally coming down. The salmon are going home!"

"Oh, wow....Well, it's about damn time!" she said. And we both laughed. I was happy for her that the dam removal was approved in her lifetime. Next, I called my dad, and we both cried.

Afterward, I joined the PacifiCorp executives for a late lunch to celebrate. We broke bread together and toasted to our collective accomplishment. They were so much more comfortable here, surrounded by other privileged businessmen, dining at a DC power lunch location, than they were on the River bar at Blue Creek just months before. I couldn't blame them; I was at ease now that FERC had approved dam removal. We had managed to align the rights of nations, nature, and business into a $515 million deal that would be the largest river restoration project in history. They had come a long way since that day at Blue Creek two years ago.

Meanwhile, on the Klamath River, the tribal people at Johnson's bar, many of whom were the protesters who had aggressively protested the same men with whom I shared a table, celebrated their victory.

CHAPTER 20

Klamath Dam Removal

▲▲▲
▼▼

2023

Immediately following the FERC approval, crews from the Klamath River Renewal Corporation (KRRC) and contractors for dam decommissioning and River restoration moved onto the Klamath River Renewal Project site, formally known as the Lower Klamath River Hydroelectric Project. The entire project includes almost twenty thousand acres of riparian land surrounding the four Klamath dams and accompanying reservoirs straddling the states of Oregon and California. The lowest dam is Iron Gate, followed upriver first by Copco 2, then Copco No. 1, then the J.C. Boyle Dam. The dams were built between 1911 and 1964.

In this area, rolling hills from the Klamath Siskiyou mountain range fell away to the River, which wound its way through the lower elevations on the mid-Klamath. This area is the traditional lands of the Shasta, Modoc, and Karuk Nations. Each dam was located where the hills and River met in a canyon that could be bound together by a dam. These locations also happened to be ideal fishing locations. In the early 1900s, there were plans to build dams throughout the entire

River that were thwarted for various reasons, including one just above Blue Creek by the village of Ah-Pa that would have been disastrous.

In September 2023, I walked down a steep gravel road headed toward the Klamath riverbed. We were at the former Klamath Hydroelectric Project site, which had existed for 112 years as a power production facility comprised of four dams spanning forty miles of River. Ownership of the hydroelectric project had been transferred to the KRRC. As we continued down the road toward the River, Mark Bransom, CEO of KRRC, stopped me about twenty feet from the water's edge. I couldn't see the water yet. I only heard the gentle roar of the water flowing. I was with the board of directors of KRRC, for which I was the Yurok Nation's representative. We were walking down a road that had been recently cut down the hillside to the River's edge, next to Copco 2 Dam. I had been to the project area just a month before to celebrate the beginning of Klamath dam removal with KHSA stakeholders and federal leadership, including Secretary of Interior Deb Haaland, my former teacher's aide at the PLSI program. Now, twenty years later, she was the first Indigenous Secretary of the Interior.

"I don't know if you remember," I said, standing in front of her holding her hand in gratitude, "my journey to representing the Yurok Nation on dam removal started at PLSI, that summer with you."

"Oh, I remember!" the Secretary said, with pride in her eyes, wrapping me in a hug.

"It's remarkable for me to have started that journey with you and to end it with you as the Secretary of Interior. Thank you for supporting Klamath dam removal," I said.

"We have hardly done anything here. You all did the work."

I nodded and we hugged again. This was perhaps the first positive interaction any member of my family had had with a Secretary of the Interior. It was not lost on me that we had come so far from Uncle

Ray's days of violence, abuse, and violations of our legal rights by past Secretaries of Interiors.

Now, just a month after this conversation, there were twelve of us walking cautiously down a freshly cut road, wearing yellow hard hats and neon-green construction vests. The sun brightly shone down on the road's path, lighting our way. A large yellow dump truck emerged from a sharp bend in the road heading away from the River toward us, carrying a load of concrete chunks. Copco 2 was being removed.

"Everybody to the left side of the road, please," directed Mark Bransom, CEO of the KRRC. The Board had been briefed about the safety protocols associated with our visit to the active construction site. There would be construction crews and equipment actively working during our trip. We were advised to be careful, stay out of the way, and follow directions.

The board members moved quickly to the left side of the road that overlooked the hillside and its descent to the River. The dirt on the hillside and road were freshly exposed and maintained a fair tan-brown color mixed with a few sedimentary small rocks. Scattered on the roadside were piles of large gray boulders and the vegetation surrounding the road had been cleared. The road crossed back and forth, winding down the steep hillside to the water's edge, where a flat platform had been made and was occupied by a large construction crane, bulldozer trucks, and skidders. The road was wide enough for one large construction truck and had pullouts here and there to allow passage. Working on the River's edge were three excavators scooping up river rocks and moving them into piles.

A large dump truck passed us. Its engine was loud and the road broke underneath its large tires. It was big, strong, and bold as it moved up the steep hillside with ease carrying a heavy load. Its driver sat in the cab about fifteen feet above the road and waved. We were all impressed and appreciated the briefing about how to safely navigate this active construction site.

"Are you ready to see it, Amy?" Mark asked.

"Where is it?"

"Just over this ledge."

My heart raced. I would see it soon. I held my breath. The dirt from cutting the road had been pushed to the Riverside edge of the new road, creating a ledge that stood about four feet tall and blocked the River below from view. The ledge was loose dirt and unstable.

"Here, take my hand," Mark said, offering me his hand.

I took it and he guided me up the ledge. With a few stable steps and the strong support of Mark's hand, I saw it. Or saw where it had been. I gasped, my hand over my heart.

Twenty feet below where Mark and I stood, there was the footprint of where Copco 2 Dam had been. For ninety-eight years, the concrete dam had held back the flow of the River's life force so the power companies that owned it could profit from using the River to create hydropower to electrify Oregon, California, and Idaho. It had been a defensive wall standing thirty-three feet tall. Water releases were controlled by a pump house on the south side of the dam that were so minimal, the river was dewatered. Bushes, and even small trees, grew in the middle of what should have been a free-flowing River.

Behind the dam, the water had been trapped. It boiled and turned and coiled, begging to follow gravity downriver, only to be impounded by an impenetrable concrete wall. Blocked and trapped, the water was invaded by phosphates and nitrogen. They sucked the oxygen out of it, creating perfect conditions for the spread of parasites and toxic blue-green algae blooms that turned the water a bright artificial green. No creature could pass to the other side of the border, coming from upriver, and for almost one hundred years no fish had made it to this part of the River, blocked by downriver dams. This stretch of River had been a dead zone.

Now, the River flowed. Where the concrete wall had stood, the water flowed freely, just like it had for thousands of years.

The water remembered where to go and what to do. It filled the River's bed like a down comforter, the drops of water settling softly around the River's sides, filling the spaces with what was meant to be there: clean, cold water. The water moved swiftly and gingerly, flowing downriver. The Riverbed and water seemed to be caressing, comforted by their reunion. The River channel was twenty feet wide and no trees or brush stood in the middle. Even though it had been blocked for almost one hundred years, the River knew exactly what to do. It remembered too, seemed to be relieved. Like an irritating splinter had been removed and now the River enjoyed the comfort of existing how the Creator intended it to. It was beginning to heal. It was beautiful.

Observing this below me, I was overwhelmed with profound and complex emotion. Poppy George, a Karuk KRRC Board Member, Mark, and I stood on the ridge. I felt like royalty observing her homelands restored. I cried. I was surrounded by the other board members and was embarrassed by my reaction. I couldn't stop. I just cried.

I thought of my ancestors and of my family, Great-Grandma Geneva, Uncle Ray, Grandma Lavina, my dad, and aunties and uncles. They had fought so hard. Their identity and way of life had been criminalized and the law used against them as a weapon of genocide and ecocide. Their land, water, fish, personal rights, religion, and even their children had been stolen from them. When they fought back, they were beaten, prosecuted, and detained. Even when they won — in the highest court in the land — the colonizer would not allow them to exercise their rights, even though they were legally valid. I wished they were all standing there with me seeing our beloved River beginning to heal.

Perhaps they were there with us from the other side. While my great-grandmother Geneva had passed away in 1986, she had been with me my whole life and was especially close to me since the 2002 fish kill. When she visited me in that dream and packed the medicine around me, she gave me the protection of the Indian way. I had worn it like invisible armor through law school, the bar exam, and every meeting, court case, and negotiation I had attended on behalf of the Yurok people. It had given me the power of the Indian way. Her medicine, her belief in prayer and determination to exercise her responsibility to take care of Yurok Country, which she had passed down through the generations, had led me and the Nation to this moment. I cried for her because she would have been so happy. She would have felt like she had finally fulfilled her responsibility to fix the world.

Uncle Ray passed away almost exactly one year before the first dam on the Klamath was removed. I cried for him because he had sacrificed so much. He was labeled a renegade, a felon, a criminal. He had been prosecuted and targeted his entire life by the federal and state governments just for exercising his Indian fishing rights. His strength and determination led to some of the Yurok Nation's greatest legal victories, which were relied upon to compel dam removal. The ugliness of the fight had broken him, and he lived hard and sad. He would have been proud and relieved to know the dams were coming down and the fish would run free up the River.

I cried for my grandma, my father and mother, and my aunties and uncles who'd risked their lives to carry on the family responsibility in the first covenant, protecting Yurok Country, sovereignty, and legal rights. They had kept fishing and stayed on the land and water even though it was dangerous and deeply traumatizing because they were prosecuted by both the federal and state governments, even though their legal rights were the supreme law of the land.

Looking at the River run free, I felt the trauma of every generation of my family since the invasion of white settlers into Yurok Country swell up through my belly and into my throat. A part of me felt guilty that I was the generation to witness dam removal. I had continued the family's fight, armed with a law degree and license to practice law. I fought my battles with words that formed legal arguments based on my uncle's arrests and the family's prosecution and court cases, which I either wrote or spoke in the comfort of courtrooms and conference rooms. I stood comfortably on my family's shoulders. I existed because of them. Yet, I was able to witness the fruit of their dangerous labor. In that great moment of release, the tears of six generations of my family flowed through me, healing historical trauma that was deeply embedded in our DNA.

Inherited anger runs deep through my family because we have suffered from generations of genocide, assimilation, and oppression. The pain and anguish of historical trauma are passed down through the DNA and through stories. We are born with the impact of trauma. Imagine coming into this world angry about things you didn't experience.

Standing there, these thoughts and emotions moving through me, I watched my River flow free where a dam once stood. It was breathtaking and almost unbelievable. I breathed in the air that moved over the former dam site and down the River and up the hill to where I stood. A flood of tears began to release my inherited anger and my grief over the fish and my sister. In its place a scar formed over my heart. I felt my own healing begin. I would never be the same girl who moved in with Grandma twenty summers before. I was more now. The grief, the people I worked with, the fight, and now, the accomplishment filled me with deep peace and gratitude. Peace because restorative justice had been served. Gratitude to all our many partners who had answered the Creator's call. This is what it felt like to be a *steward*. This is what it felt like to fix the world. I wondered, in that moment of profound revelation and healing, *Is it possible to reverse trauma from past generations? Can the souls of previous generations who have passed heal through my healing? Can they finally rest in peace knowing our River will be restored and future generations will be able to continue the Yurok fishing way of life?*

I believe they can. I believe they rest in a deeper peace knowing our River is healing.

CHAPTER 21

Fire in the Hole

◀◀◀◀◀◀◀◀◀◀◀◀◀◀◀◀◀◀◀◀◀◀◀◀◀◀◀◀◀◀◀◀◀◀◀◀◀◀◀

2023

J anuary 2024 marked the beginning of the almost simultaneous removal of the remaining three Klamath dams. A complex plan, approved by FERC and various federal agencies, facilitated dam removal. The plan was to start by draining the reservoirs behind the dams in January using explosives to blow holes in the bottom of each dam and insert tunnels to provide temporary passage for the water to drain and then the River to flow through until the dams were removed. Next, work would proceed to remove Copco 2, J.C. Boyle Dam, and then, lastly, Iron Gate Dam, the largest and farthest downriver. The project had to be completed by September of 2024 and there were strict limitations on when in-stream River work could be completed to minimize impacts to aquatic species. It was a very ambitious construction project, schedule, and budget. A dam removal project on this scale had never been done. Any mishap could cause delay and more money, and fuel the arguments of our opponents, who continued to challenge our cause. These were mostly people who were afraid of change, mostly related to converting the reservoirs back to a River.

On a cold day in January, construction began. I met Mike Belchik, the Yurok Nation biologist whom I had worked with now for decades, at the River just below Iron Gate Dam. I wanted to pray for the River. I brought my angelica root, the same type of root my great-grandmother Geneva used for prayer, and a lighter. We walked together to the River's edge one hundred yards below Iron Gate Dam. The water flowed meagerly, a dark green, as if it was tired. I looked upriver at the dam. The structure made of red (iron) rock rose 173 feet high from the River channel as if to tell the River creatures, *Don't even try passing by me.* It was intimidating. Its red rock looked violent, as if it had absorbed one hundred years' worth of salmon blood from the brave salmon that had died trying to pass its gate.

Mike helped me light the root. The smoke rolled over us and dissipated down the River. I listened to the River. While I know the River is wiser than humans, and does not likely experience human emotions, I believe it communicates in ways we can understand. I felt its anticipation and concern about the arrival of construction crews and equipment. It did not know why they had arrived. It was suspicious and worried it would be hurt more.

I felt compelled to comfort the River and wondered, *What is my most powerful tool to protect the River and the construction workers?* It came to me: my great-grandmother's Yurok song, which I had learned from an old recording of her singing. I started to sing her song. I sang to make medicine to help the River. Then I prayed. I wanted the River to know all this construction was for its benefit. I told the River the reservoirs would be drained and the dams would be removed. I told it that it could run like a River again. I told it that soon the salmon would run to places they hadn't been in more than a hundred years. I told the River it would feel better soon. I told it that it had a free-flowing future. I made my medicine. Mike prayed too.

Then, dam decommissioning began.

《《《

Phase one was to drain the reservoirs by blowing holes in the bottom of the remaining three dams for the water to flow through.

The first explosion targeted Copco No. 1, the first dam, built in 1911. Standing 132 feet tall and 415 feet wide, the dam was wedged between Copco 2 and J.C. Boyle. This stretch of River had been devoid of anadromous fish, their migration blocked by the series of dams. Water flows above and below fluctuated with releases for power production, leaving this stretch of River heavily industrialized and lifeless. The explosion was designed to make way for a tunnel through which the River could flow while the dam was removed. Though safety protocols kept us from witnessing the blast firsthand, we could witness a wave produced by the explosion from the reservoir's release — a freedom wave. It would be no ordinary rush of water; instead, we would witness the River beginning to reclaim itself.

I joined a group of Yurok and Karuk leaders on a ledge about twenty-five feet above the River, overlooking a stagnant, desolate stretch of water about two hundred yards long, less than a quarter mile below the dam. There, the water was so low that the riverbed rocks were exposed, and what little water remained moved lethargically, its surface a lifeless black. There was no sound of rushing water, no insects, no birds — only silence. The River seemed utterly devoid of life.

We all noticed this bleak reality and chose to focus on the relief that was to come. Nervous laughter and jokes filled the air as we waited for the wave. Someone suggested singing an Indian song to bless what was about to unfold. A Karuk Tribal Council member,

Kenneth "Binx" Brink, began with a beautiful, powerful song that soothed us all. Then the Yurok vice chairman, Frankie Myers, followed, his voice carrying through the stillness. As he finished the first verse, a soft roar began to rise from the distance. The shallow, sluggish water below us started to rise. He began the second verse, the water rose, and then it appeared. His song summoned the water.

About a hundred feet upriver, the wave came into view — a five-foot-tall force of water stretching the entire width of the River, surging fast and loud, rushing toward us. It moved with unwavering confidence and a fierce life force, as if it had been waiting a hundred years to break free. It felt as though this water was alive, flowing with the unstoppable strength of Mother Nature, marching toward its liberation.

We stood in awe as the water rose before us, growing stronger with every moment until the full force of the wave roared past. Its energy was overwhelming, consuming the riverbed and everything in its path. With this surge, life returned to the stretch of River before our eyes.

We hollered and cried as we witnessed the River being reborn, running with a vengeance to reclaim its former glory. And how glorious it was.

The following month, the reservoirs behind the dams were drained. These reservoirs had inundated 2,200 acres of River channel and riparian land for more than a century, transforming this large stretch of River into man-made lakes that harmed water quality and increased water temperatures throughout the rest of the River. The timing of drawdown (draining of the reservoirs) was heavily managed to mitigate impacts to the River. Around 5 million cubic yards of sediment from behind the dams was released and caused temporary water-quality problems that were heavily monitored by teams of tribal, federal, and state scientists.

As soon as the reservoirs were drained, the River revealed itself. It was a remarkable transformation. Instantly *the water remembered* and found its way into its historical channel to once again run as a River. Mother Nature helped by contributing rainstorms that increased the flows, flushing out sediment from the footprint of the former reservoir. This was astonishing. There had been a decade-long drought, and no one knew how long it would take for the accumulated mud and sand to clear. It seemed to happen in an instant, as if the River, eager to return to its place, could not wait another moment to cleanse itself.

Crews of restoration experts, including Yurok tribal members like my brother, Will Bowers, led crews to reconnect creeks and tributaries to the newly restored River channel to build salmon and aquatic species playgrounds. More than nineteen billion seeds of native species were either hand-seeded by Yurok tribal members or dropped from helicopters on the land in the former reservoirs. Thousands of acorn seeds were planted to grow oak trees. Acorns are a first food for Yurok and other Indigenous groups in the lower Klamath Basin, and planting these trees means food security for future generations. By the spring of 2024, the seeds were already blooming, covering the former inundated land with a vibrant beautiful green, and orange poppies, and the River ran proudly.

《《《

The second phase was to deconstruct the dams, which began in February 2024. Each dam had a separate crew, and they worked daily to expedite removal of the dams to meet the ambitious schedule. Each crew coordinated construction activities together for safety and River protection.

For my birthday in March, I arranged to attend a blast of Copco No. 1. The goal of this explosion was to dismantle one side of the dam.

Workers had already drilled a series of holes about five feet apart and filled them with dynamite, all connected by detonators that ran hundreds of feet away.

While we waited for crews to finish preparing for the explosion, we toured the Copco powerhouse, an industrial-looking building located on the north side of the River immediately below the dam. The powerhouse had been stripped of easily removable equipment. All that remained were the massive turbines and copper generators, each standing over thirty feet tall, that River water passed through to generate power. It struck me that for almost a hundred years all the water that flowed through Brooks Riffle and Rek-woi — water that my family and I had fished and swum in — had passed through that massive dirty metallic turbine and then through a series of pipes to be spit out into the River. What pollutants from that turbine might now be in my body, in my children's bodies, or in the bodies of the fish in the River?

After several hours of preparation, the crews were ready to detonate.

"Amy, do you want to ignite the detonator?" asked the project manager. He was asking me if I wanted to blow up the dam. I jumped for joy. There was nothing I wanted more in that moment. My day dreams from back on the River bar were coming true.

"Yes!" I eagerly replied.

The small circular silver detonator had been set up under a three-sided iron shelter big enough for four or five people, placed in the middle of the shelter on a large flat rock. I was told that there would first be a five-minute warning, then a one-minute warning, and then a brief countdown from five to one. At zero, I was to yell, "Fire in the hole," and stomp on the detonator with force.

I stood next to the detonator about to explode with excitement. I heard the horn and the five-minute warning. I said a silent prayer that all would go well.

One-minute warning.

This is for my ancestors, I thought.

The project manager counted down to one.

"Fire in the hole!" I slammed my foot down on the detonator with the force of six generations of injustice fueling my action.

Boom! Air, wood, rock, and steel from the dam exploded fifty feet into the air. I watched huge rectangular steel rods sail into the sky and then fall to the River bar. Then a thick cloud of smoke and dust covered the dam site.

"Happy birthday!" my colleague yelled.

When the dust settled, we walked down to the dam site. The blast was successful. The entire north side of the dam was now broken into pieces of concrete, twisted steel rebar, and dirt. The next day, after the area was checked for safety issues, crews would use excavators and dump trucks and begin to haul off the debris. Soon the entire dam would be gone.

It took seven years to build Copco No. 1 and five months to remove it with thirty-two explosions. We later learned the one I detonated was one of the largest explosions for the entire project. It will likely be the biggest emotional release of my life.

《《《

The last dam to fall was Iron Gate. Its removal was particularly historic because the River would finally reclaim itself, flowing unobstructed for the first time in more than a century. The Iron Gate Dam, the dam closest to the River's mouth, is located 190 River miles from my village. It is a 173-foot-tall, 740-foot-wide earthen dam faced with red rock. On the north side is a massive concrete spillway where salmon frequently die trying to get past the dam. Rotting and drying in the sun, baked to the concrete of the spillway, their carcasses are often visible at the dam site. An eerie reminder of the fatal consequences of this dam. On the south side, two pipes spill out to the main stem River, and the top of the dam is wide enough to drive a dump truck over it. The entire ugly brutalist structure appears out of place. It looks painful to the River, like a broken bone sticking out of an arm. It looks like a bad idea — and one that we no longer have to believe in.

The construction to remove the dam began in midsummer. This was an earthen dam made of rocks from a nearby hill. To remove the dam, the rocks were scooped up, loaded into dump trucks, and hauled and dumped at the hill they came from. Every day for ten hours a day, dump truck load after dump truck load of rocks from the dam were removed.

While construction workers labored, we prayed. A week before Iron Gate Dam was to be breached, the Boat Dance was held, one of the three World Renewal Ceremonies. During the Boat Dance, dancers stand in Yurok redwood canoes singing sacred songs and traversing over a riffle 145 miles from Iron Gate Dam. If the boat makes it over the riffle safely, then it's a sign the upcoming year will be good. If there is trouble, like the dancers fall or a canoe tips, it's a sign of a bad year to come. For the safety of the dancers, a higher level of flow than what is prescribed is required. Since the dance was revived in the 2000s, the Nation has had to fight with the Bureau of Reclamation (BOR) to release the water for the dance. It's usually a nasty fight.

In 2020, the Trump administration denied the Nation's request for flows, claiming there wasn't sufficient water. The next day, unexpectedly and unscheduled, the BOR increased agricultural water deliveries by the same amount as was needed for the Boat Dance. I was still general counsel for the Yurok Nation, and my office sued the federal government, claiming that their reasoning for denying the Nation's request for flows was arbitrary and capricious and in violation of the Nation's rights. In 2023, I settled the case. In the agreement, the federal government recognized the Nation's water rights included ceremonial flows and committed to providing the flows upon the Nation's request. This was one of the first instances of the federal government recognizing ceremonial water flow as part of tribal water rights.

The first occasion to test their commitment was 2024. A week before Iron Gate Dam was to be breached, the BOR and the Nation worked with the dam removal contractors to schedule flow releases to support the dance. The federal government stuck to the agreement. The BOR released the water that flowed through the dam's drainage tunnel, pushing out sediment trapped behind the dam. This reduced the amount of sediment that would have been released during the breach of Iron Gate Dam, which reduced the potential negative impact to the River. It was a beautiful combination of tribal rights advancing the restoration of the River and aquatic species.

When the canoes made it over the riffle safely during the Boat Dance, we all took it as a sign that the dam removal would go well. Over the past twenty years, the dance leaders — many of whom were grassroots activists and tribal leaders for the Undam the Klamath Campaign — took courageous steps to revive the ceremonies. By combining ceremony, culture, activism, and law, their leadership has guided us into the next era of the Yurok people. Even Grandma is now satisfied that the World Renewal Ceremonies' medicine and protocols are strong. We are working to bring back the World Renewal Ceremonies in Rek-woi.

Shortly after the conclusion of the Boat Dance, on August 26, five days after we celebrated the ninth birthday of my second son, Keane, the Iron Gate Dam was scheduled to be breached to reconnect the River for the first time in more than a hundred years. I realized I had been fighting for this moment longer than he had been alive. At eight o'clock in the morning, Ashley, my sister whom I had fished with my entire life and who was now working with me at Ridges to Riffles (R2R), stood with me and a small crowd of people at the base of Iron

Gate Dam. What was left of the dam was almost level with the water behind it upriver. Behind the dam, the River channel was about thirty feet higher than the River channel below the dam. It was anticipated that construction crews would remove enough rock from the dam within a few hours to lower the dam below the River level upriver and cause the water to flow over the dam into the main channel of the River. There was much excitement and anticipation. We waited.

Then it happened. An excavator scooped up a large pile of red rock, lifted its arm, dumped the load, and repeated. Then the sparkle of water appeared where only red rock had been. It was so small it looked like a lone star above a night sky over a big city. It was barely visible, but the crowd knew it was water and gasped.

"Here it comes!" hollered a Karuk tribal member, Leaf Hillman, who had been a leader of the Klamath Dam Removal grassroots campaign and a former Vice Chairman of the Karuk Nation.

The excavator took a few more scoops, lowering the level of Iron Gate Dam and widening the water's path. Gradually, the water moved farther downriver over the dam. *It remembered how to flow and where to go.* It slowly saturated the remaining part of the dam, heading toward the downriver channel. Finally, downriver and upriver reconnected through a stream of prosperity when the water met at the base of the former Iron Gate Dam. The River was free.

The crowd roared and cheered. I stood arm-in-arm with Ashley in tears. Our family had waited generations to reconnect this River. We were the lucky generation to watch it happen. Molli Myers, Karuk tribal member and grassroots leader of the dam removal effort, whom I worked with at R2R, hugged her colleagues in gratitude. Brian Johnson, Trout Unlimited California Director and KRRC Board President who had fought hard for dam removal for over twenty years, cried.

Later that day, past Yurok leaders, including Auntie Sue and her husband, Uncle Leonard, and my boys came to witness. Looking down at the former Iron Gate Dam site, Uncle declared it was like the dams were never even there. Indeed, the dams were hardly there when considered in the timescale of the River's life.

I woke up that morning to a dammed River and fell asleep that night to a River that flowed freely for the first time in one hundred years. I slept well. I expect all the dedicated people who worked on Klamath dam removal for decades rested well too.

J.C. Boyle was removed by August 2024.

On September 30, 2024, the Klamath River's journey toward restoration reached a powerful milestone: the removal of all four dams. More than 441 feet of steel, rock, concrete, clay, and rebar from four different dams were removed. With Iron Gate Dam alone, 1 million cubic yards of dam material was removed in twenty-five thousand truckloads with forty yards' holding capacity. This material that once blocked the River's flow was recycled, returned to the earth, or repurposed. Dam removal was completed on time, within budget, and consistent with the terms of the permits. With their removal, the River began to heal, restoring balance and the lifeways of those dependent on its vitality.

Now the River flows freely for 263 miles from its headwaters above Upper Klamath Lake to its reunion with the ocean at Rek-woi. Salmon returning to the tributaries now have access to over 450 miles of spawning habitat they'd been blocked from for over one hundred years. In October 2024, the leader of the fall chinook salmon run was spotted on sonar technology passing the former Iron Gate Dam site. By November hundreds of salmon had gone past the former dam sites into Upper Klamath Lake and its tributaries in Oregon for the first time in more than one hundred years. By November, thousands of salmon had passed the former dam sites. They spawned.

In June 2024, 2,800 acres around the former Copco No. 1 and No.

2 Dams were returned to the Shasta Indian Nation, the area's original inhabitants.

Twenty thousand acres in the former hydroelectric project area will be restored through multimillion-dollar restoration projects, and have been reseeded with nineteen billion native seeds, and hundreds of thousands of trees and shrubs have been planted within the former reservoirs to provide habitat for bears, deer, eagles, and much more.

The magnitude of this work is impossible to describe in words. It's remarkable. While there is still more work, for now, we will rest knowing the world is renewing itself before our eyes. May we all be a witness.

Afterword
Balance

◀◀◀◀◀◀◀◀◀◀◀◀◀◀◀◀◀◀◀◀◀◀◀◀◀◀◀◀◀◀◀◀

2024

The lessons from Klamath dam removal are critical now because the relationship between humans and nature is out of balance across the planet. Klamath dam removal proves that humans can work with nature to create a thriving future on planet earth.

Dam removal is just the beginning. Restoration projects to rebuild the historical ecological function of the Klamath Basin around the former dam sites, reservoirs, and tributaries will continue through 2028. My nonprofit, the Ridges to Riffles Indigenous Conservation Group, will work to increase tribal capacity throughout the basin, restore habitat and natural water flows, and make agriculture sustainable while restoring Indigenous lifeways and resources in the basin. Importantly, we will observe the River's healing by spending time on the water. We will watch it heal and listen to it. Already what we are witnessing defies conventional science. Its rate of recovery will surpass our scientific hypothesis and theories because our human metrics cannot comprehend the River's strength and resilience.

The goal is to increase the ecosystem's resiliency to support all biodiversity, humans included. This is perhaps one of the largest nature-based solution projects in the world thus far. I am confident that Klamath dam removal will prove that nature-based solutions work. As the Klamath ecosystem becomes more resilient and stronger, it will be able to support more life. It has already proven that nature-based solutions are profitable. Klamath dam removal was cheaper than installing fish ladders, which was required by law, and brought $515 million into the economy. Proving that nature-based solutions through large-scale restoration are not only environmentally critical but also economically viable. They are in the public interest. The brilliance of Klamath dam removal was that we were able to place equal value on the rights of Indigenous peoples, nature, and business in a $515 million dollar comprehensive settlement agreement.

This business model supports the creation of a global regenerative economy, one that is based on restoring ecological functions through habitat restoration while making a profit. This challenges the outdated belief that industrializing nature is the only path to prosperity. Instead, Klamath dam removal shows that deindustrializing, healing natural systems, and upholding Indigenous rights are good for business, communities, and the planet.

It also served justice. The Klamath dams embodied the legacy of the dark underbelly of the founding of this country that supported the industrialization of nature at the expense of Indigenous peoples, the environment, and marginalized communities. The ecological consequences of colonization, while devastating, need not be permanent. Dam removal sends a clear message: Indigenous rights, leadership, and lifeways are not obstacles to progress — they are critical tools for sustaining life on earth that we all should embrace. Dam removal can end the colonial era on the Klamath River and begin a new era of healing through restorative justice. This starts with mutual respect for the rights of Indigenous peoples, nature, and business.

The path forward is following Indigenous leadership and respecting Indigenous knowledge and lifeways.

My family and Nation should not have had to fight state and federal governments and power companies for two centuries to protect our rights, which are the supreme law of the land under the US Constitution. It was a grave enough injustice that the country stole 99.72 percent of Yurok land, polluted our waters, and killed the species we depended upon. The meager yet critically important rights we retained should have been protected in the development of the Klamath Basin and the country. The Creator gave us those rights. Our ancestors secured them in the unratified treaty and then in the executive orders creating the reservation. But the federal government allowed a system to develop that destroyed our resources, criminalized our identity and way of life, and weaponized the law to control and eradicate us. Generations of my family had to sacrifice our lives and our well-being just to continue our way of life. We did it because that is our duty to the Creator. We also did it for future generations.

The Yurok and Karuk, along with the other Indigenous peoples in the Klamath Basin, were guided by our worldview that supported *world renewal* by restoring balance between nature and humans. Humans are a part of nature, not separate, and must work to restore it. We exercised our responsibilities with strategic precision. We failed repeatedly, and history, precedent, money, power, and time were all against us. One of the richest men in the world was against us. Yet, somehow, against these impossible odds, the Indigenous peoples from the Klamath Basin's unfaltering commitment, strategic partnerships, and legal and political strategizing led us to our goal. Their vision of how the basin worked and what it looked like predevelopment was the light that led us forward. Their bravery and leadership pulled others into the movement and made them believe a free-flowing future was possible for the Klamath and future generations.

The World Renewal ceremonies and medicine guided this process. The first dam was removed just after the twentieth anniversary of the first complete modern World Renewal Ceremony and the fish kill. There is no denying that the medicine of the dance worked. While no one would wish for the salmon to have died, it was their deaths — their sacrifice — that catalyzed generations of people to come together to heal the Klamath River. Indeed, there was not one single champion of the Klamath Dam Removal. Instead there are thousands of champions who worked tirelessly for decades or lifetimes toward the goal of dam removal.*

While our partners, the states, PacifiCorp, and other entities, may not have been aware of it, our efforts were enhanced because we were working toward restoring the balance between the natural world and humans, advancing the first covenant between Yurok — and perhaps all humans — and the Creator. The medicine was working with us. The dams caused the humans to take too much from the natural world because they harmed the River, which disrupted the balance. Removing the dams restored the balance because the human use of the River would no longer harm it. The brilliant minds working on Klamath dam removal were aided by the Creator and good medicine because we were working toward restoring balance, which resulted in healthy ecosystems that could better support humans and all other species.

Further, Klamath dam removal proves that marginalized communities like mine can lead movements for historic wide-ranging ecosystem changes that can result in the more equitable distribution of resources, wealth, and power. Using this example, we can see that the overall health of our Nation, our people, and our ecosystems can be uplifted, and that allowing more voices, perspectives, and experiences

---

* The author acknowledges there are many champions not mentioned in this book and sends gratitude and respect to them.

to contribute to our democracy is empowering. In this way, we can create a more perfect union.

The historical systemic compromise of Indigenous rights is and always has been a threat to democracy because it is unconstitutional and morally wrong. The strength of a nation is best measured by how it treats marginalized and underprivileged populations. We are strong enough to uplift Indigenous peoples. We can no longer afford to destroy Indigenous rights and the resources upon which those rights are exercised in service of power and money, in part because more than 80 percent of the world's remaining biodiversity is on Indigenous land. In the United States, Indian reserved rights are the supreme law of the land and are entitled to the highest protection and prioritization of the law. Rather than an impediment to "progress," Indian rights often include requirements for habitat and environmental protection that are powerful tools for positive change and environmental advocacy. These rights should be uplifted to the benefit of us all and the planet.

Now that the dams are gone, perhaps soon along the River bar Yurok people, including me and my three sons, will be fishing and enjoying a restored homeland. Already, Indigenous youth, including my niece Keeya Wiki, have made the first descent in a kayak of the entire Klamath River. My son Keane and I joined them at the headwaters and last forty miles of the River. The River water and riparian areas are cleaner than I have ever seen in my lifetime. The River is fierce, stronger than I have ever known it to be. Keeya, along with my boys, will be the first generation of my family, since the arrival of white people, with the privilege *to simply enjoy a healthy River and not have to fight.* This is freedom. It may not be the freedom my great-grandmother enjoyed, but it is still a beautiful freedom.

These peaceful moments stem from the River existing in peace. Only when nature is at peace — in balance without harm — can humans truly experience peace. May Klamath dam removal prove that, even in a post-colonized world, we don't have to live out of balance. Together, when we place equal value on the rights of Indigenous peoples, nature, and business, we can fix the world.

This is a pathway to peace.

My great-grandmother lived by this credo. Her wisdom and influence are timeless and surpass life and death. Following her guidance, I found my path, which allowed me to play a part in the healing of my River, culture, and family. There is no higher calling of my life force, other than raising my three sons to continue our fishing way of life.

Having witnessed this historic effort, I believe all humans have ancestral knowledge in our blood about what it was like to live on a healthy planet. The Indian way is still here. The medicine is still here, in you and me. In all of us. We can restore the balance. We can renew the world.

The water remembers, and so can we.

Acknowledgments

Many people helped me with this book: Lavina Bowers, Bill and Diane Bowers, Sue and Leonard Masten, Stephanie and Josh Stanton, Janet Wortman, Deb Yturralde, Ashley Bowers, Geneva Wiki, George Foreman, Abby Abinanti, Ash Davidson (to whom I now owe a kidney), Kim Cross, John Echohawk, Congressman Jared Huffman, Abigail Dillen, Molli and Frankie Myers, Mike Belchik, Lori Hodge, Hope Masten, Lynda Mapes, Glenn Stout, Brian Johnson, awok Charles Wilkinson, the Yurok Nation, and Ridges to Riffles Indigenous Conservation Group.

A special thank-you to my parents and boys, Brooks, Keane, Tobiyahz, and Daniel Cordalis, for supporting me while I wrote this book. A special thank-you to Mark Tauber, Tracy Sherrod, Cara Bedick, Peyton Young, and the Little, Brown team for believing in this book and going above and beyond to bring it to life.

Notes

1 Lavina Bowers, interview by the author, June 2020; Geneva Mattz, interview 1, August 29, 1984, tape 1, side 1. The story and dialogue in this chapter come from these sources.

2 Native American Smithsonian Museum, Indian-United States Treaty Exhibit, 2023.

3 Geneva Mattz, interview transcript, interview 2, September 25, 1984. The dialogue in this part of the chapter is from this interview.

4 Geneva Mattz, interview transcript, interview 3, January 29, 1985. The dialogue in this part of the chapter is from this interview.

5 Arnett v. Five Gill Nets, Mattz, 48 Cal. App. 3d 454 (1975).

6 Geneva Mattz, interview 1, August 24, 1984, tape 1, side 2, p. 30.

7 U.S. Department of Commerce, National Oceanic and Atmospheric Administration, National Marine Fisheries Service, Pacific Fishery Management Council, Supplement to the Final Environmental Impact/Fishery Management Plan for Commercial and Recreational Salmon Fisheries off the Coasts of Washington, Oregon, and California including Proposed Amendments and Appendices for 1979, Portland Oregon, 1978–1979, at 7–9.

8 *Depleted Chinook Salmon Runs, Id.*

9 *Depleted Chinook Salmon Runs,* p. 3. Gary L. Rankel, *Depleted Chinook Salmon Runs in the Klamath Basin Drainage* (Arcata, CA: US Fish and Wildlife Service, Fisheries Assistance Office, 1980), p. 12.

10 Pacific Fishery Management Council, Final Fisheries Management Plan for Commercial and Recreational Salmon Fisheries off the Coasts of Washington, Oregon, and California Commencing in 1978, Portland Oregon, at 13,1978.

11 U.S. Department of Commerce, National Oceanic and Atmospheric Administration, National Marine Fisheries Service, Pacific Fishery Management Council, Supplement to the Final Environmental Impact/Fishery Management Plan for Commercial and Recreational Salmon Fisheries off the Coasts of Washington, Oregon, and California including Proposed Amendments and Appendices for 1979, Portland Oregon, 1979.

12 Gary L. Rankel, *Depleted Chinook Salmon Runs in the Klamath Basin Drainage* (Arcata, CA: US Fish and Wildlife Service, Fisheries Assistance Office, 1980), p. 12.

13 Diane Whipple Mattz, Interview 11, June 11, 1968, tape I, side I. The scene and dialogue in this chapter are from this interview.

14 Mattz v. Arnett, 412 U.S. 481 (1973).

15 *Id.* at 497.

16 *Id.*

17 https://americanindian.si.edu/nk360/pnw-fish-wars/backlash.

18 Jose A. Del Real, "Sick River: Can These California Nations Beat Heroin and History?," *New York Times,* September 4, 2018, https://www.nytimes.com/2018/09/04/us/klamath-River-california-nations-heroin.html; Thadeus Greenson, "Yurok Nation Declares Emergency After Rash of Suicides," *North Coast Journal,* January 24, 2016, https://www.northcoastjournal.com./NewsBlog/archives/2016/01/24/yurok-nation-declares-emergency-after-rash-of-suicides.

19 https://ktvz.com/news/government-politics/2020/11/17/klamath-River-deal-revives-plan-for-largest-us-dam-demolition/.

20 US Federal Energy Regulatory Commission, 1095th Commission Meeting Transcript, November 17, 2022, p. 6, available at https://www.ferc.gov/media/commission-meeting-transcript-november-2022.

21 *Id.* p. 12, November 17, 2022.

22 *Id.*

23 *Id.* pp. 18–19.

About the Author

Amy Bowers Cordalis is a Yurok tribal member, attorney, environmental advocate, fisherwoman, and cultural practitioner committed to restoring Indigenous rights and sovereignty and advancing environmental justice. She is the cofounder and executive director of the Ridges to Riffles Indigenous Conservation Group, a nonprofit dedicated to the protection of tribal cultural and natural resources.

She played a key role in the historic agreements to remove four dams along the Klamath River, the largest River restoration project in history, and spearheaded the legal effort to declare personhood rights for the Klamath River, making it the first River in North America to have such status. In addition to her legal work, Cordalis advocates for cultural revival and tribal self-determination. Her efforts to defend tribal sovereignty, promote sustainable practices, and heal ecosystems align with a sacred mandate to restore harmony with the natural world. She views this work as essential to dismantling colonial systems of oppression and fostering environmental justice. Recognized as one of *Time* magazine's one hundred most influential climate leaders and internationally by the United Nations, as a recipient of the Champion of the Earth Award, she inspires action to protect the planet while honoring the Creator's design for balance and harmony.

Amy resides in Southern Oregon, where she enjoys spending time with her family fishing, being outdoors, and exploring.

To support Klamath River restoration and Indigenous-led conservation, consider donating to the Ridges to Riffles Indigenous Conservation Group at www.ridgestoriffles.org.